The law workbook: Developing skills for legal research and writing

Suzanne Gordon, BA, DEA, D Jur.

Sherifa Elkhadem, BA, LLB, LLM

2001
EMOND MONTGOMERY PUBLICATIONS LIMITED
TORONTO, CANADA

Printed in Canada.

Edited, designed, and typeset by WordsWorth Communications, Toronto.
Cover design by Susan Darrach, Darrach Design.

We acknowledge the financial support of the Government of Canada through the
Book Publishing Industry Development Program (BPIDP) for our publishing activities.

National Library of Canada Cataloguing in Publication Data

Gordon, Suzanne (Suzanne Elizabeth)
    The law workbook : developing skills for legal research and writing

(Working with the law)
Includes bibliographical references.
ISBN 1-55239-084-5

    1. Legal research — Canada.   2. Legal composition.   I. Title.   II. Series.

KE250.G67 2001   340'.07'2071   C2001-902172-0

*In appreciation of the expertise of the librarians at Osgoode Hall Law School,
and their work to maintain an outstanding library and support
to students, faculty, and the public;*

with thanks to our parents and friends for their encouragement; and

to Chris for his helpful comments.

*Suzanne Gordon
Sherifa Elkhadem*

Contents

CHAPTER 4   CASE-BRIEFING SKILLS: HOW TO READ A COURT CASE LIKE A LAWYER   123

CHAPTER 5   SKILLS OF LEGAL ANALYSIS: HOW TO USE THE LAW TO SOLVE PROBLEMS AND PREDICT OUTCOMES   187

Preface

This workbook provides exercises that show students how to read, research, and analyze problems like a lawyer. The exercises focus the student's attention on the skills used to discern relevant information, to identify legal questions, to research effectively, and to resolve legal problems.

The purpose of this workbook is to provide students of law with an opportunity to practise and hone their research and analytical skills. Intended as an introduction to legal research methodology, the workbook attempts to use plain language to introduce legal terminology and concepts. It offers an overview of the various methods of solving legal problems, the research sources available, and how to use research effectively.

The idea of using a workbook to teach legal research and writing is inspired by the questions and interests of students and instructors in the Legal Research and Writing Program at Osgoode Hall Law School, York University. We wanted to provide more opportunity for students to practise and develop their skills. The workbook begins at a basic level and gradually introduces students to the more difficult task of using the law to solve problems and answer questions. Our objective is to allow students to develop and hone a reliable methodology to use when tackling legal problems.

We are grateful to Dale Brawn for his contributions to this project and for working with us to develop the concept of a law workbook. Over the years, we have benefited greatly from the encouragement, assistance, and expertise of the law librarians at Osgoode Hall Law School, especially Marianne Rogers, Head Reference Librarian, and Louise Tsang, Reference Librarian. Louise has also worked closely with us to develop the chapter and materials on electronic researching skills.

CHAPTER 1

Analytical skills: How to analyze problems and identify legal issues

IDENTIFY THE RELEVANT FACTS

When lawyers are presented with a problem to solve or a "fact situation" to examine, they analyze the situation in terms of the legal questions that are raised. A clear understanding of the facts is an important first step in this analysis. Lawyers are trained to look for certain information when they read the facts and to summarize lengthy descriptions of events.

One method of searching quickly for relevant facts is to determine which facts are essential to the story. To test the relevance of a particular fact, decide whether its presence or absence changes the outcome of the story.

When reading problems or legal material, use the following steps to identify the key facts:

1. Divide a fact situation into **key words and concepts** to identify **Key People**, **Events**, or **Actions**, **Places**, and **Objects**.

2. Provide a short description for each of the key people. Usually, a description of their occupation, profession, or the type of relationship they have with someone else is sufficient.

3. Determine how the situation arose. Write a short statement that describes what action or activity gave rise to the problem.

4. Decide if place or location is important. Write a short statement that explains why.

5. Determine whether any physical objects are relevant to what happened. Write a short statement that explains how they are relevant.

Read the following fact situations and identify the key facts.

> **Tip:** In law, "legal persons" include people like you and me, as well as organizations, corporations, and institutions such as banks, companies, and charities. When you identify "key people" in a problem, be sure to include both human and corporate entities.

EXERCISE 1   Mr. Jones and Ms Smith

On September 1, 1995 Susan Smith and her son David moved into an apartment managed by Andrew Jones. At that time, Ms Smith, a single mother, signed a one-year lease. When it expired, the lease was renewed when Ms Smith verbally advised Jones of her intent to continue as a tenant. The last renewal took place on September 1, 2000. Two weeks after Ms Smith advised Jones of her intention to remain in the apartment for another year, Misty Nance, the 15-year-old daughter of one of the other tenants living in the building, told her mother that David had sold her some drugs. The transaction allegedly took place in the parking lot of the apartment building. Constable Couples, a beat cop responsible for patrolling the area in which the Smiths reside, saw Misty speaking with David. When David left, the constable noticed that a foil package had fallen from Misty's pocket. Constable Couples walked over, picked it up, and asked Misty if it belonged to her. Misty admitted that it did and that the package contained drugs. Constable Couples immediately charged her with possession of a drug, and on September 22, 2000, she pleaded guilty to the offence. David denied selling Misty any drugs, but was charged with trafficking. Those charges, however, were thrown out at trial because of a technical error made by the arresting officer.

Misty's mother was upset by what happened, and blamed David for getting her daughter into trouble. When Mr. Jones returned from holiday several days after Misty's court appearance, Ms Nance told him what David had done. Mr. Jones promptly confronted Ms Smith, and told her that he was going to give her a notice of termination because he believed that David had sold drugs on the apartment building premises. That notice was delivered to Ms Smith on September 28, 2000. No similar notice was given to the Nance family, although Ms Nance had already advised Jones that she and her family were moving to New Brunswick at the end of September.

On the date of the alleged incident involving David and Misty, David was 16 years old and had been using drugs for at least two years. He missed school regularly to hang out with friends, and on several occasions had been escorted home in a drugged state by the same police constable who witnessed the alleged drug transaction. On his 16th birthday, David had been caught with two marijuana joints in his pocket, and pleaded guilty to a charge of possession of narcotics. This charge is his only conviction.

Before Mr. Jones gave Ms Smith notice to vacate, Ms Smith had been an ideal tenant. On one occasion while she was away, however, David threw a party that quickly became rowdy, and some tenants complained. David apologized to Mr. Jones and the tenants, and no other complaints have been made. Since the charge of trafficking was thrown out, David has been receiving treatment for his drug problem, and has not missed any classes at school. His treatment has included a two-week stay in hospital, ongoing counselling, and regular talks with his older sister, an architect.

Ms Smith is worried that if she is forced out of her apartment, she will not be able to afford similar accommodation. She is currently renting her two-bedroom apartment for $425 a month. She earns extra money toward her rent by doing odd jobs around the building for Mr. Jones.

Identify the relevant facts

1. List the key **people** involved in this case and provide a short description for each person.

   For example:

   — Ms Smith: tenant, mother of David Smith.

   Comment: It does not matter that Ms Smith is a single mother. This detail does not alter the story in any way.

   List any other key people.

   Susan Smith ✓ & Son David

   Apt. manager - Andrew Jones ✓

   Constable Couples — witness ✓

   Misty Nance — ⊅ (Is it relevant to eviction?)
   _No_

2. Identify the key **events** that took place.

   For example:

   — David Smith: Ms Smith's son, charged but not <u>convicted of trafficking</u>.

   — Constable Couples: arresting officer, asked Misty what was in the package he observed fall from her pocket.

   List any other key events.

   { _Ms Smith intention to stay on for another (Tenancy agreement)_
   { _year (No contract) — Eviction Notice ✓_
   Charge of Misty's possession of drugs
   No lease — David caught with Marianan joints ✓

3. Describe any important **objects**.

For example:

A foil packet containing drugs belonging to Misty Nance.

Comment: The foil packet is an important piece of evidence. Misty Nance claims that she bought the package from David Smith.

List any other significant objects.

Evidence - Favourable for David Landlord

proof for illegal activities on (the premises

Eviction Notice

_____

4. Is the **place** where this event occurred important? Why or why not?

For example:

David Smith allegedly sold drugs from the parking lot of his mother's apartment building.

Comment: Location matters here since the landlord, Mr. Jones, may have reason to evict any tenant breaking the law on apartment premises.

List any other places that are important.

Residential Property - Is the parking

lot is a part of the premises

_____

_____

Assess the significance of the events that took place

1. List the complaints that Mr. Jones has against Ms Smith.

   Sale of Drugs Alleged
   Previous will party — Was there
   Escorted home by police — Don't need
   police on premises — Don't know if had lease knew
   Were these problems notified
   to the Landlord .

2. List the facts that are important to determine the reasonableness of these complaints.

   Police Involvement —
   Disturb the quiet enjoyment of other tenants

3. What facts might Ms Smith rely upon in response to Mr. Jones's complaints?

   David is changed his attitude..
   Always pay rent on time
   Excellent tenant in the past
   (Charges dropped) material evidence

EXERCISE 2 Ms Ravji and the Ashtar Estate

Ms Ashtar passed away in 1970. She and her husband had enjoyed 15 years of happy marriage. They had two children — a boy and a girl who were just 4 and 6 at the time when Ms Ashtar lost her struggle with breast cancer. They had been an ideal family. Both parents were active members of their community. As leaders of the block parents' association on their street, they had strong friendships with neighbours. The family had a busy schedule. Both parents worked, taking turns driving their children to and from day care and school, as well as to extra activities such as swimming and gym lessons.

Everything changed after Ms Ashtar died. Mr. Ashtar was devastated. For the next three years, he was severely withdrawn, engaging in little or no social activity. He even cancelled his children's activities. His depression was very hard on the children, who were too young to understand the strange change in their father's behaviour. It made them miss their mother even more.

The neighbours tried to help. They stopped by to visit on occasion, and offered to take the children to movies and other special events. One of these neighbours was a single parent, Ms Ravji. Often she would stay for coffee while her children and the Ashtar children played together. Ms Ravji and Mr. Ashtar became close friends, and over time Mr. Ashtar began to look forward to her visits. She lifted his spirits, and soon he began to live his life again. In 1974, they agreed to try living together, bringing their two families together. It seemed like a huge risk to take at first. Neither one wanted to re-marry at the time. Later, they had a child together, and Ms Ravji stayed at home to raise the five children. Although they never married, their life together was a happy one and they lived together many years.

Mr. Ashtar died in June 1998. Unfortunately, Mr. Ashtar had intended to write a will, but had found the whole process to be a painful reminder of the depression he suffered after his wife passed away. Ms Ravji, always sympathetic and supportive, did not press him to deal with the matter. She was confident he would address the matter in his own time. Mr. Ashtar died intestate (without a will) on June 1, 1998.

Ms Ravji has just found out that, under the provisions of the Alberta *Intestate Succession Act*, she will not receive anything from Mr. Ashtar's estate since they were never married. The section of the Act that refers to the spouse of an intestate does not include persons living in a common law relationship. Ms Ravji finds herself in tremendous financial difficulty as a result. She gave up work when she moved in with Mr. Ashtar to raise their children. Although she has led an active life as a mother, supportive partner, and dedicated community volunteer, she has no savings or assets of her own.

Identify the relevant facts

1. List the key **people** and provide a short description for each person.

Appointment of Estate trustee

___3/___

~~(MR Ashter 1998 Died)~~   *Bring application*

Ms Ravji   *2004*

3 kids · from MR Ashter & incl. (1.)

Ontario Home 400,000 }his
cottage 180,000 }New
Savings 60,000
Now — 2,000
Joint Act.

2. List only those **actions, places,** or **objects** that are directly relevant to Ms Ravji's claim for survivor status under the Alberta *Intestate Succession* Act.

Having a child common law —

Support to deserted man & his family

Enhance the spirit of the family funckly

① Death of MR Ashtar — (Common law Spouse)

Issues → Did MR Ashtar deliberately fail to make a will?

+ Is there a law of statutory duty to provd for her?

Assess the significance of the events that took place

1. What is the basis of Ms Ravji's complaint?

Failure to provide a will / make arrangement for her support
" " " support for Ms Ravji
Discussion

↓ Provide support for him and the children

social & psychological

2. List the facts that you believe provide essential information required to resolve the problem.

Not married

Lic Together 24 year   — Financially ruined

Had a child   — Estate ability to pay to maintain Standard of Livin

Maintain the household.

Out Job to stay home with the childn — Her

Career Potential loss of experience —

Age and health / measures available for the dependat

to become self-supporting

EXERCISE 3 Green Acres

Jeb Green and his wife Iris have four children, Randy, Bruce, Daisy, and Jake. Jeb Green has operated a nursery all his life. In addition to his greenhouse operations, the nursery grows trees and shrubs to supply major retail nurseries. It's a family business. Iris and Jeb worked together to establish the business, and the children were always expected to help out with chores, and to work in the fields and greenhouses in the summer. The business has a popular roadside retail operation, but the main revenues are generated from supplying the trades and larger retail operations.

In 1970, on his accountant's advice, Jeb incorporated Green Acres Ltd. and transferred the nursery's assets to the company. The capital of the company consists of 20,000 class A voting common shares and 20,000 class B voting preferred shares. Upon incorporation, Iris, Randy, Bruce, and Jake Green received 200 common shares. Jeb Green was issued 1,000 preferred shares. Jeb was also given 200 common shares but these were never issued. At the time, the rest of the children had chosen not to participate in the family business in an active manner.

According to the company's bylaws, any shareholder wishing to sell his or her shares must sell to the other shareholders at fair market value. In 1976, Bruce left the farm, and his 200 common shares were sold to Jeb and Iris Green and their son Jake. Each of the purchasers receiving 66, 68, and 66 shares, respectively.

Jake worked at the nursery without salary for the next six years. During that time, he and his parents saw the business through a difficult time. Each of them made certain financial loans to the corporation. Then, Jake's wife decided not to return to full-time work after having their first child. At that point, it was agreed that Jake should begin to receive a monthly salary. He and his wife were also provided with a small home near his parents. At around this time, Bruce Green's business failed, and he returned to work at the nursery. It was not long before old rivalries between Bruce and Jake became unbearable. Soon Jake found himself at cross-purposes with his father as well. The situation deteriorated quickly. Jeb called a family meeting; his sons' inability to work together was not only hard on family life, but ruining the business. Jake arrived at the meeting angry and upset. He could not understand why his father seemed to side with Bruce so readily. He was nothing less than blunt when he told his parents that he felt used and poorly treated. He announced that he was quitting and left the house. He did not return to discuss the matter.

The other shareholders accepted Jake's resignation as a director and employee of the company, but they did not give their notice to this effect to him immediately. They hoped that the matter could be resolved amicably. Jake never came back and even though he lives next door to his parents, they have not spoken. Jake is informed of the shareholder's meetings every year, but he refuses to attend unless he is given formal notice of the meetings through his lawyer. He did not appoint another person to act as his proxy, as permitted by the Saskatchewan *Business Corporations Act*. The situation has upset Iris so much that she does not want Jake living next door anymore.

Although he has resigned as a director and employee of the company, Jake refuses to sell his shares to his family, as they now wish. He alleges oppressive and unfairly prejudicial treatment under ss. 207 and 234 of *The Business Corporations Act*.

Identify the relevant facts

1. List the key **people** and provide a description for each person.

Assess the significance of the events that took place

1. List the **actions, places,** or **objects** that are relevant to Jake's complaints against the other shareholders.

2. List the **actions, places,** or **objects** that explain the other shareholders' position and that might be used to justify their actions.

_____

_____

_____

_____

_____

_____

_____

3. What information might be useful in determining a solution to the dispute between Jake and the other shareholders?

_____

_____

_____

_____

THE LAW WORKBOOK: Developing skills for legal research and writing

EXERCISE 4 Romeo and Juliet

Romeo and Juliet fell in love in spite of the horrible feud between their families. Determined to live their lives together, they decided to elope to avoid objections to their marriage. On Friday, July 13, 2000, they packed their bags, loaded Romeo's motorcycle and set off at about 6 a.m. to be married by a justice of the peace in a neighbouring town, two hours away. It was a clear morning and the couple took their time along the winding country roads, enjoying the sunrise over lush pastures.

At 7:30 a.m. the sun had risen and it was already a swelteringly hot day. Juliet complained to Romeo that wearing full-face helmets and leather motorcycling suits on such a day was unbearable. Even though the state laws would have allowed it, Romeo would not let her ride on the back of his bike without the protection of her full-face helmet and motorcycle suit.

As Juliet admired the beautiful, open fields, something dark moved in the side ditch. She cried out to Romeo when she saw a large dog about to leap out in front of the bike. The dog seemed to spring from the ditch, running directly into the path of the bike. Romeo responded quickly, swerving sharply to miss the dog. As he did so, Juliet was thrown from the back of the motorcycle. Her body skidded across the road. When Romeo went to her, he found her body lying like a rag doll in the ditch on the other side of the road. She was barely conscious. The frightened dog continued running, leaping over a fence and disappearing into the next field. Out of the corner of his eye, Romeo observed that the dog had a leash trailing behind it.

Earlier that same morning, Dean Pelletier awoke as usual to begin training and grooming the show dogs boarded at his kennels. When he was done at about 7:15 a.m., he prepared to take his own Doberman, "Shadow," on a morning walk. Shadow was highly excitable and had never been a well-disciplined dog in spite of Dean's best efforts. A client drove up to the kennel gates just as Dean had finished attaching Shadow's leash. Dean dropped Shadow's leash for a moment while he opened the gates to let in the car. Shadow took off in a flash. Dean immediately called the local police and set out to find his dog. Constable Chekim found Shadow at 9 a.m., playing in a nearby field. By that time, Chekim was also aware of the motorcycle accident. But Shadow showed nothing that would indicate that he had been hit by a motorcycle. There was, however, one eyewitness to the accident. A retired commercial flight pilot was out early that same morning in his ultralight aircraft. He had been flying low over Pelletier's kennels just as Pelletier was preparing to take Shadow on his morning walk. He saw the dog flee and followed its path. From his plane, he saw the dog shoot out from the ditch and across the path of Romeo's motorcycle. The pilot could not be certain whether the bike had actually hit the dog.

The doctors who set Juliet's broken hands and wrists and tended to her broken ribs said that it was the leather gear and full-face helmet that saved her from the most gruesome of motorcycle injuries. Judging by the way she fell face first, the helmet had saved Juliet from severe facial injuries. Even so, she must take six months off work and may never be able to use her hands with ease again. As a self-employed writer, she stands to lose the career of her dreams. Moreover, to meet her mortgage payments and therapeutic needs, Juliet estimates she requires $20,000 in the short term.

Identify the relevant facts

1. List the key **people** involved and provide a short description for each person.

Juliet – free lance writer

Romeo –

Pelletier – Dog owner Kennel

Piolet - Key witness

Officer – Timing

Assess the significance of the events that took place

1. What complaints do Romeo and Juliet have against Dean Pelletier? –>

Negligence – (Exercise action or not?)

careless.

Need to know state of law as it is today and how does it apply

2. List only those **actions, places,** or **objects** that might be used to support these complaints.

Hwy Act

Negligence Act.

Dog Owner Liability Act

Kennel Act

Issues –> in form of Question –

Was Romeo negligent - in the way he or contributed. –

Who is liable - Did Peltier liable – for Action of doberman

Is there a limitation – What is the standard of negligence with kennel operators.

Find out about Romeo -

3. What facts might Dean Pelletier rely upon to excuse what happened?

ASSESS THE SIGNIFICANCE OF THE FACTS

Lawyers learn to focus on the essential facts. These are the facts relevant to the legal problem at hand. These "key" facts are called "material" or "determinative" facts. Being able to summarize the "material facts" or essential information in a few lines is an important skill.

The material facts tell a cold story — one that may exclude background information required to appreciate the circumstances of a particular problem or dispute. For this reason, lawyers also identify "background" or "mitigating facts." These facts shade or colour the appreciation of the main events and circumstances.

Other times, the material facts may not include all the information required to solve the problem. Facts that help to formulate a solution or remedy are known as "remedial facts." For example, in a case where financial compensation is sought for an injury, the cost of care may not be relevant or "material" to the story about how the injury occurred. This information is an important detail, however, and probably relevant to a court's assessment of damages. Similarly, information about family circumstances or patterns of behaviour may be important details that a court might take into consideration in sentencing. Learning to identify relevant background and remedial facts is an important skill.

EXERCISE 5   Remedial facts

Based on the problem you have just read in exercise 4, list any remedial facts that might be important to Juliet's case.

_____

_____

_____

_____

_____

IDENTIFY THE RELEVANT LEGAL ISSUES

Once a lawyer understands what has happened, the next step is to determine the nature of the legal problem and the legal questions to be answered. The identification of the legal questions or issues raised by a particular set of circumstances provides an outline for researching the problem (see researching skills in chapter 2). In addition, just as the research lends further insight into the relevant legal issues, so too the statement of legal issues clarifies the essential or material facts. Once the legal issues have been identified, you may have to revise your assessment of the important facts.

The following steps outline one way to identify legal issues.

Step 1   Identify the problem

One method of determining the legal issues raised in a problem is to identify the **general question(s)** that must be answered in order to resolve the problem or dispute. You have practised identifying these general questions in the preceding exercises. The next step is to determine whether the general question is one that raises a **legal question or issue**.

For example:

- A driver collides with a cyclist. The problem is that the cyclist wants to recover the costs of damages and injuries sustained. This problem raises general questions about who is at fault and who is responsible for the injuries or damages. The general questions also raise legal questions about a driver's responsibility to act carefully toward others on the road.

- A businessperson decides to cancel an order of eggs and not to pay for the shipment already on its way. The cancellation causes a problem for the supplier who has already incurred the costs to deliver the eggs. The problem raises general questions about who should pay for the egg order. This general question raises legal questions about one party's contractual obligation to another.

- A restaurant owner has advertised his grand opening as featuring his trademark blueberry pancake brunch. On the morning of the opening, the restauranteur went to the supermarket to buy fresh blueberries. The blueberry shipment was delayed and the supermarket had none in stock. The restauranteur had no choice but to endure the embarrassment and cost of rescheduling the opening. Now, the restauranteur wants to sue the blueberry supplier for failing to deliver the blueberries to the supermarket.

    The problem raises general questions about whether the blueberry supplier is responsible for the restauranteur's misfortunes. Certainly, one feels sorry for the restauranteur. Unfortunately, the supermarket makes no guarantees regarding its inventory. Furthermore, there is no direct legal relationship between the berry supplier and the restaurant owner. In the absence of such a relationship, the restauranteur has no legal claims on the berry supplier. Although the situation raises general questions about what should have happened, the questions are not legal ones. It is important to remember that not all problems are legal problems, and that not all wrongs have a legal solution or remedy.

Legal questions or issues identify those problems that may be resolved through legal means. A court may hear such problems, and the remedy or solution may be found in legislation, regulation, case law, or precedent. These types of problems are said to have "legal merit" or to be "justiciable." Courts will not rule on problems that are without "legal merit."

Step 2 Isolate the governing legal principles or doctrines, and categorize the area of law

Law is best understood as a tapestry of legal doctrines and concepts that act as bridges toward the resolution of problems and disputes. Identifying the central legal problem is the first step in assessing the applicable primary legal doctrines or concepts. The next step is to categorize the nature of the legal problem to determine which category of law governs the doctrines or concepts.

For example, when a problem involves an individual's duty to be careful toward another, legal issues relevant to the legal doctrine of "duty of care" are raised in circumstances where there is a question of wrongdoing. This legal doctrine can only be appreciated and applied fully when the category of law governing the situation is identified. For this reason, it may be necessary to revisit the material facts to identify the appropriate category of law.

In exercise 4, the "duty of care" implied is a specific legal concept or "legal term of art" that falls under the legal category of tort law. Under tort law, the "duty of care" triggers a specific analytical framework that outlines a series of questions to be followed in solving the legal problem. (See figure 1.1.) The framework provides a methodology for assessing the parameters of an individual's legal responsibility toward others. Chapters 2 and 3 outline the skills used to research legal terms of art and to identify the applicable methodology.

Primarily, legal problems fall into broad categories of law. Figure 1.2 identifies these basic categories and some of their main subcategories.

FIGURE 1.1 LEGAL DOCTRINES: THE BRIDGE BETWEEN PROBLEMS AND THEIR LEGAL SOLUTIONS

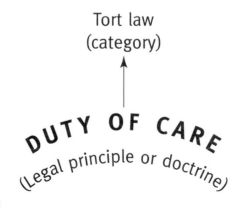

Tort law
(category)

DUTY OF CARE
(Legal principle or doctrine)

Situation:
Driver collides
with a cyclist

General problem:
Who is at fault;
who is responsible

FIGURE 1.2 CATEGORIES OF LAW

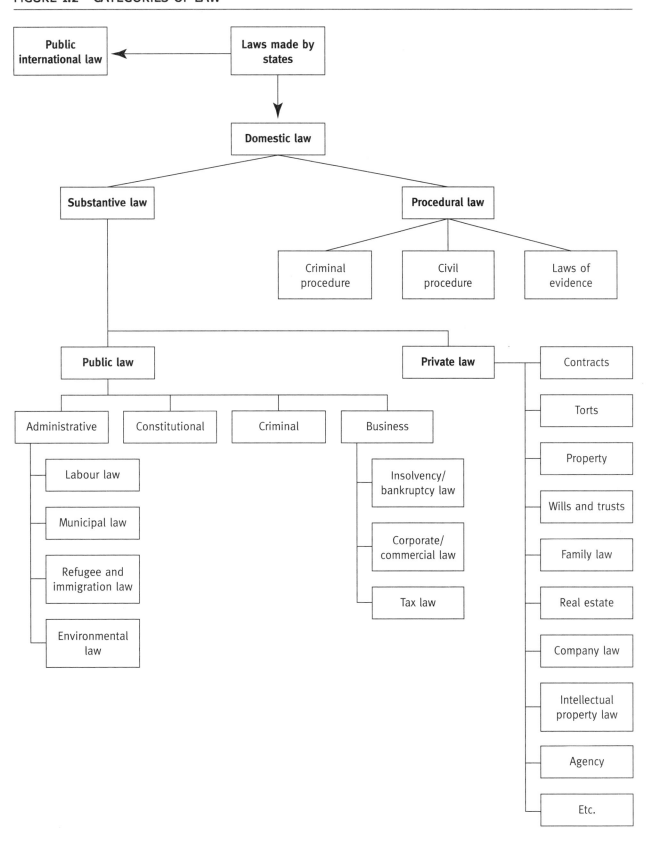

EXERCISE 6   *Higgs v. City School*

Material facts

Ben Higgs has dislocated his hip. A classmate (Taylor) came up behind Ben Higgs, lifted him off his feet, carried him a distance of about 20 feet and dropped him on a patch of ice on the schoolyard of the City School.

There were four teachers outside on duty supervising the break period. None of the teachers saw the incident or knew anything about it until some of the other students told Mr. Herlick. Mr. Herlick ran across the ice and reached Ben before he had a chance to get up.

Ben was in tears, but refused Mr. Herlick's assistance and refused to see the school nurse. Mr. Herlick helped him up and escorted him into the classroom. He insisted that Ben go to see the school nurse. The nurse treated Ben quickly, finding his injuries to be superficial. Later, Ben's parents took him to the family doctor. X-rays taken by the family physician confirmed that the boy's hipbone was dislocated.

Remedial facts

The doctor found that the injury sustained was not caused entirely when Taylor dropped Ben on the ice. In her opinion, most of the injuries were caused when Ben walked on his leg. The weight on his leg was likely to have caused the more severe condition that required hospitalization.

Demonstration

Assess the relevant facts

1. Identify the key facts.

    a. Key people and institutions:

        The City School — school that Higgs attends

        Ben Higgs — injured student

        Mr. Herlick — teacher

        Taylor — student who dropped Higgs

    b. Event:

        Ben Higgs was injured when another student picked him up and dropped him while playing in the schoolyard.

    c. Place:

        Schoolyard of the City School.

    d. Object:

        No objects were involved.

Assess the relevant legal issues

2. Identify the problem.

   Ben sustained injuries for which he wants compensation.

3. Identify the general questions:

   a. Is anyone or anything responsible for Ben's injuries?

   b. If so, who or what caused the injuries?

   c. To what remedy, if any, is Ben entitled?

4. Isolate the governing legal principles or doctrines.

   This problem raises questions about the legal principle of one's responsibility to another.

   At this point, a lawyer needs to know what legal terminology or "term of art" best expresses the concept of responsibility raised in this problem. To express this precisely, it is often necessary to identify the area of applicable law.

   (Chapter 2 explains how to research legal terms of art and categorize legal problems. See especially sections on *Library of Congress Catalogues*, legal dictionaries, and the *Canadian Encyclopedic Digest* for examples).

5. Categorize the area of law.

   This type of responsibility or "duty" falls into the category of tort law. The concept of "duty" in tort law is expressed as "duty of care."

6. Frame the problem as a series of questions that must be answered to resolve the problem. There are several questions that might be asked to determine who is responsible for Ben's injuries, for example:

   Is Taylor responsible?

   Is Mr. Herlick responsible?

   Is the City School responsible?

   Is Ben responsible?

   AND,

   If the school or Mr. Herlick or Taylor are responsible for Ben's injuries, did Ben contribute to his own injuries when he refused assistance and insisted on walking to the school?

   AND,

   Are schools generally responsible for accidents that occur on their property?

   If so, did the school take proper precautions to prevent such an accident from occurring?

   Such a preliminary assessment of the important facts and legal issues is important research preparation. Note that legal questions may break down into several legal issues. Keep in mind that you will refine and reorganize the legal questions in a manner that reflects the analytical approach courts have used to address similar problems. Research will help to confirm the material facts, any background or remedial facts, as well as the relevant legal issues.

EXERCISE 7 Mr. Kuresh

Mr. Mori Kuresh was born on August 2, 1954. He is a citizen of the former state of "Pann." He entered Canada on October 5, 1990 and was recognized as a "Convention refugee" by the Refugee Division of the Immigration and Refugee Board on April 10, 1991.

The neighbouring state of "Neverland" invaded Pann in 1989 and began oil exploration on sacred Pann burial grounds. To suppress resistance, the authorities of Neverland require all religious and cultural activity in Pann to operate under a licence. Few licences are granted. In addition, Pann artists and religious leaders are imprisoned and tortured frequently. Before coming to Canada, Mr. Kuresh was a well-known journalist in Pann. Upon his arrival in Canada, he sought out members of the Canadian Pann community who assisted him in his adjustment to Canadian life. In the summer of 1991, Mr. Kuresh applied for landing in Canada under the provisions of the *Immigration Act*, which allow recognized Convention refugees to apply for permanent residence status.

Shortly after his arrival in Canada, Mr. Kuresh began working with the International Pann Movement (IPM), and eventually became the fundraising coordinator for that organization. He also acted as a coordinator for a cultural community centre for Pann-Canadians. He held these positions until his detention by Canadian immigration authorities on September 18, 1995.

The Canadian Security Intelligence Service (CSIS) monitors terrorist groups in Canada. CSIS alleges that the IPM operates in Canada as a front organization for the Freedom Fighters of Pann (FFP). In that role, IPM exists for the purpose of fundraising, propaganda, and procurement of material on behalf of FFP. FFP is an organization alleged to engage in terrorist activities against Neverland and surrounding countries. CSIS alleges that Mr. Kuresh is a high-ranking member of the FFP in contact with the international leadership of the FFP, collects funds on behalf of the FFP in North America, and procures FFP materials, some of which may have military application.

On the basis of CSIS allegations, the solicitor general of Canada and the minister of citizenship and immigration completed a certificate alleging that Mr. Kuresh is inadmissible to Canada on security grounds under s. 40.1 of the *Immigration Act*. They claim that Mr. Kuresh obtained refugee status "by wilful misrepresentation of facts" and lacks credibility. This certificate prevented the finalization of Mr. Kuresh's application for landing status in Canada on the grounds that Mr. Kuresh fell into three of the inadmissible classes found within s. 19 of the *Immigration Act*, which states:

— clause 19(1)(e)(iv)(C), "persons who there are reasonable grounds to believe are members of an organization that there are reasonable grounds to believe will engage in terrorism";
— subparagraph 19(1)(f)(ii), "persons who there are reasonable grounds to believe have engaged in terrorism"; and
— clause 19(1)(f)(iii)(B), "persons who there are reasonable grounds to believe are or were members of an organization that there are reasonable grounds to believe is or was engaged in terrorism."

Mr. Kuresh denies membership in FFP and the allegations that he was involved in terrorist activities before coming to Canada and that he obtained refugee status by misrepresenting his situation to Canada authorities.

Identify the relevant facts

1. List the key **people** and provide a description for each person.

_____

_____

_____

_____

_____

_____

_____

2. Identify the **actions, objects,** or **places** relevant to Mr. Kuresh's claims.

_____

_____

_____

_____

_____

_____

_____

_____

_____

_____

Identify the relevant legal issues

1. List the complaints the Canadian authorities have against Mr. Kuresh.

   _____

   _____

   _____

   _____

   _____

2. What legal principles or doctrines are likely to apply to such complaints?

   _____

   _____

3. What category of law is likely to apply?

   _____

   _____

4. What are the relevant legal questions or issues?

   _____

   _____

   _____

   _____

5. What facts might provide important background or remedial information relevant to the legal issues raised?

   _____

   _____

   _____

   _____

   _____

EXERCISE 8 Mr. Fuentes and Steel & Wheels Inc.

Mario Fuentes became a Canadian employee of Steel & Wheels Inc. in 1961. He began as an engineer and was soon promoted to chief engineer. He retired as vice-president of production in April 30, 1987. Mr. Fuentes was eligible to participate in the company's pension plan. He was enrolled in the company pension fund in 1962. He has received pension benefits from the company pension fund since 1987.

In 1943, Steel & Wheels Inc. created a pension fund for certain of its employees and agents to be administered pursuant to a certain plan. The plan called for contributions to be made by member employees and by Steel & Wheels Inc. These contributions were to form part of the pension fund used to provide pension benefits to the member employees or their designated beneficiaries upon termination of employment, retirement, or death. By way of a written trust deed dated July 1, 1971, Steel & Wheels Inc. transferred the pension fund to three trustees who were to administer the fund and reserves in accordance with the terms of the trust deed and the terms of the pension plan as amended from time to time. The trustees were the Bank of Manitoba; Smith, Jones and Barley Securities; and the Global Manager's Fund Group.

Subsequently, the trustees charged with administering the fund have been replaced from time to time, and the terms of the trust deed and the plan have been amended. On April 24, 1973, Steel & Wheels Inc. amended the plan so that s. 30 provided:

> Subsequent to the date at which payments of annuity or disability benefits commence, increments in such payments in the form of annuity elected, if applicable, will be granted not more frequently than annually. For payments that commenced prior to January 1, 1973, the aforesaid increments will be effective with the first payment in 1973 and every April thereafter. For payments commencing after December 31, 1972 such increments will commence with the payment received in April subsequent to the month of retirement and will be effective yearly thereafter.
>
> The amount of the aforesaid increments shall be as the Company may from time to time determine and will be related to the investment performance of the Steel & Wheels Inc. Assurance Company Canadian Employees' Pension Fund.

On October 23, 1990, Steel & Wheels Inc. amended the plan, deleting the indexing provisions found in s. 30 and replacing them with provisions under which Steel & Wheels Inc. provided itself with the right to exercise complete and total discretion with regard to the calculation of pension increments. There was no express reference to the increments being related to the investment performance of the fund. On December 1, 1993, Steel & Wheels Inc. again amended the plan to provide that the maximum amount of allowable pension increments was to be tied to the Consumer Price Index as published by Statistics Canada.

Mr. Fuentes believes that, as a result of these amendments, he is not receiving the benefits to which he is entitled under the pension plan. He claims that Steel & Wheels should have been paying annual increments based on the investment performance of the pension fund to those employees who started with the company after December 31, 1943 and retired between January 1, 1982 and October 22, 1990. Under the new scheme, Steel & Wheels has failed to pay these annual increments.

Another method of identifying the relevant facts is to identify the key facts according to the legal issues raised. This time, identify the legal issues first. Assess the facts that are material, background, or remedial based on whether the information is required to answer the legal questions raised.

Identify the relevant issues

1. List the complaints Mr. Fuentes has against Steel & Wheels.

_____

_____

_____

_____

_____

_____

2. What legal principles or doctrines are likely to apply?

_____

_____

3. What category of law is likely to apply?

_____

_____

4. What are the relevant legal issues?

_____

_____

_____

_____

_____

_____

Identify the relevant facts

1. List, by name, each of the key **people** and provide a description for each.

_____

_____

_____

_____

2. Identify the **actions, objects,** or **places** relevant to Mr. Fuentes's claims.

_____

_____

_____

_____

_____

_____

_____

_____

_____

_____

_____

3. What facts might provide important background or remedial information relevant to any of the legal issues raised?

_____

_____

_____

_____

EXERCISE 9   Rucz family

As a young boy, Aaron Rucz had two dreams: he wanted to become a dentist and to live in the west. A citizen of Romania, he completed high school, attended technical school for a year, and then attended medical school. In Romania, a dentist must first qualify as a medical doctor and then as a dentist. Mr. Rucz practised dentistry in Romania from 1973 to 1977. He met Helen Lutka, also a Romanian citizen, in December 1972 at the university coffee shop while he was completing his internship in medicine. She told him of her family's plans to move to Israel later that year. Although she would soon be moving away, Mr. Rucz courted her. As planned, Ms Lutka moved from Romania to Israel with her family, where she obtained employment as a draftsperson. She earned the sum of 1,800 Israeli new shekels (ILS) per month in 1977.

From June 1973 to November 1976, Mr. Rucz travelled from Israel to Romania every six months to visit Helen. They both petitioned the appropriate authorities on several occasions for permission to marry, as was then required by Romanian law. On six separate occasions their petitions were denied. Helen lobbied tirelessly to obtain the necessary permission, which they received finally in August 1976. The couple was married in Bucharest on November 17, 1976. Two weeks later, Helen returned to her home in Israel. Four months later, having received permission to emigrate from Romania, Aaron joined his wife in Israel under her sponsorship.

Within three months of his arrival in Israel in May 1977, he decided unilaterally to leave that country. He found out that if he became a citizen of Israel, it would be impossible for him to claim refugee status for the purpose of emigrating to a western country. He had learned that the only likely way of emigrating to the west quickly was to become a voluntary intern in a refugee camp for an unspecified period of time. He also learned that couples with children often received easier entry into western countries. In August 1977, he left Israel for Greece, leaving Helen behind. She remained in Israel for approximately one month, during which time she settled her financial affairs. She then resigned a tenured position, which she held at the University of Negev, and joined Aaron in Greece. She became pregnant a few months later. They lived in a refugee camp in Greece for approximately nine months. Late in May 1978 they arrived in Toronto, and on August 20, 1978 their son was born.

After they arrived in Toronto, Aaron needed to become proficient in English in order to obtain a licence to practise dentistry. For one year, he took intensive English classes while Helen went to work. On weekends and evenings, Aaron worked as a dishwasher and a waiter. Helen took jobs on the assembly line in a factory, as a beautician in her home, and as a hairdresser. In 1979 Aaron obtained employment at a dental lab, and in December of that year he was employed at the Toronto General Hospital Dental Clinic at a salary of $18,000 per annum. During this time he continued his efforts toward passing examinations to obtain his licence to practise dentistry in Ontario. He succeeded in obtaining his licence in May 1981. Although the family was poor and without assets, they believed the dental licence opened a door to a brighter future.

Two days after Mr. Rucz was notified that he was qualified to practise dentistry in Canada, he informed his wife that he wanted a divorce. In negotiating a settlement, Ms Rucz claims that the dental licence is property into which both she and her husband paid.

Identify the relevant issues

1. List the complaints Mrs. Rucz has against her husband.

_____

_____

_____

_____

2. What legal principles or doctrines are likely to apply?

_____

_____

3. What category of law is likely to apply?

_____

_____

4. What are the relevant legal issues?

_____

_____

_____

_____

Identify the relevant facts

1. List, by name, each of the key **people** and provide a description for each.

_____

_____

_____

_____

2. Identify the **actions, objects,** or **places** relevant to the legal issues raised in this dispute.

_____

_____

_____

_____

_____

_____

_____

3. What facts might provide important background or remedial information relevant to any of the legal issues raised?

_____

_____

_____

REFERENCES

The Business Corporations Act, RSS 1978, c. B-10.

Canadian Encyclopedic Digest (Scarborough, ON: Carswell), available in book form and CD-ROM.

Immigration Act, RSC 1985, c. I-2.

Intestate Succession Act, RSA 1980, c. I-9.

Library of Congress Subject Headings, 23rd edition (Washington, DC: Library of Congress Cataloguing Distribution Service, 2000).

Research skills: How to find the applicable laws

INTRODUCTION: HOW TO RESEARCH A LEGAL PROBLEM

Lawyers must be experienced researchers. Expertise lies in knowing how to analyze problems and how to find information relevant to a solution. Above all else, legal research must be timely, accurate, and comprehensive. Following a research checklist guarantees that all the relevant resources are checked and that the research is up to date. As a guide, the checklist serves as a helpful reminder of how to begin research in a new or unfamiliar area of law. The checklist below provides a methodology for researching a problem. It may not always be necessary to follow every step outlined here; however, the steps are a good reminder of the materials that should be consulted.

THE RESEARCH CHECKLIST

Define the research area

IDENTIFY SEARCH TERMS   Step 1

Think about the main questions raised in the problem. Then make a list of the key words and concepts. These words can be used as "search terms" to research the problem and to find the relevant law, or the law "on point."

CHECK SEARCH TERMS WITH THE LIBRARY OF CONGRESS   Step 2
SUBJECT HEADINGS

Ensure that the search terms will produce results. Check the key words and concepts you have identified against the list of searchable terms found in the *Library of Congress Catalogues*, a multivolume, cataloguing system.

In hard copy, these catalogues comprise five volumes of alphabetically arranged library search terms. The catalogue may also be accessed online through the computer cataloguing systems of most law libraries. The catalogue lists common legal terms and their synonyms. The synonyms are ranked according to their proximity to the original term. Abbreviations are used to indicate the utility of various synonyms. For example:

UF = used for

BT = broader term

RT = related term

SA = see also

NT = narrower term

The symbol "**May Subd Georg**" means that place names may follow the heading.

Sources of research

There are primary and secondary sources of research. In legal research, primary sources comprise those documents (cases and legislation) that have legal force and effect. Primary sources have the force of law. Documents that have the potential to affect parties' legal rights and obligations directly are said to be "legally binding." It is true, however, that while some sources of law are binding, others are merely "persuasive." The difference between the two is the extent to which the rule or principle in question must be strictly applied or followed.

Secondary sources are all the "other" legal resources from which no legal right or obligation results. Although these documents have no direct legal impact, they may help to clarify, interpret, and comment on the law. Secondary sources may be encyclopedic summaries of the law or publications of opinion (such as academic commentary and critique, including textbooks, journal articles, newspaper reports, and case comments). For this reason, secondary sources are not legally binding, but the information or opinion expressed may have persuasive value or offer insight into potential legal arguments, questions, or issues.

Secondary sources are an excellent starting point for research because they provide an overview or synopsis of a legal area or subject. Often, secondary sources present the researcher with not only a useful synopsis of the law, but also a list of the most relevant primary sources.

Step 3

SECONDARY SOURCES: STARTING POINT FOR RESEARCH

Some useful secondary source materials are:

- case digests
- law digests
- legal periodicals
- looseleaf services
- conference and seminar materials
- law reform commission reports
- textbooks
- legal dictionaries

PRIMARY SOURCES: RESEARCHING THE LAW

Once a legal area is identified, then the primary sources of law — legislation and cases — can be researched. Use the summary below as a reminder of the steps to ensure thorough, complete, and up-to-date research results.

Binding legislation

Step 4

Make sure that you have identified all the relevant and applicable federal, provincial, or municipal legislation.

- Determine whether any **provincial** statutes govern over the problem.
- Determine whether any **federal** statutes govern over the problem.

Update the legislation

Step 5

Update the relevant sections of the Act to check whether there have been any recent changes in language, amendments, or repeals that may affect the problem.

- Check to see if there is any pending legislation that, if adopted and brought into force, would change how the law applies to the problem at hand.
- Updating the legislation is often called "noting up" the legislation.

Trace back the legislation

Step 6

Trace back the section of the legislation to its original enactment date.

- Make a note of all the previous versions of the section.
- Look up each of these citations to see how the courts have interpreted the section and developed the law over time.
- Tracing back the legislation is commonly called "backdating" the legislation.

Legislation judicially considered

Step 7

Find out how the courts have applied the legislation.

- If there are statutory provisions that govern over the problem, check to see how the courts have applied these provisions in previous, relevant cases.
- If there are cases in which the courts have looked at these statutory provisions, be sure to find the most recent cases.
- Assess the significance of precedent cases. Check to see whether these cases have been appealed to a higher court level or considered in subsequent cases by the same or different courts.

Binding cases

Step 8

Make sure that you have identified all the relevant, applicable case law. To ensure that you have found all the relevant cases:

- Do a topic search in the relevant abridgment or digest series.
- Complete a "words and phrases" search.

Step 9	**Update the case law**
	If you find a relevant case, update the case to check whether it has been appealed.

Step 10	**Cases judicially considered**
	Assess the persuasiveness of the case law.

- For each relevant case, find out how the courts have applied this case in subsequent cases.
- Update any cases that have judicially considered the primary case.

Step 1   Define the search

Chapter 1 demonstrates how to identify key words, concepts, and legal issues. Key words and concepts establish the initial parameters for research by helping to identify possible search terms. For the best results, ensure that search terms used in research correspond to those used by libraries and other cataloguing and indexing services.

Step 2 Check search terms with the Library of Congress subject headings

EXERCISE 1

Find a list of synonyms from the Library of Congress subject headings for the following key words and legal concepts.

Example:

1. Find relevant Library of Congress terms to research the legal concept of "responsibility."

   Method: Look up "responsibility" in the catalogue.

   Answer: For: responsibility, criminal   Use "criminal liability"

   For: responsibility, legal   Use "liability"

   Other relevant synonyms: accountability, obligation, ethics, duty

2. Find relevant Library of Congress terms to research family law.

   _____

   _____

3. Find relevant Library of Congress terms to research the legal concept of "restraint of trade."

   _____

   _____

4. Find relevant Library of Congress terms to research the legal concept of "deportation."

   _____

   _____

5. Find relevant Library of Congress terms to research the legal concept of "divorce."

   _____

   _____

6. Find relevant Library of Congress terms to research the legal concept of "equality."

   _____

   _____

THE LAW WORKBOOK: Developing skills for legal research and writing

Step 3   Check secondary sources

Check secondary sources for an overview of the applicable area(s) of law. Some of the more commonly used sources of secondary research are described below.

Digests

Legal digests are legal summaries. There are two types of digesting services provided by the major legal publishers in Canada: the case digests and the law digests.

CASE DIGESTS

Case digests provide a series of case summaries on points of law. The best examples of Canadian case digests are the main volumes of the *Canadian Abridgment*. The *Canadian Abridgment* is one of the most popular and most useful research tools in Canada. It is an encyclopedic tool that offers a series of different services, among which the case digesting volumes are central. These digests may also be found online or in CD-ROM form.

LAW DIGESTS

Law digests provide a series of summaries on a particular area of law. The best example is the *Canadian Encyclopedic Digest* (CED). The *Canadian Encyclopedic Digest* is a looseleaf, multivolume binder service that contains statements on the status of law in about 159 legal subjects. The binders are organized alphabetically by subject and by title.

There are two CEDs, one for Ontario law known as the CED (Ont. 3rd), which focuses on Ontario and federal law, and one for the law of the western provinces known as the CED (West 3rd), which focuses on the law in the four western provinces and incorporates the law from the territories as well as important federal laws. Both CEDs also cite decisions from other common law provinces, the United Kingdom, and other jurisdictions relevant to a particular subject matter. Since the CED is a looseleaf service, new legal developments are incorporated on a regular basis to keep the digest up to date. The CED is also available on CD-ROM.

Legal periodicals

Legal periodicals contain academic and often critical writing on areas of law, cases, legislation, or books and treatises. There are two broad categories of legal periodicals: general and topical. Many legal periodicals may be searched using both print and online catalogues.

As with all secondary source material, periodical literature is not "binding"; however, it may be used as "persuasive authority." The degree of persuasiveness will depend on the subject matter covered, the reputation of the writer, the relevance of the critique, and the timeliness of the examination.

Do not assume that a periodical or article contains an exhaustive reference to all the governing cases or relevant legislation. Authors are likely to highlight only the most germane and significant primary sources of law. Similarly, the research should not rely solely on another author's analysis or interpretation of a particular legal matter. Most legal articles are written from a particular perspective and with a particular purpose. Always read the primary sources of research.

Looseleaf services

Looseleaf services are legal research tools that are published in binder form so that they may be updated regularly. Their currency makes them an ideal researching tool.

Not all looseleaf services are organized in the same way. Depending on the publisher, the binder services may have different internal accessing and referencing steps. Most looseleaf services contain an easy-to-use index or table of contents, as well as an instruction guide on how the service is organized.

To determine the currency of the looseleaf inserts, look at the bottom of the page inserted. The information on the page will be accurate and current to the date on the page. As for the looseleaf service as a whole, the binder will have a time-stamp somewhere on the first few pages indicating when the entire looseleaf binder was last updated.

Conference and seminar materials

Groups, organizations, and schools that hold conferences or conventions will sometimes record and publish their materials. These publications often include helpful summaries of specific and topical areas of law. Conference, seminar, and convention publications may provide helpful legal synopses, and are often written by legal experts. To access such material, search for it as you would any other secondary source material, using one of the bibliographies or indices to secondary source material, such as the *Canadian Abridgment's Index to Canadian Legal Literature*, also available in both print and online versions.

Law reform commission reports

Law reform commissions are independent legal bodies that tackle areas in need of legal attention or reform. Their work is usually of an investigative nature and published in committee reports of findings and recommendations. These reports can be useful because they set out the status of the law, what areas need attention or reform, and the process by which reforms should be initiated and carried out. Access law reform commission reports in the same way as any other secondary source literature.

Textbooks

A textbook provides the reader with a more in-depth coverage of an area of law (rather than the "snapshots" that are provided by law reviews and legal periodicals).

Legal dictionaries

There are a number of legal dictionaries, among which *Black's Law Dictionary* and *Osborn's Legal Dictionary* are the most commonly used. A legal dictionary works like any dictionary, providing definitions for commonly used legal phrases, concepts, and expressions. "Words and phrases" guides work in the same way, and also show how certain terms and phrases have been judicially considered.

The following exercises introduce the secondary sources of research.

EXERCISE 2

Use the *Canadian Encyclopedic Digest* to answer the following questions.

Example:

1. What is the purpose of bankruptcy legislation?

   Method: Go directly to the binder or online service of the *Canadian Encyclopedic Digest* (CED) in the law library. Use the Index Volume (or online tables) to examine how subjects and topics are broken down. Find the section that deals with "Bankruptcy" and note the volume number of the CED that contains this topic. The volumes are organized alphabetically, according to subject heading. Use the table of contents, available for each subject, to find the appropriate paragraph. Note that the table of contents refers to sections, using the symbol "§" and not page numbers. There are also tables, such as the Table of Statutes, that direct you to discussions of specific legislation.

   Answer: *"One of the purposes of the Act [bankruptcy legislation] is to permit an honest but unfortunate debtor to obtain a discharge from his or her debts, subject to reasonable conditions. The Act [bankruptcy legislation] was also passed to provide for the orderly and fair distribution of the property of a bankrupt among his or her creditors on a pari passu basis."*

2. Define the term "insolvency."

   _____

   _____

   _____

   _____

   _____

   _____

3. Define the tort of defamation.

   _____

   _____

   _____

   _____

   _____

   _____

4. What is the difference between libel and slander?

_____

_____

_____

_____

_____

_____

_____

5. What are some of the most common prohibited narcotics according to the *Narcotics Control Act*?

_____

_____

_____

_____

_____

_____

_____

6. Provide the name and chapter of a statute that defines "trafficking" and "selling" of controlled drugs and substances.

_____

_____

_____

_____

_____

_____

EXERCISE 3

Use the *Index to Canadian Legal Periodicals* or *Canadian Legal Literature* to answer the following questions. You may use either the bound copy or the online version.

Example:

1. Cite a 1982 article dealing with derivative works in Canadian copyright law.

   Method: Alphabetically organized and presented in annual volumes, the *Index to Canadian Legal Periodicals* is arranged so that the information may be searched in five ways: by subject index, by author index, by book review index, by a table of cases, and by a table of statutes.

   Identify the key words that define the search. Use the facts of the problem or case to isolate broad categories. Use these categories to narrow down the search. For example, in the sample question above, knowing the date helps to narrow the search to a particular year. "Article" indicates that you want to find an article, and not a case or statute. "Canadian copyright law" tells you the area of law of interest; "derivative works" tells you more about the particular kind of article for which you might be looking.

   We looked in the 1982 volume under the subject index "Canadian copyright law" for articles written about derivative works. The full name of the periodical is given in the table of periodical names at the front of the book.

   Answer: W.J. Braithwaite, "Derivative Works in Canadian Copyright Law" (1982-83), 7 CBLJ 191.

   (CBLJ = Canadian Business Law Journal)

2. Cite a 1983 article dealing with professional education and the university.

   _____

   _____

3. Cite a 1986 article written by Clayton Ruby that deals with sentencing.

   _____

   _____

4. Cite a 1987 article by J.G. Kirkpatrick on the subject of the role of the trustee under a trust deed in Quebec civil law.

   _____

   _____

5. Which 1990 article was authored by Constance Backhouse?

   _____

   _____

6. Cite a 1999 article on the subject of gender and judicial appointments.

_____

_____

7. Cite a 1990 article dealing with the early years of former Chief Justice Bora Laskin.

_____

_____

8. Cite a 1991 article on the Saskatchewan *Representation Act*.

_____

_____

9. Find an article that appeared in 2000 on protecting aboriginal folklore.

_____

_____

10. Cite a 1988 article on Meech Lake that discusses the concepts of "distinct society" and "identity."

_____

_____

EXERCISE 4

Use the legal dictionaries to define the following terms. Cite the legal dictionary used.

Example:

1. *Caveat emptor*:

   Answer: "Let the buyer beware." <u>Black's Law Dictionary</u> also explains the rule: "This maxim summarizes the legal rule that a purchaser must examine, judge, and test for himself or herself."

   From: B.A. Garner, ed., <u>Black's Law Dictionary</u>, 7th ed. (St. Paul, MN: West Group, 1999).

2. *Adverse possession*:

   _____

   _____

   _____

   _____

3. *Consideration*:

   _____

   _____

   _____

   _____

4. *Res ipsa loquitur*:

   _____

   _____

   _____

   _____

5. *Notwithstanding*:

   _____

   _____

   _____

   _____

6. *Bona fide*:

_____

_____

_____

_____

7. *Prima facie*:

_____

_____

_____

_____

8. *Violenti non fit injuria*:

_____

_____

_____

_____

THE LAW WORKBOOK: Developing skills for legal research and writing

Step 4 Check the legislation: Statute research

WHAT IS LEGISLATION?

Legislation is also referred to as an "act," a "statute," or a "statutory instrument."

Act

An act is a piece of legislation that

- is one of the two primary sources of law in a common law system;
- has passed successfully through the "reading" process of either the federal Parliament or the provincial legislatures; and
- is considered legally binding in terms of all its rights and obligations as soon as it comes into force.

Regulation

A regulation is a piece of implementing law that is also referred to as "subordinate legislation" or "delegated legislation."

The term "regulation" is the generic term given to rules, regulations, orders, by-laws, or proclamations made by an authority (governor in council, minister, government department, or judicial or quasi-judicial body) under the terms of an enabling act of either the federal or provincial Parliament.

A regulation derives its powers from its enabling legislation. Where a piece of legislation may set out general objectives to be achieved, a regulation operationalizes those objectives. Regulations are the nuts and bolts of the law. In addition, since regulations are not subject to the same parliamentary "reading" process as legislation, they may be enacted more quickly.

To find the text of a regulation passed pursuant to an act, look up the regulation in the *Consolidated Regulations* volumes that are printed by both the federal and provincial levels of government.

Since regulations are physically located in separate government documents and consolidations (and only general reference is made to them in the empowering act), they may be overlooked easily in research. Since regulations may be replete with enforcement, implementation, and sanctioning details, such an oversight can have disastrous consequences.

Bill

A bill is a piece of legislation in draft form. When a proposed piece of legislation is first tabled before Parliament for debate and reading, it is called a "bill." As it moves through the legislative process, the document has no legal force. A bill becomes law when it receives its final reading and is given royal assent to come into force. It is then known officially as an "act."

To table a bill or a piece of legislation

To "table" a bill before Parliament means to introduce it to the members of the House (or the Senate) for general discussion and debate. Tabling a bill initiates the "reading" process.

Reading legislation: The legislative reading process

To "read" a bill means to examine, discuss, debate, rewrite, and redraft it. Before a bill can progress to the next level of reading, parliament (or the legislature) must vote to accept the bill.

A federal bill must go through three readings in the federal House of Commons and three readings in the federal Senate before becoming a legally binding act. (See figure 2.1.) At the provincial level, a bill is submitted to three readings of the provincial legislature before it becomes legally binding. (See figure 2.2.)

Coming into force

An act becomes legally binding and enforceable when it "comes into force." A bill does not automatically become a legally binding act upon receiving third reading. There are three ways that a bill can be declared official and come into force:

1. *Royal assent*   The statute may provide that the act, or specific sections of it, "come into force upon Royal Assent." If an act is silent as to when it comes into force, the presumption is that it comes into force upon receiving royal assent (the final approval of the Queen or her representative). This presumption is set out in both the federal and provincial interpretation acts. The governor general or the lieutenant governor gives royal assent in a ceremony at which justices and legislative representatives are present. Royal assent is the quickest way that a bill can become an act. Royal assent is official acknowledgment that the bill has passed through the requisite parliamentary reading process.

2. *Specifically designated date*   The statute may provide that the act, or specific sections of it, will come into force on a particular date. For example: "This Act will come into force on September 9, 1998."

3. *Proclamation*   The statute may provide that the act, or specific sections of it, will come into force "on a date to be set by proclamation." Proclamation is the most arduous and involved manner by which a bill, or portions thereof, become a legally binding statute. This is because specific proclamation dates do not appear on the face of the act. Thus if you encounter an act that either in its entirety or in certain provisions states that force and effect is to be "on a day to be set by proclamation," you must do extra research to check for such proclamation.

    Proclamations can be found in: (1) Table of Public Statutes; (2) *Canada Gazette*, part III; or (3) *Canada Statute Citator*.

WHAT IS FEDERAL LEGISLATION?

Legislation that is passed by the federal houses of Parliament is known as federal legislation or as a federal act or statute. There are two houses of the federal Parliament — the House of Commons and the Senate. In most cases, a bill must go through three readings in each House of Parliament before it can be declared "an act."

How does a federal bill become a federal act?

When a document is first brought up for discussion at the federal level, it is usually "tabled" first in the House of Commons; subjected to three readings in that House before being tabled for three readings in the Senate.

Typically, with a few rare exceptions, all bills are tabled, read, and debated and voted upon in the House of Commons before going on to the Senate (where the entire process is repeated). Because most bills are tabled first in the House of Commons, they will have, as part of their title, a "C" designation. For example, Bill C-45, *A Bill Respecting General Amendments to the Criminal Code of Canada.* The "C" indicates that the bill was first tabled in the House of Commons. In the rare instance when a bill is tabled first in the Senate, the bill will have an "S" designation as part of its title. The "S" indicates that the Senate first introduced the bill for reading and debate.

Federal regulations

Federal regulations implement objectives of federal legislation and are adopted pursuant to federal acts.

WHAT IS PROVINCIAL LEGISLATION?

Legislation that is passed by the provincial legislature is known as provincial legislation or as a provincial act or statute. Unlike the federal parliamentary structure in which there are two houses of Parliament, there is only one house at the provincial level. Consequently, for a provincial bill to become a provincial act, it need only go through the three-stage reading process once — in the one provincial legislature.

Provincial acts mirror federal legislation in how they are tabled for debate and how they proceed through first, second, and third reading. Similarly, provincial legislation "comes into force" in one of three ways: by royal assent, by stipulated date, or by proclamation.

Provincial regulations

Provincial regulations implement objectives of provincial legislation and are adopted pursuant to provincial acts.

FIGURE 2.1   PASSAGE OF A BILL THROUGH PARLIAMENT

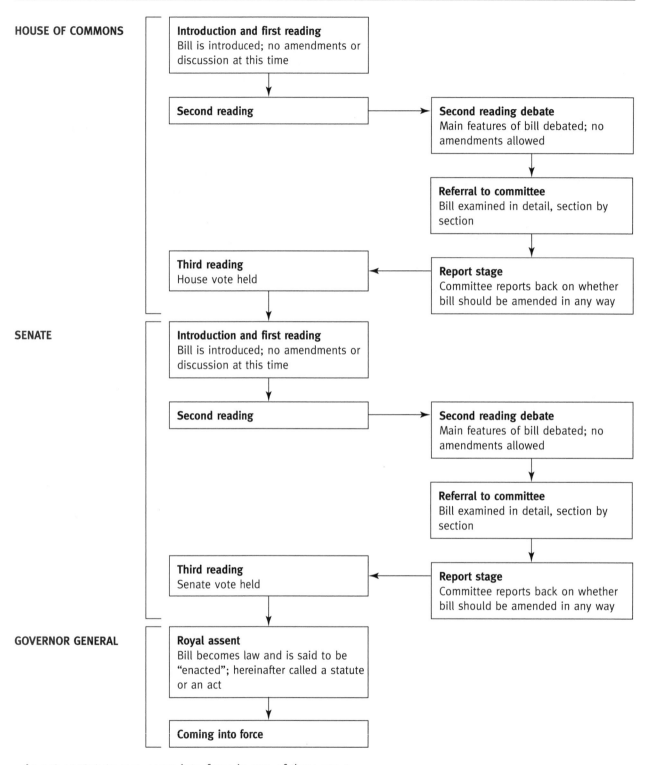

HOUSE OF COMMONS

Introduction and first reading
Bill is introduced; no amendments or discussion at this time

Second reading

Second reading debate
Main features of bill debated; no amendments allowed

Referral to committee
Bill examined in detail, section by section

Third reading
House vote held

Report stage
Committee reports back on whether bill should be amended in any way

SENATE

Introduction and first reading
Bill is introduced; no amendments or discussion at this time

Second reading

Second reading debate
Main features of bill debated; no amendments allowed

Referral to committee
Bill examined in detail, section by section

Third reading
Senate vote held

Report stage
Committee reports back on whether bill should be amended in any way

GOVERNOR GENERAL

Royal assent
Bill becomes law and is said to be "enacted"; hereinafter called a statute or an act

Coming into force

An act or statute may come into force in one of three ways:

1. *Royal assent*   Royal assent brings the act into force; no further steps necessary
2. *Particular date* The act comes into force on a date specified expressly within the text of the statute
3. *Proclamation*   The act comes into force on a date to be announced later (further research will be required, either online or through printed updates)

Note: Different sections of the statute may come into force at different times.

FIGURE 2.2   PASSAGE OF A BILL THROUGH A PROVINCIAL LEGISLATURE   49

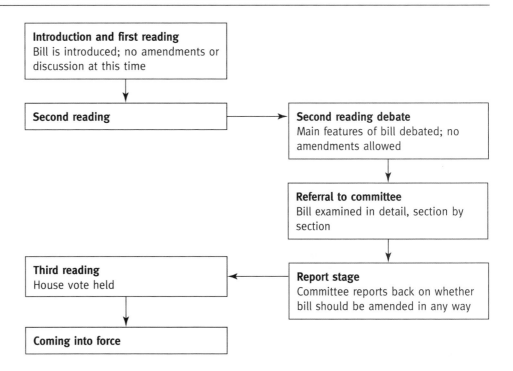

An act or statute may come into force in one of three ways:

1. *Royal assent*   Royal assent brings the act into force; no further steps necessary
2. *Particular date* The act comes into force on a date specified expressly within the text of the statute
3. *Proclamation*   The act comes into force on a date to be announced later (further research will be required, either online or through printed updates)

Note: Different sections of the statute may come into force at different times.

THE PUBLICATION OF STATUTES

The sessional volumes

After each session of Parliament (at both the federal and the provincial levels), the Queen's Printer publishes the full text of all of the acts that were passed during that session. These acts are published officially by chapter number in a sessional (non-cumulative) volume of statutes. Sessionals are designated by year (and there may be situations where there is more than one sitting per year).

In the citation of the act, reference to the sessional volumes is denoted by an "S" (for "statutes"). For example, the sessional Statutes of Ontario are cited as "SO." The sessional Statutes of Canada are cited as "SC."

The revised federal statutes

The sessional statutes of Canada are periodically consolidated (marshalled together, alphabetically organized, edited to incorporate all amendments and repeals to date, indexed, and arranged in an encyclopedic manner). The last time the Federal Revision Commission did this was in 1985. Consequently, the most current consolidation is the *Revised Statutes of Canada*, 1985 (RSC 1985). This series consolidates all public federal statutes still in force as of December 31, 1984.

In the consolidation exercise, the Federal Revision Commission is given "editing" powers to consolidate and to organize all legislation, to alter the numbering and arrangement of acts, to alter any language, to preserve a uniform mode of expression, to make minor clarifications, to harmonize the English and French versions, and to correct grammar.

Once the consolidation exercise is completed, the revised or consolidated acts are proclaimed. The revision thus becomes the definitive version of the federal statutes (subject to any later amendments or repeals made in subsequent sittings of Parliament, which will be denoted by a sessional citation, such as: "as amended by SC 1990, c. H-5)."

Revised provincial statutes

The provincial statutes are also marshalled together, organized alphabetically, and consolidated.

As with its federal counterparts, a Provincial Revision Commission may omit any enactment that is not of general application or is obsolete. It may alter the numbering and arrangement of any act, it may harmonize language and punctuation, and it may clarify and reconcile inconsistent enactments or grammatical errors.

The Provincial Revision Commission prints those acts and their amendments in the form in which they are then in force and omits any acts or parts of acts that have been repealed or that have ceased to be in force.

Once the provincial revision is completed, the revised statutes are brought into force by proclamation and become the definitive version of the statutes (subject to any amendments or repeals made in subsequent sessions of the Legislative Assembly).

The revision is the definitive and authoritative source for the statute. All legislation must be cited to the latest consolidation of the statute.

THE LAW WORKBOOK: Developing skills for legal research and writing

FIGURE 2.3   LEGISLATIVE CITATION

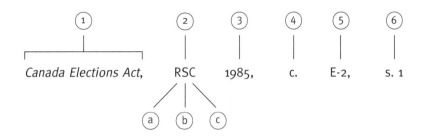

Components of the citation:

(1)   Full title of the act is always in italics. Use the short title when it is given in the statute.

(2)   Name of the statute reporter.

    (a)   R = Revised

    (b)   S = Statutes

    (c)   C = Canada (name of jurisdiction)

(3)   Date of the most recent consolidation.

(4)   Lowercase "c" is the abbreviation of "chapter."

(5)   Chapter abbreviation is followed by the capitalized alphabetical ("E") and numerical ("2") listing of the chapter in the index to the consolidation.

(6)   Lowercase "s." is the abbreviation of "section," followed by the section number. Note: "ss." refers to "sections."

HOW TO CITE A STATUTE

All citation for legislation follows a similar pattern (see figure 2.3 above). For detailed notes on how to cite various types of legislation, refer to proper citation guides such as *The Canadian Guide to Uniform Legal Citation*, often called the *McGill Guide*.

FIGURE 2.4   HOW TO READ A STATUTE

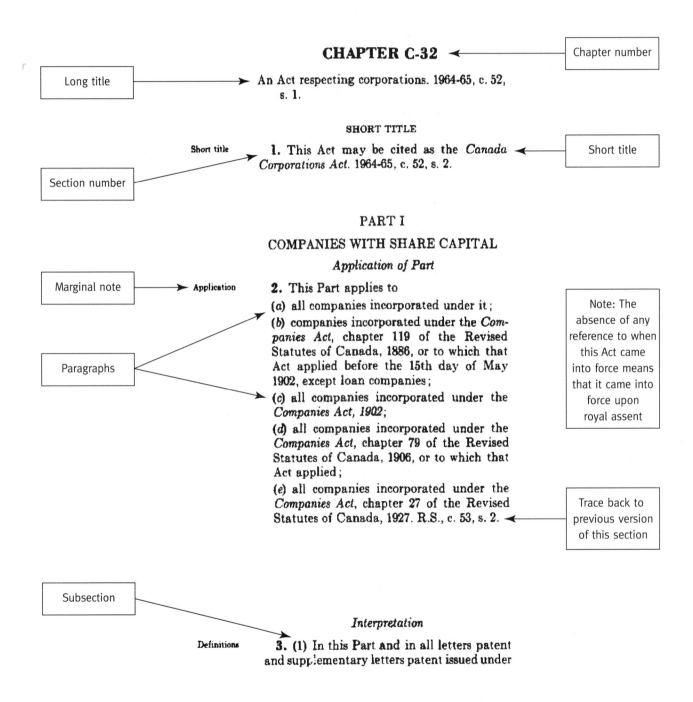

CHAPTER C-32   ← Chapter number

Long title →   An Act respecting corporations. 1964-65, c. 52, s. 1.

SHORT TITLE

Short title → Section number

1. This Act may be cited as the *Canada Corporations Act.* 1964-65, c. 52, s. 2.   ← Short title

PART I

COMPANIES WITH SHARE CAPITAL

Application of Part

Marginal note → **Application**

2. This Part applies to

(*a*) all companies incorporated under it ;

(*b*) companies incorporated under the *Companies Act,* chapter 119 of the Revised Statutes of Canada, 1886, or to which that Act applied before the 15th day of May 1902, except loan companies ;

Paragraphs →

(*c*) all companies incorporated under the *Companies Act, 1902*;

(*d*) all companies incorporated under the *Companies Act,* chapter 79 of the Revised Statutes of Canada, 1906, or to which that Act applied ;

(*e*) all companies incorporated under the *Companies Act,* chapter 27 of the Revised Statutes of Canada, 1927. R.S., c. 53, s. 2.   ← Trace back to previous version of this section

Note: The absence of any reference to when this Act came into force means that it came into force upon royal assent

Subsection

Interpretation

Definitions

3. (1) In this Part and in all letters patent and supplementary letters patent issued under

HOW TO INTERPRET A STATUTE

Statutory interpretation rules are tools of legal persuasion, used to support a particular interpretation with regard to the meaning and intent of a statute. Like most tools of legal persuasion, these rules may be used by lawyers and judges to support a particular interpretive approach. Thus, the rules point to a methodology of interpretation.

It is also possible that the rules of statutory interpretation contradict each other. As methodology, it is conceivable that when two valid rules are applied legitimately to the same situation, different interpretations may result. In general, however, statutory rules of interpretation can be used very persuasively, especially in formulating legal argument. Below are the most basic rules of statutory interpretation.

The literal or plain meaning rule

The "literal rule" states that if the statutory words are plain and unambiguous, they must be construed in their ordinary sense. This rule holds true even if such plain language interpretation leads to an absurdity or injustice. Although the rule is quite inflexible and uncompromising, it does provide a high degree of certainty, reducing the scope for argument.

When applied, this rule does not allow reference to any extrinsic tools of interpretation — only the words of the statute can be used to establish meaning. Accordingly, the literal rule may be of little use in deciding the exact meaning of contemporaneous legislation.

The golden rule

This interpretive method is almost identical to the literal rule except that it aims to prevent interpretations that would lead to absurdities, injustices, or contradictions.

Typically, one begins with the literal or plain meaning rule. If its application leads to an absurdity, then the golden rule permits the ordinary sense of the words to be modified *but only to the extent of rectifying the absurdity or inconsistency, and no more.*

The mischief rule

The mischief rule originated in 1594 and examines four questions:

1. What was the common law before the making of the act?

2. What was the mischief and defect for which the common law did not provide?

3. What is the remedy or method devised by Parliament for resolving the mischief or defect?

4. What is the specific remedial legislative intention (the legislative objective behind the legislative change or modification)?

Stated in more contemporary terms, the mischief rule attempts to unmask parliamentary intention. It attempts to ascertain the defect that Parliament sought to correct by passing the particular legislation. When this defect is identified, the statute can be interpreted and applied to achieve parliament's objectives.

There is still some disagreement about what extrinsic material a court may use when assessing the intent of Parliament. Traditionally, it was preferred that the courts stay within the "four corners" of an act, using only the official text as a reference for assessing the preferred interpretive method. As courts have become more activist, they have sought out extrinsic aids (external sources such as books, articles, and policy statements) as interpretive tools.

HOW TO FIND THE RELEVANT ACT

Figure 2.5 outlines the steps used to find legislation.

FIGURE 2.5   FINDING THE RELEVANT ACT

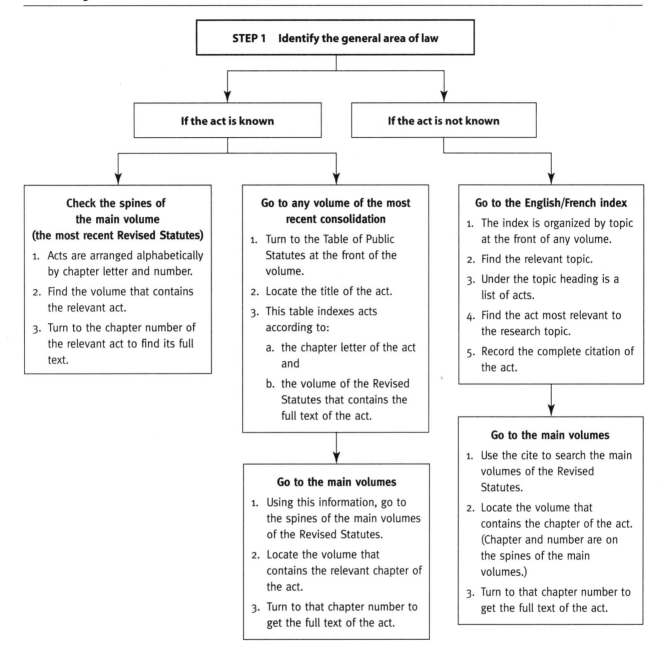

STEP 1   Identify the general area of law

If the act is known

If the act is not known

Check the spines of the main volume (the most recent Revised Statutes)

1. Acts are arranged alphabetically by chapter letter and number.
2. Find the volume that contains the relevant act.
3. Turn to the chapter number of the relevant act to find its full text.

Go to any volume of the most recent consolidation

1. Turn to the Table of Public Statutes at the front of the volume.
2. Locate the title of the act.
3. This table indexes acts according to:
   a. the chapter letter of the act and
   b. the volume of the Revised Statutes that contains the full text of the act.

Go to the English/French index

1. The index is organized by topic at the front of any volume.
2. Find the relevant topic.
3. Under the topic heading is a list of acts.
4. Find the act most relevant to the research topic.
5. Record the complete citation of the act.

Go to the main volumes

1. Using this information, go to the spines of the main volumes of the Revised Statutes.
2. Locate the volume that contains the relevant chapter of the act.
3. Turn to that chapter number to get the full text of the act.

Go to the main volumes

1. Use the cite to search the main volumes of the Revised Statutes.
2. Locate the volume that contains the chapter of the act. (Chapter and number are on the spines of the main volumes.)
3. Turn to that chapter number to get the full text of the act.

STEP 2   Identify the statutory section(s) governing the problem being researched

1. Follow the process in step 1 to find the relevant act.
2. Locate the full text of the act.
3. Read the marginal notes. Marginal notes provide a kind of running commentary on the statute. They are not an "official" part of the text (they have no legal effect). They are research tools to assist in locating relevant sections of legislation.
4. Use the marginal notes to identify the applicable section(s).
5. Read the section entirely to ensure that it is applicable to the problem being researched.

EXERCISE 5

Provide the name of the act for each of the following statutes:

Example:

1. RSC 1985, c. C-24

   Method: See figure 2.5.

   Answer: <u>Canadian Multiculturalism Act</u>

2. Part I of the *Constitution Act, 1982*, being schedule B to the *Canada Act 1982* (UK), 1982, c. 11, s. 15(1).

   _____

3. RSC 1985, c. T-11

   _____

4. RSO 1990, c. D.16

   _____

5. SC 2000, c. 26

   _____

6. SPEI 1994, c. 67

   _____

7. SC 1999, c. 8

   _____

8. RSBC 1996, c. 242

   _____

9. SS 1989-90, c. C-7.2

   _____

10. SA 1995, c. R-4.5

    _____

EXERCISE 6

Find and cite the relevant statute.

1. Provide the full cite for the Ontario *Human Rights Code*.

    _____

2. Cite the amendments that have been made to the Ontario *Human Rights Code*.

    _____

3. Cite the provincial statute that establishes the white trillium as the floral emblem of Ontario.

    _____

4. a. Cite the federal act that refers to copyright protection.

    _____

    b. Cite the section that deals with the conditions for obtaining copyright.

    _____

5. Cite the Ontario statute that governs over the addition of fluoride to the water supply.

    _____

6. Cite the section of a federal act that provides that copyright in a work exists during the life of the work's author, and for 50 years following his or her death.

    _____

7. Provide a complete citation to the appropriate section and subsection of an Alberta statute that protects consumer rights and allows for consumer complaints and grievances.

    _____

Steps 5 and 6   Update and trace back the legislation

See figure 2.6 for the steps used to update (panel A) and backdate (panel B) legislation.

THE LAW WORKBOOK: Developing skills for legal research and writing

FIGURE 2.6   UPDATING AND BACKDATING LEGISLATION

A. Update statutory section(s) (check for amendments or repeals)

Use the most recent sessional volume

OR

Use the Table of Statutes

1. The Table of Statutes is at the back of the volume. Acts are listed alphabetically in the left-hand column of the table. Look through this listing to find the relevant act.

2. Look at the right-hand column to find a list of amendments or repeals pertaining to this act.

3. Read through this list to see whether the act has been affected by amendments or repeals.

4. If it has, look up the citations in this column to see whether the relevant section is affected.

Use the provincial or federal Statute Citator

1. The Statute Citator arranges acts alphabetically. Find the volume that deals with the relevant act.

2. Turn to the statute and look under its main title for a listing of all repeals and amendments.

3. Read through this list to see whether the act has been affected by amendments or repeals.

4. If it has, look up the citations in this list to see whether the relevant section is affected.

B. Backdate statutory section(s) (find the original enactment date)

Locate the applicable statutory section(s)

(see figure 2.5)

Locate the historical citation

Read through the relevant section of legislation to check for a historical citation at the end of the text. This citation will look something like:

RSO 1970, c. 212, s. 5   OR   1926, c. 41, s. 4

This citation means that the section in question can be traced back to an earlier version in the previous consolidation of the Act — in this example, RSO 1970.

This citation means that the section in question can be traced back to an earlier version in sessional volumes of the statutes — in this example, the 1926 Sessional Volumes for Ontario.

Locate the next historical citation

1. Find the next most recent version of the section being researched. Read through the section to check whether there is another reference to an earlier version of the section at the end of the text.

2. If there is a citation, look it up using the chapter and number references of the statute to locate the next version of the section.

3. Repeat these steps until the original enactment of the section is found.

EXERCISE 7

Trace back and update the following statutory provisions.

1. Find the *Landlord and Tenant Act*, RSO 1990, c. L.7, s. 107(1)(b).

   a. Trace the section(s) or subsection(s) back to the original enactment date.

   _____

   _____

   _____

   _____

   b. Update the section(s) or subsection(s) indicating whether there have been
   any amendments or repeals since the 1990 consolidation.

   _____

   _____

   _____

   _____

2. Find the *Occupiers' Liability Act*, RSO 1990, c. O.2, ss. 3(1), (2), (3).

   a. Trace the section(s) or subsection(s) back to the original enactment date.

   _____

   _____

   _____

   _____

   b. Update the section(s) or subsection(s) indicating whether there have been
   any amendments or repeals since the 1990 consolidation.

   _____

   _____

   _____

   _____

3. Find the *Human Rights Code*, RSO 1990, c. H.19, ss. 5(1), (2).

    a. Trace the section(s) or subsection(s) back to 1981.

_____

_____

_____

_____

    b. Update the section(s) or subsection(s) indicating whether there have been any amendments or repeals since the 1990 consolidation.

_____

_____

_____

_____

4. Find the *Department of Environment Act*, RSC 1985, c. E-10, s. 4(1).

    a. Trace the section(s) or subsection(s) back to the original enactment date.

_____

_____

_____

_____

    b. Update the section(s) or subsection(s) indicating whether there have been any amendments or repeals since the 1985 consolidation.

_____

_____

_____

_____

5. Find the *Defamation Act*, RSA 1980, c. D-6, s. 5.

    a. Trace the section back to the original enactment date.

_____

_____

_____

_____

    b. Update the section indicating whether there have been any amendments or repeals since the 1980 consolidation.

_____

_____

_____

_____

4. Find the *Civil Service Act*, RSNB 1973, c. C-5, s. 9.

    a. Trace the section back to the original enactment date.

_____

_____

_____

_____

    b. Update the section indicating whether there have been any amendments or repeals since the 1973 consolidation.

_____

_____

_____

_____

Step 8 Identify the binding case law

> **Note:** A knowledge of how to find case law is needed to do judicial considerations. For the purposes of this workbook, it is necessary to introduce how to identify the binding case law before showing how to do judicial considerations. The research steps are therefore introduced out of sequence.

STRUCTURE OF THE COURTS

The court structure in a common law system is hierarchical. If the grounds for appeal are accepted, the judgment of a lower court may be taken to a higher court for a ruling. In Canada, cases are heard first by a judge or a judge and a jury presiding at trial. There are strict rules about when a lower court's decision can be appealed. For example, the purpose of an appeal is to review questions of law, not fact. An appeal court will not rehear evidence. Instead, it will accept the factual record of the trial court, which was in the position to hear witness testimony and evidence directly. The appeal court thus accepts the trial court's assessments of credibility and accuracy. An appeal court usually comprises a three-judge panel, who may deliver joint or separate judgments.

For matters that are heard initially at the administrative board level (such as workers' compensation matters, human rights issues, labour arbitration, and immigration cases), there is also a right of "judicial review" to the provincial appeal court. Although similar to an "appeal," "judicial review" is an administrative concept. While the right to appeal developed as a common law concept, the concept of judicial review is statute-based, and each administrative body has its own mandate set out in an empowering statute.

The final level of appeal in Canada is the Supreme Court of Canada (SCC). Right of appeal to the Supreme Court is not automatic. The Supreme Court grants permission or leave to appeal based on its assessment of the national significance of a case and the potential contribution to existing law. Recognizing the high personal stakes in criminal law matters (imprisonment, financially significant sanctions, and social stigma), the Supreme Court usually grants leaves to appeal on matters of criminal law.

It is important to note which level of the court rendered the decision in a case, and to find out whether a decision has been appealed. If the case has been appealed to a higher court, it is important to know whether the higher court agreed or disagreed with the lower court's decision. This information is essential to determine the jurisprudential weight of a particular case. Effective research of case law finds out how important one decision is to the outcomes of subsequent cases — in other words, how "binding" or "persuasive" the precedent case is.

Figure 2.7 shows the structure of the Canadian court system.

Trial court
Decision-making functions

A judge or a judge and jury preside at trial. The trial judge has three primary responsibilities:

1. Hear the facts and evidence.
2. Determine the governing law.
3. Apply the law to the facts.

The role of counsel

1. Argue the case on behalf of the client.
2. Establish the factual record.
3. Submit arguments regarding:
   a. the correct facts and
   b. the applicable legal principles.

Appeal court

The appeal court judge has three primary responsibilities:

1. Hear legal arguments.
2. Determine whether the lower court applied the law correctly.
3. Decide whether to reverse the trial judgment, uphold it, amend portions of it, or send the matter back to the trial division for retrial.

FIGURE 2.7   STRUCTURE OF THE CANADIAN COURT SYSTEM

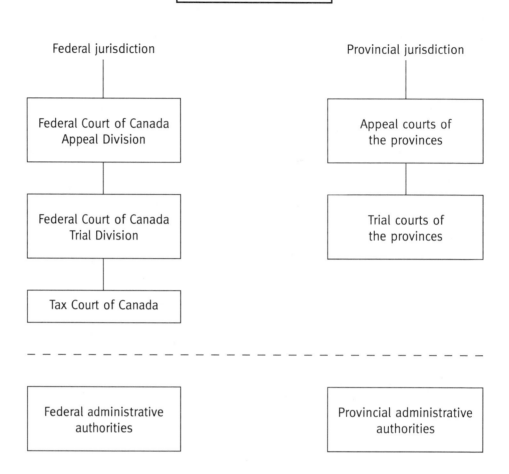

The Supreme Court of Canada and the Federal Court of Appeal

Based on its powers under s. 101 of the *Constitution Act, 1867* to establish "any additional Courts for the better Administration of the Laws of Canada," Parliament established two national courts in 1875. One was a general, national court of appeal, known as the Supreme Court of Canada. The other was a national court with jurisdiction over claims involving the federal Crown, known as the Exchequer Court. Subsequently, the jurisdiction of the Exchequer Court expanded, giving the court mandate over such matters as copyrights, patents, and interprovincial railways. In addition to these two courts, Parliament also created two other important federal courts: the Court Martial Appeal Court (established in 1959) and the Tax Court of Canada (previously known as the Tax Review Board), established in 1983.

After 1971, the Exchequer Court became known as the Federal Court of Canada and was restructured to have two divisions: a Trial Division and an Appeal Division. The jurisdiction of this Federal Court was expanded to include mandates over decisions and orders of federal boards, commissions, and other tribunals.

THE SUPREME COURT OF CANADA

Even after the establishment of the Supreme Court of Canada in 1875, the final court of appeal in Canada remained the Judicial Committee of the Privy Council (PC) in the United Kingdom until December 23, 1949, when Parliament adopted legislation to abolish Privy Council appeals.

The Supreme Court of Canada hears appeals from the Federal Court of Appeal and from provincial courts of appeal (including Quebec). The court is composed of nine judges, three of whom are required by statute to come from Quebec. By convention, three of the remaining positions are filled by judges from Ontario, two from the western provinces, and one from the Atlantic provinces. Usually, the position of chief justice alternates between a French-speaking and English-speaking judge. There must be five judges presiding to constitute a quorum to hear a case.

FEDERAL COURT OF CANADA

In 1971, the Federal Court of Canada replaced the Exchequer Court. This court inherited the jurisdiction of the Exchequer Court and was given additional jurisdiction, including the power to review the decisions of federal agencies.

The Federal Court does not have the exclusive jurisdiction to hear all cases involving federal law. Generally, Parliament has been content to leave the provincial courts with the jurisdiction to preside over federal as well as provincial issues (for example, criminal law).

Federal Court — Trial Division

The Trial Division of the Federal Court has exclusive jurisdiction with respect to relief claimed against the federal Crown including contracts and torts (for example, if an RCMP officer used unreasonable or unnecessary force on an individual, that individual would have a tort claim against the federal Crown). The Trial Division can also hear appeals under the *Citizenship Act*, the *Income Tax Act*, and the *Excise Tax Act*. It also hears patent, trademark, copyright, and admiralty cases.

Federal Court of Appeal

The Appeal Division hears appeals from the judgments of the Trial Division. It also hears appeals of decisions of federal administrative boards, commissions, and agencies. In turn, decisions of the Federal Court of Appeal may be appealed to the Supreme Court of Canada.

Tax Court of Canada

Established in 1983, the Tax Court is a federal court intended to expedite the hearing of those matters of federal legislation pertaining to the *Income Tax Act*. The Tax Court is really a specialized Trial Division of the Federal Court and its decisions may also be appealed to the Appeal Division of the Federal Court.

Provincial courts

SUPERIOR COURTS (SECTION 96 COURTS)

Each province has superior courts of general jurisdiction with a trial and an appellate division. The names of these courts vary from province to province. These provincial courts are general courts with unlimited jurisdiction and unlimited powers to administer the law, except where their jurisdiction is limited by a particular statute or federal law. These courts hear criminal matters, some family law matters — such as divorce, custody, and support — and most civil matters. These provincial courts are established under s. 96 of the *Constitution Act*. For this reason, they are sometimes known as "section 96" courts.

COUNTY OR DISTRICT COURTS

Some provinces have courts whose jurisdiction is limited by territory to a local county or district, as well as by subject matter. These courts are of a lower rank than the provincial courts. They hear intermediate civil cases and some of the less serious criminal cases (the most important criminal cases being reserved for the superior courts).

INFERIOR COURTS

Below the county and district courts are the provincial courts, whose judges are provincially appointed and paid by the province. Small Claims Court is an example of an inferior court. This court hears minor civil disputes under a legislated monetary value set out in the provincial *Small Claims Act*.

Provincial and federal administrative authorities

ADMINISTRATIVE FUNCTIONS

At the federal and provincial level, governments enact legislation that creates and regulates the function of various administrative and quasi-judicial bodies. Under such legislation, claims are adjudicated by tribunals or commissions composed of adjudicators or arbitrators.

These administrative boards are often engaged in fact-finding missions. Like courts, however, these administrative bodies preside over adversarial disputes. The general principle is to create a specialized body to deal with a certain area of the law. In theory, administrative tribunals deal with issues faster and somewhat more informally than do the courts.

In addition to carrying out their adjudicative functions, such administrative bodies also make policy, provide services, investigate, research, and educate. The decisions of an administrative tribunal are subject to judicial review by (superior) courts (through prerogative writs such as *certiorari*). Federal administrative bodies are subject to review by the Federal Court of Canada. Provincial administrative bodies are subject to review by the superior court of the province (or the highest provincial appellate court).

As the common law developed over time, the superior courts issued official notices (known as "writs") that prevented lower courts or officials from exceeding their jurisdictions or forced them to exercise their legal mandates.

CASE LAW REPORTING

The common law system is based on the premise that like cases should be decided alike. For this reason, a court is generally bound by the earlier decisions of a higher court within the same jurisdiction. Since cases are a primary source of law, it is extremely important for courts and legal practitioners to be able to access written judgments of previous cases as soon as possible. Law reporting plays a pivotal role in the legal process.

There is little logic to the case-reporting system, especially in Canada. There is extensive duplication between both paper-based and online reporting services. The art of researching a case is to avoid repetition without leaving gaps.

Report series are classified as official, semi-official, and unofficial. **Official reports** are authorized by the court whose decisions they report (Supreme Court Reports, Federal Court Reports). **Semi-official reports** are privately published but have a measure of authority through custom and practice (for example, Ontario Reports). **Unofficial reports** are unauthorized publications by private organizations. This classification is important for the citation of "parallel reports" (the same case reported in different report series), and dictates the order of preference among reports if there is a discrepancy (that is, the most official report is cited first; online series are usually cited last).

Reported decisions

Law book publishers obtain copies of judgments as soon as they are filed with the court authorities. The publisher reviews the judgments and categorizes them by subject, by area, and by court. The judgments are then sent to the editors of the individual law report series, or to computer editors responsible for entering judgments onto online databases.

Not all cases are included in law reports or online databases. Generally, the editors exclude cases that do not raise any important or significant rules of law. Furthermore, law reports do not give a complete record of the court proceedings. For example, counsels' arguments are not usually reported in full. The case reporter records only the decision of the court and the reasons given.

It is customary to preface these reported judgments with an editorial summary of the case, known as a "headnote." These "headnotes" are not part of the official text of the case. As editorial comment or summary, they should be used with caution. While some "headnotes" provide excellent summaries, others are notoriously misleading and sometimes even inaccurate. It is important to read the entire decision and to rely only on the official text of the judgment. On Quicklaw, these headnotes are available by clicking on "DRS Summary."

There are several publications that "digest" or "summarize" cases soon after they are released (there are both paper and online services). The full reasons for judgment of these cases may not be available immediately, but the summaries give a useful synopsis of the main facts and issues of the case.

Canadian law reports are grouped into national, regional, provincial, and topical reports. These groupings include many specialty reports that have increased in number as specialization by lawyers has increased. Law reports published by the same law book publisher have uniform indexing features that often make research more convenient.

Unreported decisions

There are some judgments that are not reported in paper form in any of the published series. Most online databases (such as Quicklaw), carry unreported decisions. Citations for these unreported decisions use "docket numbers" (for example, file no. 20815) and are different from reported case citations. (See the "Unpublished Decisions" and "Unreported Decisions" sections in the *Canadian Guide to Uniform Legal Citation*.)

THE MAJOR PUBLISHED REPORTS

The Supreme Court Reports and the Federal Court Reports

From 1875 to 1922, full-text judgments of both the Supreme Court of Canada and the Federal (previously Exchequer) Court could be found in two reporter series entitled *Reports of the Supreme Court of Canada* and *Reports of the Exchequer Court of Canada* (cited as SCR and Ex. CR).

From 1923 to 1969, the full-text judgments of these two courts were published together in the series known as the *Canada Law Reports*. There was, however, a separate set of volumes for each court, known respectively as the *Canada Law Reports: Supreme Court* and the *Canada Law Reports: Exchequer Court*.

From 1970 onward, the term *Canada Law Reports* was no longer used. Cases from these two courts began to be published in both official languages (in side by side columns on each page). Since 1970, the reports became known respectively as the *Canada: Supreme Court Reports* and the *Canada: Exchequer Court Reports*. After the coming into force of the *Federal Court Act* in 1971 (which enacted the name change from the Exchequer Court to the Federal Court), this series became entitled the *Canada: Federal Court Reports* (cited as FCR).

Canada-wide reporter series

There are reporter series that cover decisions from each province and territory as well as from the federal level. Available in both paper and online form, these services offer reporters and databases of national scope in which publishers have included Canadian decisions of legal significance.

Regional reporter series

There are certain paper and online series that report cases from a particular geographic region in Canada (such as the *Western Weekly Reports*). The individual publishers of these series will include only those cases of legal significance and importance.

Provincial reporter series

Decisions from provincial courts are also reported in paper and online form. Publishers of provincial reports will again include only those cases that may have a legal impact or that discuss a novel or significant legal concept.

Topical reporter series

Not only are reporters and databases divided by court, province, or region, but there are also reporters covering a specific subject matter or topic (for example, *Family Law Reports*, *Motor Vehicle Reports*, *Dominion Tax Cases*). Because of their scope, topical reporters and databases may duplicate cases that are reported in either national or provincial reporters.

CASE CITATION

The following is a brief explanation of how to read a case citation. For a complete discussion of proper Canadian citation style, please refer to the *Canadian Guide to Uniform Legal Citation* (commonly known as the *McGill Guide*).

Components of a case citation

Figure 2.8 illustrates and explains the components of a case citation. Specific rules govern the way these components are put together. Knowing where to put periods, commas, round and square brackets, and abbreviations is crucial to correct legal citation. In addition, it may be important to include extra information in the citation, such as "parallel citations" to indicate the different law reports in which the same case appears, as well as the "case history." The case history provides the citations for each level of court that heard the case.

FIGURE 2.8   COMPONENTS OF A CASE CITATION

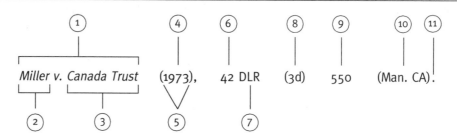

(1) Style of cause: The title of a case identifies the parties to the case. The style of cause is either italicized or underlined.

(2) The plaintiff's name is listed first.

(3) The defendant's name is listed second. On appeal, the style of cause used to change if the defendant appealed the lower court decision. Under such circumstances, the defendant would be listed first as the appellant, and the plaintiff would become the respondent. If the plaintiff at trial appealed the decision, there would be no change in the order of the style of cause. This practice is no longer followed. Now, the style of cause remains the same, with no changes to the order in which the parties' names appear, regardless of how many appeals are involved.

(4) The date of the decision indicates when the court released or published its reasons for judgment.

(5) Round brackets or parentheses are used to indicate the date the case was decided. Square brackets indicate the year of the case reporter.

(6) The volume number of the case reporter.

(7) The publication source in which the case is reported. Abbreviations of the title of the case reporter series are used.

(8) The edition number of the case reporter.

(9) The page number of the first page of the text of the case.

(10) The jurisdiction and the court level where the case was decided. If the jurisdiction or court level is evident in the name of the case reporter (such as the SCR — the *Supreme Court Reporter*), there is no need to repeat information.

(11) The citation ends with a period. In this example, there are no parallel citations given. If there were parallel citations, a comma would replace the period, followed by another citation. The style of cause is not repeated. Specific rules govern the way these components are put together. While there may be slight variations in publisher styles, knowing where to put periods, commas, round and square brackets, and abbreviations is crucial to correct legal citation. For this reason and to encourage the use of a consistent style, we refer users of this workbook to the *McGill Guide*. (It should be noted, however, that the citation style used in this workbook follows Emond Montgomery house style, which differs from *McGill* style in that Emond style italicizes the "v." and omits periods in capital-letter abbreviations.)

Case history

To note the case history:

1. note the court level and provide parallel citations; and

2. indicate how the higher court treated the lower court's decision of the case, using standard symbols.

The two most commonly used symbols are:

- aff'd = affirmed   The decision was affirmed on appeal or on reconsideration, or application for judicial review was refused; used to indicate the *subsequent* history of the decision.

- rev'd = reversed   The decision was reversed on appeal or on reconsideration; used to indicate the *subsequent* history of the decision.

Other symbols may be used to indicate the following:

- aff'g = affirming   Same as affirmed; used to indicate the *prior* history of the decision.

- rev'g = reversing   Same as reversed; used to indicate the *prior* history of the decision.

- amended   Correction of wording of decision by the decision maker to conform to intended meaning.

- add'l reasons   Additional explanations given for the decision.

- allowed leave to appeal/refused leave to appeal   Indicates whether permission to appeal to an appellate court was granted or not.

- reconsideration or rehearing   Indicates whether application for reconsideration or rehearing of decision by the same court is granted or refused.

- referred for further clarification   The decision was referred back by an appellate court to the lower court for further consideration or clarification.

- set aside or quashed   The decision was negated, removed, or not followed.

- var'd   The decision was varied or modified by either the decision maker or an appellate court without reversing the result.

The treatment signals denote the relationship between the first case cited and each of the subsequent or prior decisions listed.

Examples of citations

1. *Gwyer Inc. v. Jaworski* (1994), 6 OR (2d) 388 (Prov. Ct.).

   The case involves a dispute between a corporation (Gwyer Inc.) and an individual (Jaworski). The case was decided in 1994, but because the date is part of the style of cause (in round brackets), it is not necessary as an aid to locating the case. The number "6" shows that the case is located in that volume of the report series, and "(2d)" shows that it is in the second edition of the series. The letters "OR" refer to the name of the series, *Ontario Reports*. Because only Ontario cases are reported in this series, there is no need to indicate the jurisdiction at the end of the citation. The name of the reporter provides no indication of which court heard the case. The court level is therefore indicated in parentheses.

2. *Miller v. Canada Trust Co.* (1981), 33 Nfld. & PEIR 107, 93 APR 107 (Nfld. Dist. Ct.).

   The case was decided in 1981 and published in volume 33 of the *Newfoundland and Prince Edward Island Reporter*, beginning at page 107. The same case is also reported in volume 93 of the *Atlantic Provinces Reports*, beginning at page 107. The reference to the Newfoundland District Court indicates the jurisdiction and court level that heard the case.

3. *R v. Brown* (1982), 41 AR 69, 1 CCC (3d) 107 (CA), aff'd [1985] 2 SCR 273, 21 CCC (3d) 477, 21 DLR (4th) 761, 40 Alta. LR (2d) 193, [1986] 1 WWR 97, 62 NR 241.

   This case involves the Crown, as indicated by the letter "R" in the style of cause. From the citation, it is immediately clear that the case was heard both by the Court of Appeal and by the Supreme Court of Canada. There are also parallel citations for both the Court of Appeal and the Supreme Court of Canada decisions. For example, the appeal decision is reported at volume 41 of the *Alberta Reports* and volume 1 of the *Canadian Criminal Cases*. The Supreme Court decision is reported in volume 2 of the *Supreme Court Reports* for the year 1985, as well as volume 21 of *Canadian Criminal Cases*, volume 21 of the *Dominion Law Reports*, volume 40 of the *Alberta Law Reports*, volume 1 of the *Western Weekly Reports* for the year 1986, and volume 62 of the *National Reports*. The symbol "aff'd" appears before the citation of the Supreme Court decision, indicating that the Supreme Court "affirmed" the lower court decision (Court of Appeal).

EXERCISE 8

Identify the information that the following fictional case citations provide.

1. *Neuman Ltd. v. Smythe* (1998), 92 Sask. R 23 (CA).

   _____

   _____

   _____

2. *Grey-Bruce Snowmobile Trails Inc. v. Morris* (1997), 151 DLR (4th) 646, 103 OR (3d) 398 (CA).

   _____

   _____

   _____

3. *Dubuc v. Cameron*, [1996] 2 SCR 343, 4 Man. R (2d) 45.

   _____

   _____

   _____

4. *Garibaldi v. Southridge Foundation Inc.* (1996), 71 OR (3d) 322, 27 CCC (2d) 56 (CA), rev'g (1994), 11 DLR (3d) 511 (QB).

   _____

   _____

   _____

5. *Parker v. Gordon* (1997), 7 CCLT 233 (BC SC), aff'd (1999), 15 CCLT 122 (CA) [leave to appeal to SCC refused 15 September 2000].

   _____

   _____

   _____

EXERCISE 9

Make up citations for the following fact situations.

1. A case involving the Saskatchewan Government Employees Union reported in the *Saskatchewan Reports* at page 89 of volume 191. Judgment in the case was handed down by the Saskatchewan Court of Queen's Bench on February 17, 2000.

_____

2. The case of George Palek and Eleanor Hanson whose suit was heard by the Alberta Court of Appeal in 1997 and reported the following year in volume 54 of the third edition of the *Dominion Law Reports* at page 29.

_____

3. A case involving Michel Benoit reported in volume 122 of the third edition of *Canadian Criminal Cases* at page 105. The decision was rendered in 1998 by the Quebec Court of Appeal.

_____

4. A Prince Edward Island case of a man who was charged for failing to submit to an ALERT test. The final appeal was heard by the Supreme Court of Canada in 1991 and reported at page 139 of volume 3 of the 1991 *Supreme Court Reports*, and also in the fourth edition, volume 110 of the *Dominion Law Reports*, at page 241.

_____

5. A case involving Air Canada and the minister of transport heard by the Federal Court of Canada — Trial Division and published in volume 165 of the *Federal Trial Reports* at page 60 in 1999.

_____

EXERCISE 10

Find the following cases and complete the citations.

1. [1947] 1 DLR 417 (PC).

   _____

2. 42 DLR (3d) 550 (Man. CA).

   _____

3. 67 OR (2d) 385.

   _____

4. 14 DLR (3d) 110.

   _____

5. 47 DTC 1004.

   _____

6. (1999), 1 MPLR 11 (Ont. Ct. J).

   _____

7. (1997), 63 LAC (4th) 256 (Can. LB).

   _____

8. (1997), 18 RPR 213 (Ont. Ct. J).

   _____

Step 7 Judicial consideration of legislation

Legislation and cases should not be read in isolation. The only way to understand the impact of a piece of legislation is to examine how the courts have interpreted and applied the Act in question. For the same reason, it is important to find out how the courts have treated a particular decision. Researching the "judicial consideration" of legislation and cases is an important step in assessing the impact that a particular law or case is likely to have, and how the courts are likely to apply the legal principles in question. Research is never complete until the courts' treatment of a particular act or case has been verified.

STATUTES JUDICIALLY CONSIDERED

Follow the steps outlined below to research the judicial consideration of legislation.

1. Update the section of legislation in question to ensure that you are working with the most recent version of the legislation and that you know when and how the section has been amended. Working with the most recent version of the legislation ensures that you will find the most recent cases.

2. Trace back the section of legislation to its original enactment date. Make a note of all of the previous versions of the section. Look up each of these citations individually to see how the courts have interpreted the section over time.

The most useful bibliographical tool for this research is the *Canadian Statute Citations* (CSC) volumes of the *Canadian Abridgment*. These volumes are indexed alphabetically and according to jurisdiction. They list all federal and provincial statutes. Find the volume that deals with the legislation in question and look up the citation. The *Canadian Statute Citations* lists all the cases in which courts have judicially considered a piece of legislation. The *Canadian Statute Citations* is organized alphabetically by statute. Each statute is subdivided into its sections, under which the cases that have considered the section are listed. Figure 2.9 summarizes these research steps.

The *Canadian Abridgment* uses the following *Canadian Statute Citations* treatment symbols to indicate how the courts have considered the legislation:

- **U** = unconstitutional   Where a section of a statute has been found by the court considering it to be unconstitutional or invalid, in whole or in part.

- **C** = considered   Where a section of a statute has been analyzed or interpreted in a particular case.

- **P** = pursuant to   Where a proceeding was undertaken pursuant to a section of a statute.

- **R** = referred to   Where a section of a statute has been mentioned by the court, but no comment made.

FIGURE 2.9   JUDICIAL CONSIDERATION OF LEGISLATION

STEP 1   Trace back the section

Have a complete list of the legislative history of the relevant section, dating back to its first enactment. (See figure 2.6.)

STEP 2   Locate the Canadian Statute Citations

The *Canadian Statute Citations* (CSCs) are part of the *Canadian Abridgment* series. These are grey hardcover books that are organized alphabetically and according to jurisdiction.

STEP 3   Locate the relevant CSC volume

Using the historical citations for the section:

1. Turn to the pages in the appropriate volume that covers the act in question.

2. Take the earliest (oldest) citation for the relevant section.

3. Flip through the pages to find this citation listed on the upper corners of the pages.

4. Find the appropriate page and glance down the column to see whether the section in the historical citation is mentioned. If it is, there may be a list of cases that have judicially considered this early version of the section. The symbol before the case name indicates how the section was considered in that case. If no cases are listed, then no cases judicially considered the section.

5. Repeat the steps above for each historical citation of the section. As a final step, check whether the most recent version of the section has been judicially considered.

STEP 4   Update using the softcover supplement

Repeat steps 1–3 using the softcover (paperback) supplement to the CSCs.

EXERCISE 11

Using the *Canadian Statute Citations* volumes of the *Canadian Abridgment*, list the number of times and how the following statutory sections have been judicially considered.

Example:

Using the *Canadian Statute Citations* volumes of the *Canadian Abridgment*, find out how many cases have judicially considered the *Canada Bankruptcy Act*, RSC 1970, c. B-3, s. 95(5).

Two cases have judicially considered the Act:

C = <u>Re Ogden Enterprises Ltd.</u> (1982), 22 NBR (2d) 344, 39 APR 344 (QB).

   This case "considered" the section in question.

R = <u>Rogers v. Thorne Riddell Inc.</u> (1982), 41 CBR (NS) 184 (Alta. QB).

   This case "referred" to the section in question.

1. Using the *Canadian Statute Citations* volumes of the *Canadian Abridgment*, find out how many cases have judicially considered s. 107(1)(b) of the Ontario *Landlord and Tenant Act*.

   _____

2. Using the *Canadian Statute Citations* volumes of the *Canadian Abridgment*, find out how many cases have judicially considered s. 3 of the Ontario *Occupiers' Liability Act*.

   _____

3. Using the *Canadian Statute Citations* volumes of the *Canadian Abridgment*, find out how many cases have judicially considered s. 5 of the Ontario *Human Rights Code*.

   _____

4. Using the *Canadian Statute Citations* volumes of the *Canadian Abridgment*, find out how many cases have judicially considered s. 106 of the New Brunswick *Insurance Act*.

   _____

5. Using the *Canadian Statute Citations* volumes of the *Canadian Abridgment*, find out how many cases have judicially considered s. 254 of the *Criminal Code of Canada*.

   _____

EXERCISE 12

Using the *Canadian Statute Citations* volumes of the *Canadian Abridgment*, list the cases that have considered the following legislation. Provide a complete citation and indicate how the legislation was considered.

1. The *Immigration Act*, RSC 1985, s. 77 [amending SC 1992, c. 49, s. 68].

_____

_____

_____

_____

2. The *Forest Act*, RSBC 1960, c. 153.

_____

_____

_____

_____

3. The *Marital Property Act*, SNB 1980, c. M-1.1, s. 1 dealing with the subject of "marital debts."

_____

_____

_____

_____

4. The *Business Corporations Act*, SA 1981, c. B-15, s. 115 and s. 140.

_____

_____

_____

_____

Steps 9 and 10 Update the case law and check for judicial consideration of the case law

Good research identifies the relative importance of a particular court decision by studying how other courts have used the decision. If other courts have followed or applied the decision to solve subsequent problems, the decision in question is considered to be a "strong authority." If, however, other courts have made a point of not applying the decision or "distinguishing" it, then the case may not be a strong or convincing precedent.

Follow the steps outlined below to update the case law and to research judicial consideration of the case law.

1. Find the complete citation for the case. Check whether the case has been appealed and make sure that you have the most recent citation for the case.

2. To record a complete history of the full judicial consideration of the case, search each individual citation separately (that is, do a separate search for the trial decision and a separate search for the appeal decision). This step can also be done using the "Quickcite" function on Quicklaw.

The most useful bibliographical tool for this research are the *Canadian Case Citations* (CCC) volumes of the *Canadian Abridgment*. These volumes are indexed chronologically and alphabetically. They list all Canadian cases since Confederation (1867). The listings provide full citations for all cases (including all parallel citations), plus a list of judicial considerations (all subsequent cases that have considered the case at issue). The CCCs also list all foreign judgments that were judicially considered by Canadian courts.

To use the *Canadian Case Citations*, find the volume that deals with the year in which the case was decided. Use the alphabetical breakdown on the spine of the volumes to look up the case. Figure 2.10 summarizes these research steps.

The *Canadian Abridgment* uses the following treatment symbols to indicate how the courts have considered other cases. Note that different publishers may use different symbols.

• **Affirmed**	Decision affirmed on appeal or on reconsideration; or application for judicial review refused.
• **Amended**	Correction of wording of decision by decision maker to conform to intended meaning.
• **Distinguished**	Cited decision inapplicable because of difference in facts or law.
• **Followed**	Principle of law in cited decision adapted.
• **Not followed/overruled**	Principle of law in cited decision not followed or affirmed.
• **Reversed**	Cited decision wrongly decided.
• **Considered**	Some consideration given to cited decision.
• **Varied**	Part of law in cited decision changed on subsequent consideration.

Quicklaw, an online database service, also indicates whether cases are "mentioned" or "explained."

FIGURE 2.10 JUDICIAL CONSIDERATION OF CASES

STEP 1   Locate the Canadian Case Citations

The *Canadian Case Citations* (CCCs) are part of the *Canadian Abridgment* series. These are red/burgundy hardcover books that are organized alphabetically and according to jurisdiction.

STEP 2   Locate the main CCC volumes

1. The main hardcover CCCs cover the years from 1867 to July 1998.

2. These volumes are organized alphabetically.

3. Check the spines of these volumes to find the volume that contains the relevant case.

4. Turn to the page on which the relevant case appears. Under the citation of this case there may be a list of cases that have judicially considered the case. A symbol appears before the case name in the list to indicate how the courts considered the case being researched (e.g., whether the court considered, followed, applied, or reversed the decision in the precedent case). If no cases are listed, then no cases judicially considered the case in question.

STEP 3   Update using the softcover supplement

Repeat steps 1 and 2 using the softcover (paperback) supplement to the CCCs.

EXERCISE 13

Use the *Canadian Case Citations* volumes of the *Canadian Abridgment* to answer the following questions.

Example:

How many cases have judicially considered *Laplante v. Porcupine* (1951), 2 WWR 638 (Sask. CA)?

2 cases judicially considered this case. These cases are:

— <u>Mildenberger v. Francis</u>, [1955] 1 DLR 51, 13 WWR 534 (Sask. CA) *considered* <u>Laplante v. Porcupine</u>.

— <u>Campbell v. Monet</u>, [1953] 2 DLR 220, 8 WWR 129 *considered* <u>Laplante v. Porcupine</u>.

1. a. How many cases have judicially considered *Berry v. Alberta* (1979), 23 AR 338 (CA)?

_____

    b. Give the parallel citation for *Berry v. Alberta*.

_____

    c. How many cases "followed" *Berry v. Alberta*?

_____

    d. Cite the case that "considered" *Berry v. Alberta*.

_____

2. a. How many levels of court heard the case of *Klimashewski v. Klimashewski*?

_____

    b. What was the final court disposition of *Klimashewski v. Klimashewski*?

_____

    c. Cite a case that "considered" the Manitoba Court of Appeal decision in *Klimashewski*.

_____

3. a. Give a full cite for *Bartlett v. Weiche Apartments Ltd.*

_____

    b. What court heard this case?

_____

    c. How many cases judicially considered the final court level decision in *Bartlett v. Weiche Apartments Ltd.*?

_____

EXERCISE 14

Using the *Canadian Case Citations* volumes of the *Canadian Abridgment*, provide the full citation and describe the way in which the following cases have been treated:

1. *Ball v. MacMillan Bloedel Ltd.*

2. *Kough v. Price*

3. The Queen's Bench decision in *Todoshichuk v. Marchenski Lumber Co.*

4. The British Columbia Court of Appeal decision in *Toronto Dominion Bank v. Calderbank.*

5. *Bartlett v. Brake's Construction Co.*

EXERCISE 15

Find the following case information.

1. What is the history of the case *Allan Eiserman v. Ara Farms Ltd. et al.* (1988), 52 DLR (4th) 498?

_____

_____

2. What court decided this case?

_____

3. List the cases that "follow" *Allan Eiserman v. Ara Farms Ltd. et al.* (1988), 52 DLR (4th) 498.

_____

_____

_____

_____

4. What is the history of the case *Interprovincial Co-operatives Ltd. v. Dryden Chemicals Ltd.*, [1976] 1 SCR 477?

_____

_____

_____

_____

5. List the cases that distinguished this case.

_____

_____

_____

_____

_____

_____

THE LAW WORKBOOK: Developing skills for legal research and writing

REFERENCES

Brann, A.B. (revised), *The Law Dictionary: Pronouncing Edition: A Dictionary of Legal Words and Phrases with Latin and French Maxims of the Law* (Cincinnati, Ohio: Anderson, 1997). [Note: First published in 1888 under the title *Student's Law Lexicon*; later eds. published under the title *Cochran's Law Lexicon, Pronouncing Edition.*]

Garner, B.A., ed., *Black's Law Dictionary*, 7th ed. (St. Paul, Minn.: West Group, 1999).

Gouvernement du Québec, Ministère de la justice, *Termes juridiques : vocabulaire français-anglais / Commission de terminologie juridique* (Québec: 1997).

McGill Law Journal, *The Canadian Guide to Uniform Legal Citation* (Scarborough, ON: Carswell, 1998).

Rutherford, L. and S. Bone; with contributions from C. Burke ... [et al.], *Osborn's Concise Law Dictionary*, 8th ed. (London: Sweet & Maxwell, 1996).

CHAPTER 3

Online research skills: How to search legal databases

INTRODUCTION

Most legal research exists in both electronic and paper form. Increasingly, it is becoming more efficient to conduct legal research online. To date, to ensure the accuracy and comprehensiveness of research results, it may still be necessary to do the same search using both print and electronic sources. The electronic sources, however, are developing at a rapid pace and becoming more reliable and authoritative as primary research tools. For example, it is now acceptable in certain circumstances to cite cases and legislation to online sources. If you are preparing official documents, be sure to check whether citation to electronic sources is acceptable.

In Canada, the main electronic resources are as follows:

Online

Online legal services include commercial legal research databases. Some of these commercial services provide law students with free "educational" access during their time in school. Otherwise, these services generally charge by the minute or by the hour. Examples of such services relevant to Canadian legal research are:

- Quicklaw
- Lexis-Nexis
- Westlaw

CD-ROMs

Many legal publishers make their materials available on CD-ROMs. The CD-ROMs are available at most law school libraries and sometimes through the library's Web site. To find subject-relevant CD-ROMs, you must examine a publisher's catalogue just as you would when searching for print material. Examples of some of the currently available CD-ROMs are:

- Aboriginal Land Claims
- Bankruptcy Partner

- Canadian Case Digests
- Canadian Encyclopedic Digest
- Canadian Statute Citation
- Civil Practice Partner
- Corporate Law Partner
- Criminal Law Partner
- Employment Law Partner
- Environmental Law Partner
- Family Law Partner
- Immigration Law Partner
- Legal Trac
- Security Partner
- Tax Partner
- Treaties with Canada
- Provincial Citator Services

The Internet

The Internet provides access to:

- Most legislation (see relevant government Web sites).
- Supreme Court of Canada decisions.
- Parliamentary materials such as Hansard Committee Debates and certain public policy documents.

In addition, most major law schools, law firms, government agencies and international organizations now have their own Web sites on which research may be conducted.

This chapter provides a general overview on how to use these materials. For demonstration purposes, the exercises will focus on Quicklaw searching skills, since Quicklaw is, at present, the service most commonly used in Canada.

SEARCHING STRATEGIES FOR THE INTERNET

The Internet is a global communication network through which lawyers communicate and research. The scope of Internet resources has not yet replaced law libraries, but the pool of information is expanding rapidly. The Internet is quickly becoming an indispensable research tool. Its main advantage, of course, is that it provides free access to public documents. The Web sites of university law libraries and law directories are excellent places to begin Internet-based legal research.

Law libraries and law directories*

Law libraries and law directories often organize links to helpful legal Web sites in order to facilitate online research. Some of the helpful law directories are:

- ACJNet: Access to Canada Justice
  http://www.acjnet.org
- Bora Laskin Law Library Legal Resources
  http://www.law-lib.utoronto.ca/resources/intro.htm
- Cornell Legal Information Institute
  http://www.law.cornell.edu/
- York University Law Library Law-Related Internet Resources
  http://info.library.yorku.ca/depts/lawlinks.htm

Search engines

SEARCH ENGINES/META-SEARCH ENGINES

Search engines are also called "spiders" or "crawlers." When you use a search engine, you are searching that search engine's index, not the whole Internet. Even the biggest search engines index only one-third to one-half of the Internet's public documents. Search engines visit sites periodically to revise indexes and to add sites to their databases. Some of the most popular search engines include:

- LawGuru.com
  http://www.lawguru.com/search/lawsearch.html
- Google
  http://www.google.com
- AllTheWeb
  http://alltheweb.com/
- Altavista
  http://www.altavista.com/
- Excite
  http://www.excite.com/
- Infoseek
  http://infoseek.go.com

* Information in this section was supplied by Louise Tsang, Reference Law Librarian (Osgoode Hall Law School), York University Law Library, May 2001.

- Lycos
  http://www.lycos.com
- Northern Light
  http://www.northernlight.com

Meta-search engines search several search engines at the same time. Some popular meta-search engines include:

- Metacrawler
  http://www.metacrawler.com
- Dogpile
  http://www.dogpile.com
- ixQuick
  http://ixquick.com/

LIMITS OF SEARCH ENGINES

Search engines do not search formatted files such as Adobe Acrobat portable document format (PDF) files, proprietary databases, and intranets.

USE OF SEARCH ENGINES

Search engines are useful after all other library resources (print and electronic) have been exhausted (including "law-related Internet resources" and other comprehensive sites).

Search engines are also good "fishing tools" to use when you are not sure which site will contain the relevant information.

WHICH SEARCH ENGINES TO USE

Google is for now a very popular search engine, although Dogpile and Metacrawler also produce quite adequate search results. They search most of the popular search engines such as Altavista, Infoseek, Lycos, Excite, etc. They are fast and they allow you to set the length of time you are willing to wait for a response.

EFFECTIVE USE OF SEARCH ENGINES

There are a number of searching guides available on the Internet to help a researcher in formulating the most effective and fruitful searches. A few helpful addresses are:

- "Web Searching Tips" from Search Engine Watch
  http://www.searchenginewatch.com/facts/index.html
- Quick Reference Guide to Search Engine Syntax (University at Albany Library)
  http://library.albany.edu/internet/syntax.html

For more information on search engines, check these sites:

- Search Engine Watch
  http://www.searchenginewatch.com/

- Things To Know Before You Begin Searching
  http://www.lib.berkeley.edu/TeachingLib/Guides/Internet/
  ThingsToKnow.html
- Finding Information on the Internet (UC Berkeley Library)
  http://www.lib.berkeley.edu/TeachingLib/Guides/Internet/FindInfo.html

THE INVISIBLE WEB AND SPECIALTY DATABASES

The content of these sites is stored in proprietary databases and is not indexed easily by search engines.

Useful law-related Web-based databases are included on many law library Web sites, such as the "Law-Related Internet Resources" site found at York University Law Library at:

- http://info.library.yorku.ca/depts/law/lawhome.htm

Directories of invisible Web and specialty databases

- Direct Search
  http://gwis2.circ.gwu.edu/~gprice/direct.htm

  This site is created by Gary Price from George Washington University and is strong in government, business and economics, legal, and news databases.

- InvisibleWeb.com
  http://www.invisibleweb.com

  This site contains over 10,000 databases.

- Librarians' Index to the Internet
  http://www.lii.org

  This site is a searchable, annotated subject directory of more than 7,000 Internet resources (including databases) selected and evaluated by librarians for their usefulness.

- Adobe PDF Search
  http://searchpdf.adobe.com/

  This site searches through more than a million summaries of Adobe® portable document format (PDF) files on the Web. The search results allow you to see the summaries before deciding to view the original Adobe PDF.

EVALUATING INTERNET MATERIAL

It is especially important in legal research to rely upon credible sources of information. When deciding whether or not a Web site is authoritative and accurate, start by verifying the following information:

The author or producer

- Check the site documentation
- Check the URL (uniform resource locators):
  - .com for commercial (both U.S. and Canada)
  - .edu for U.S. educational institutions
  - .gov for U.S. Government
  - .org for other organizations (U.S., Canadian, foreign/international)
- For organizational-based Web sites, check the name and professional reputation of the organization. This will provide information on the authority or expertise of the creator of the site.

Currency of the information

- Check "last updated" or "last modified" date

Veracity of the information

- Survey the other resources (print or electronic) available in the area and use only the most reliable sources.

WEB SITE RESEARCH SHORTCUTS

To be effective in your research strategy:

- Use the Web site's site map, table of contents, or index.
- Use the Web site's search engine.
- To locate quickly some keywords on a page that continues over several screens, use the "Find in Frame" on the "Edit" menu if you are working from Netscape, or the "Find (on this page)" on the "Edit" menu if you are working from Internet Explorer.

CITATION OF INTERNET MATERIAL

If you are using material obtained from the Internet, it is important to cite these materials accurately. Other researchers must be able to find the Web site again to check your research. There are several ways of citing Internet sources. A good citation style guide will show you how. It is recommended that you use either the *Canadian Guide to Uniform Legal Citation* (the *McGill Guide*) or the *Harvard Bluebook*.

CD-ROM and online search strategies

A list of keywords and concepts is a useful way to begin to construct searching terms. Both CD-ROMs and online services are organized according to "Boolean" logic. This system means that a search is constructed through a series of commands directing the computer to search for keywords or terms that appear within a defined relationship to each other. There are three main ways to relate or "connect" keywords and search terms to each other.

For example:

- **Drunk and driving**

   This command instructs the computer to search for one keyword and another. For example:

   [keyword] and [keyword]

   This searching technique will find all documents where the words "drunk" and "driving" appear in the same article, but not necessarily as the phrase "drunk driving."

- **Spouse or partner**

   This command instructs the computer to search for one word or another. For example:

   [keyword] or [keyword]

   This searching technique is useful when there are possible synonyms for a word or concept, and you want to cover all possibilities.

- **Freedom /5 speech**

   This command instructs the computer to search for one word within five words of another. In this instance, the word "freedom" must appear within five words of the word "speech." For example:

   [keyword] /n [keyword]

   where **n** is a number. Known as a "proximity connector," it will search for the idea of "freedom of speech" without limiting the search to instances where the exact phrase appears. Alternatively, the search may be structured more precisely by stipulating a closer connection between the keywords. This is done by decreasing the number of the proximity connector. For example, to find articles that deal only with the problem of drunk driving, search for the word "drunk" within two words of "driving." For example:

   drunk /2 driving

The commands used to express the relationship between searching terms are known as "connectors." Increasingly, many of the online services now provide the possibility to opt out of the Boolean system and to search using "plain" or "natural" language instead. Plain language searching allows the researcher to use narrative language (devoid of connector symbols or abbreviations) to fill in certain categories of information. The relationship between the keywords or search terms is expressed by selecting the appropriate option provided in a drop-down menu.

If properly used, the Boolean system is quite effective in pinpointing specific information. Since the plain language searches tend to be menu-driven, the exercises in this workbook focus on Boolean searching strategies. Even in Boolean search-

Important
Note the spacing between keywords and connectors.

ing, ideas and concepts may be expressed in a myriad of different ways. The exercises later in this chapter introduce the different techniques of constructing a Boolean search. Finally, although each online service uses its own system, in general Boolean searches use the following commands to represent the three main "connectors." Be sure to check with the user guide of the online service to see which command the service uses.

- To express the connector "and"

```
and     [keyword] and [keyword]
&       [keyword] & [keyword]
space   [keyword] [keyword]
```

For example:

```
drunk and driving
drunk & driving
drunk driving
```

- To express the connector "or"

```
or      [keyword] or [keyword]
|       [keyword] | [keyword]
```

For example:

```
Spouse or partner
Spouse | partner
```

- To search for keywords within a certain "proximity" to each other

```
/n      "[keyword] [keyword]" /n
@n      "[keyword] [keyword]" @n
```

where *n* is a number. For example:

```
"Freedom speech" /5
"Freedom speech" @5
```

MORE SEARCHING STRATEGIES

Many Boolean searching systems allow the researcher to search for various combinations of the same word at the same time. Often called "truncation" or "wildcard" searches, these commands direct the computer to find various conjugations of a keyword, various endings to a keyword, or various possible spellings of a word (to take into consideration, for example, a letter that may change). The symbols used for truncation and wildcard searches vary from one online service to another. Check the user guides for each service or the comparative summary tables for online database services (provided in this book on the inside back cover).

A final note: Boolean searching systems search for information in a particular order. It is important to check the user guides to see which order the particular service uses.

SEARCHING STRATEGIES FOR CD-ROMs

Most CD-ROMs are organized according to general headings in a contents window. Beside each heading there is a "**+**" sign. Double-click on the symbol to open up the table of contents of each chapter. Each subheading and category may be expanded in the same manner to show more detail. Similarly, the "**−**" sign collapses the table of contents back up to the next level. Consult the user guide for an explanation of the various toolbar functions. There is a help menu online and an instruction card to explain how to use the system. It is important to note the spacing between keywords and connectors.

Table 3.1 shows the searching strategies for CD-ROMs published by Carswell.

TABLE 3.1 SEARCHING STRATEGIES FOR CD-ROMs (CARSWELL)

To find	Connector to use	Example
[keyword A] or [keyword B]	`or` `|`	`Partner or spouse` `Partner	spouse`

[keyword A] and [keyword B]	`space`
	`&`
	`and`
		`Drunk driving`
		`Drunk & driving`
		`Drunk and driving`

[keyword A] but not [keyword B]	`not` `^`	`Property not personal` `Property ^ personal`
[key phrase]	`"[key phrase]"`	`"promissory estoppel"`
[keyword A] near [keyword B], regardless of order	`"[keyword] [keyword]"` followed by **@n**, where **n** is a number	`"duty warn" @2`
[keyword A] near [keyword B], in the order typed	`"[keyword] [keyword]"` followed by **/n**, where **n** is a number	`"duty warn" /2`
Truncation and wildcard searches		
Wildcard letter in place of a specific letter	`?`	`"depend?nt"`
Wildcard suffix in place of a specific suffix	`[root of keyword]*`	`Employ*`
Different conjugations of the keyword	`[keyword]%`	`Eat%`
Synonyms for the keyword	`[keyword]$`	`Child$`

SEARCHING STRATEGIES FOR ONLINE SERVICES

In Canada, Quicklaw is still the most commonly used online service. For this reason, this section will concentrate on Quicklaw search strategies, providing only an overview of Lexis-Nexis and Westlaw services. Each online service offers access to a number of different databases, and most services have comprehensive online database lists. It is a good idea to review what the database contains before selecting one in which to search. Often, it is a good idea to search more than one database to ensure that all possible sources and materials are accessed.

For a general comparison of the databases available in Lexis-Nexis, Westlaw, and Quicklaw, see the appendix. A comparison of the Boolean and proximity operators used to search these services is summarized on the inside back cover of this book.

Lexis-Nexis: An overview*

CONTENTS

(Based on law school password access. For a comprehensive list, check the Lexis-Nexis directory.)

- US cases, legislative materials, law reviews, bar journals
- Canadian cases, legislative materials, law journals
- UK, EU cases and legislative materials
- Commonwealth cases

SIGNING ON TO LEXIS.COM

1. Go to http://www.lexis.com/research or http://www.lexis.com > Sign on
2. Sign on with your ID
3. Enter password (usually your last name)

CONDUCTING RESEARCH

There are several options listed in the upper-left corner:

- **SEARCH** will access all Lexis-Nexis legal databases through two options:
    - **Find a Source** enables you to key in a publication name and go directly to it.
    - **Explore Sources** allows you to browse through the subject hierarchy to choose a source.

    A source must be chosen before a search can be run.

- **SEARCH ADVISOR** is for US legal materials only.
- **GET A DOCUMENT** retrieves US case law, law reviews, statutes, and regulations by citation.
- **CHECK A CITATION** (Shepard's) works with Canadian cases and with US case law, statutes, and regulations; where appropriate, it provides parallel citations, history, and citing references with analyses.

SEARCH TIPS

- Quotation marks or brackets are not necessary for phrase searching.
- Searches for both singular and plural forms of a word.
- Not case sensitive.
- Connectors:
    - **and, or, /n**   (terms within *n* terms of each other);
    - **/p**   (in the same paragraph);
    - **/s**   (in the same sentence);
    - **pre/n**   (both terms appear in the document in the same segment, and the first word must precede the second word by *n* words); and
    - **and not**   (excludes any words that follow the connector from appearing in a document).
- Truncation is **!** and the wildcard is *****.

FOR HELP

- Click the "Help" button at the top-right corner.

* Information in this section was supplied by Louise Tsang, Reference Law Librarian (Osgoode Hall Law School), York University Law Library, May 2001.

Westlaw: An overview*

CONTENTS

(Based on law school password access. For a comprehensive list, check the Lexis-Nexis directory.)

- US cases, legislative materials, law reviews, bar journals
- UK, EU cases and legislative materials
- US newspapers + *The Globe and Mail* + newspapers from other countries
- Some Canadian law journals

SIGNING ON TO LAWSCHOOL.WESTLAW.COM

- Go to http://www.lawschool.westlaw.com
- Enter password

CONDUCTING RESEARCH

There are several options on the main horizontal navigation bar and on the left frame.

- **FIND** retrieves US case law by citation, law reviews, statutes, and legislative sections by citation.
- **KEYCITE** works with US case law and statutes (not regulations) and provides parallel citations, history, and citing references with analyses.
- **DIRECTORY** allows you to browse through the subject hierarchy to choose a source. A source must be chosen before a search can be run.

SEARCH TIPS

- Quotation marks are necessary to search a complete phrase.
- Not case sensitive.
- Connectors:

— **&**	(and);
— **space**	(or);
— **/s**	(in the same sentence);
— **+s**	(the first term preceding the second in the same sentence);
— **/p**	(in the same paragraph);
— **+p**	(the first term preceding the second within the same paragraph);
— **/n**	(within *n* terms of each other);
— **+n**	(the first term preceding the second by *n* terms); and
— **%**	(not containing the term or terms following the "but not" symbol).

- Truncation is **!** and the wildcard is *****.

FOR HELP

- Click the "Help" button at the top-right corner.

* Information in this section was supplied by Louise Tsang, Reference Law Librarian (Osgoode Hall Law School), York University Law Library, May 2001.

Quicklaw: An overview*

Following are descriptions of some frequently used databases of Quicklaw.

CASE LAW

Includes Canadian cases and selected cases from the United States, the United Kingdom, the European Union, Australia, Africa, and Caribbean states.

CANADIAN CASE LAW CONTENT

Summary and digest databases examples

- **DRS**   Dominion Report Service
- **ACWS**   All Canada Weekly Summaries (for civil cases)
- **WCB**   Weekly Criminal Bulletin

Full-text databases examples

- **SCC** database (includes SCR, SCJ, and SCCA, Supreme Court Rulings in Motions for Leave to Appeal).
- There are similar databases for provincial materials. In Ontario, all the Ontario databases can be searched individually or together using the "Ontario Reports Plus" (ORP) database, which searches the Ontario Reports as well as the database of Ontario Judgments. The "Western Provinces Judgments" (WPJ) database searches decisions from western and northern Canada as well as the Supreme Court of Canada. The "Atlantic Provinces Judgments" (APJ) database searches decisions from Atlantic Canada and the Supreme Court of Canada.
- The most recent version of Quicklaw lists the contents of each database on the main menu.

Special features

- **Quickcite**: Updates cases and shows judicial consideration of a case.
- To search for statutes judicially considered: Open a database and search for all cases that have mentioned the section in question. For example, to search for judicial consideration of s. 12 of the *Canadian Charter of Rights and Freedoms*, use the following Boolean search:

  ```
  charter /2 rights /2 freedoms /p 12
  ```

  This search finds the name of the Act by describing the relationship between the words "charter," "rights," and "freedoms." It finds the instances where the name of the Act appears in the same paragraph as the number "12."
- Use **LNET** to find recent decisions and other documents newly added to Quicklaw. LNET is a comprehensive database that covers decisions from Ontario courts, the Supreme Court of Canada, and newsworthy press releases and government statements of legal significance.

STATUTES AND REGULATIONS

Includes Canadian statutes and regulations, federal US Code and selected state codes, and the South African constitution.

For Canada, you may search for all federal and some provincial legislation. There is both an entire act version and a section version.

It is also possible to search for bills and their status in the parliamentary or legislative reading process.

JOURNALS

There are about 16 Canadian law journals available on Quicklaw.

LEGAL TEXTS

Specific legal texts, provided by Irwin Law, are also available on Quicklaw.

NETLETTERS

Netletters are materials that are not indexed in the *Index to Canadian Legal Literature* database, but that may be searched on other Quicklaw databases.

LEGAL INDEXES

The two most useful Quicklaw legal indexes are:

- **ICLL**   Index to Canadian Legal Literature
- **CLSI**   Canadian Legal Symposia Index (for practice-oriented conference papers)

NEWS AND WIRE SERVICES

There are various news databases on Quicklaw. Check the most current Quicklaw database list (which is available online). For Canadian and UK research, try the following news and wire services:

Canada

- **CPN**   Canadian Press 1984-

United Kingdom

- **EN** includes
    - **IND**   *The Independent*, London
    - **TI**   *The Times*, London

TOPICAL DATABASES

You may conduct Quicklaw searches under specific topics or subjects. Again, check the Quicklaw database list for a complete index of topical databases. There are both narrow and global topical databases. A global database allows you to search simultaneously more than one database (on the same topic, or covering the same jurisdiction). For example, for Canadian topical global databases, **CRIM** ("Criminal Law Topical, Global") includes all criminal cases and criminal law texts, netletters, and journal articles.

Using Quicklaw: Overview and practice

Quicklaw has recently offered a menu-driven system. If you have Internet Explorer 5, you will find Quicklink Pro offers a very user-friendly browser service. The browser provides options for both plain language and Boolean searching.

Quicklaw makes it easy to look up specific cases. If you know the exact citation of a case, find the relevant database and click on the button for case citation searches. Fill in the information according to the Quicklaw example provided on the screen.

If you wish to search using plain language, the Quicklaw Pro screen prompts you to search for information using a template that searches according to case name, court level, deciding judge, and even counsel of record. There is a final option called "any field" that allows you to search generally. Beside each of these searching categories (or "fields" as Quicklaw calls them) is a drop-down box that allows you to stipulate the relationship between the search words.

Field searches are an effective way to find cases using specific information, such as case name, court level, judge's name, or specific date.

If you wish to use the Boolean searching system, select a database and then click on the "Boolean search" button at the top of the screen. Table 3.2 summarizes the Boolean searching techniques that can be used. There is a detailed description of these tools on the Quicklaw help menu for "query searches." A glossary of the Boolean operators or connectors appears on the sidebar of the screen, and a drop-down box at the bottom of the screen lists the operators used to search fields in the Boolean system.

Boolean searching is most effective in finding cases on general research topics or for cases on a particular point of law. Quicklaw Boolean searching looks for information that satisfies the connector commands in the following order:

    &

    % (not)

    or

    /n   **+n**   **/p**   **" "**

    [space] (implicit **or**)

A detailed description of this system is available on the Quicklaw Web site (www.quicklaw.com).

TABLE 3.2 SEARCHING STRATEGIES FOR QUICKLAW

To find	Connector to use	Example
[keyword A] or [keyword B] *Note: More than 2 keywords may be connected*	`or`	`partner or spouse` `partner or spouse or wife`

[keyword A] and [keyword B]
Note: More than 2 keywords may be connected
	`&`
	`and`
		`drunk & driving`
		`drunk and driving`
		`drunk and driving and`
		`   impaired`

[keyword] within how many words from [keyword B]	`[keyword] /n [keyword]` where **n** is a number	`duty /2 warn`
[keyword A] within the same paragraph as [keyword B]	`[keyword] /p [keyword]`	`charter /p religion`

Truncation and wildcard searches

[keyword] followed by truncation in place of different word endings	`[keyword]!`	`employ!`
[keyword] followed by suggested suffixes to find more than one specific word ending	`[keyword](suffixes)`	`employ(ment,ed,ing)`
wildcard letter in place of a specific letter	`*`	`depend*nt`

Field searches that limit the search to date, court level, case name, or citation, etc.

To limit the search to case names	`@2 [case name]`	`@2 Ing /2 Jones` restricts the search to `Ing v. Jones`
To limit the search to a specific citation	`@3 [case citation]`	`@3 1996 2 s.c.r. 507`
To limit the search to a particular year	`@4 [year]`	`@4 2001`
To limit the search to a particular jurisdiction and court	`@4 [jurisdiction] &` `[level of court]`	`@4 ontario & appeal`
To limit the search according to a judge's name	`@4 [judge's name]`	`@4 laskin`

PRACTISE WRITING BOOLEAN QUERY SEARCHES

EXERCISE 1 Using numeric proximity connectors and truncation

Using only the numeric proximity connectors and truncation, suggest a possible Quicklaw Boolean query search for the following legal terms of art.

Example:

Legal term of art:	Possible Boolean search query:
duty of care	duty /2 care
freedom of expression	free! /2 express!
administration of justice	_____
adverse discrimination	_____
adverse possession	_____
arbitrary detention	_____
assault with a weapon	_____
breach of trust	_____
burden of proof	_____
class action suit	_____
concealed weapon	_____
consensus ad idem	_____
constructive dismissal	_____
constructive lien	_____
constructive trust	_____
contributory negligence	_____
criminal negligence causing death	_____
duty to accommodate	_____
duty to warn	_____
en ventre de sa mère	_____

fee entail   _____

fee simple   _____

felony murder   _____

fiduciary duty   _____

for the purposes of trafficking   _____

free and democratic society   _____

freedom of association   _____

full answer and defence   _____

EXERCISE 2   Using "and" connectors and truncation

Using only the "and" connector and truncation, suggest a possible Quicklaw Boolean query search for the following legal terms of art.

Example:

Legal term of art:	Possible Boolean search query:
duty of care	`duty and care`
freedom of expression	`free! & express!`
illegal discharge of firearms	_____
independent legal advice	_____
justifiable homicide	_____
mandatory retirement	_____
mareva injunction	_____
moral rights	_____
occupiers liability	_____
peace order and good government	_____
presumption of innocence	_____
prima facie case	_____
principles of fundamental justice	_____
prohibited grounds of discrimination	_____
quid pro quo	_____
reasonable forseeability	_____
reasonable person	_____
res ipsa loquitor	_____
resident alien	_____
right to counsel	_____
rule against perpetuities	_____
sexual interference	_____

spousal support   _____

squatters' rights   _____

tortious interference   _____

unreasonable search and seizure   _____

vested rights   _____

PRACTISE USING BOOLEAN QUERY SEARCHES

Practise using Boolean query searches to find cases dealing with a specific set of circumstances or legal principles.

There is no one right way to construct a Boolean search. However, some methods of searching are more effective than others. With practice, Boolean searching allows you to formulate specific and detailed searches to pinpoint relevant material. The Boolean search will find sources with all the keywords in the order stipulated. The following examples illustrate how certain Boolean search commands can be used to find specific cases. Practice these strategies in the exercises that follow.

Example 1

PROBLEM

Find a 2001 case involving a Canadian resident who is not a Canadian citizen and who commits a serious criminal offence. As a result of a criminal conviction, Canada wants to deport the individual back to his home country.

SOLUTION

First, identify the keywords and concepts that may be used to construct a Boolean search command or query.

Keywords and concepts	Key facts
Person	Canadian resident
	Non-citizen
Event or action	Criminal offence
	Criminal conviction
	Deportation
Date	2001
Place	Not applicable
Object	Not applicable

From this list, suggest a possible Quicklaw Boolean query search using a combination of the "**&**" and proximity connectors, and the truncation symbol to construct a search command.

For example:

Keyword	Possible Boolean search command	Finds
Canadian resident, non-citizen	**canadian & resident & citizen!**	Cases where the words "canadian," "resident," and various forms of the word "citizen" appear, such as citizenship, non-citizen, etc.
Criminal offence, conviction	**crimin! & convict!**	Cases where any form of the word "criminal" and any form of the word "convict" appear
Deportation	**deport!**	Cases where any form of the word "deport" appears, such as "deporting," "deported," "deportation," etc.
2001	**@4 2001**	Restricts the search to those cases reported in 2001

When these search commands are strung together, they form the following possible query search:

canadian & resident & citizen! & crimin! & convict! & deport! @4 2001

This search looks for cases decided in 2001 in which the words "Canadian" and "resident" appear along with any form of the words "citizen," "criminal," "convict" and "deport."

Example 2

PROBLEM

Find a case concerning an individual arrested for possession of marijuana or, as it is known in the *Criminal Code*, "cannabis."

SOLUTION

First, identify the keywords and concepts that may be used to construct a Boolean search command or query.

Keywords and concepts	Key facts
Person	Not known
Event or action	possession, marijuana, cannabis
Date	Not known
Place	Not known

From this list, suggest a possible Quicklaw Boolean query search using a combination of the connector "**or**" and truncation to construct a search command.
For example:

Keyword	Possible Boolean search command	Finds
Possession	**possess!**	Cases where any form of the word "possess" appears, such as "possession," "possessing," etc.
Marijuana	**marij!**	Cases where any form of the word "marij" appears
Cannabis	**cannabis**	Cases where the word "cannabis" appears

When these search commands are strung together, they form the following possible search query:

possess! & marij! or cannabis

This search looks for cases decided in which any form of the word "possess" appears with any form of the word "marij" or the word "cannabis." Since "marijuana" and "cannabis" mean the same thing, this search will likely find more cases on point than if only one of these words is used.

Example 3

PROBLEM

Find a case where, after a divorce settlement, one of the parties finds out that the other party failed to disclose significant stock holdings during the initial divorce proceedings.

SOLUTION

First, identify the keywords and concepts that may be used to construct a Boolean search command or query.

Keywords and concepts	Key facts
Person	divorced party
Event or action	failure to disclose assets or stock holdings, terms of settlement

From this list, suggest a possible Quicklaw Boolean query search using any combination of proximity connectors ("**or**," "**and**," **/n**) and truncation to construct a search command.

For example:

Keyword	Possible Boolean search command	Finds
divorced party	`divorc!`	Cases where any form of the word "divorc" appears, such as "divorcee," "divorced," "divorcing," etc.
failure to disclose assets or stock holdings	`failure /2 disclose /2 asset!` `stock`	Cases where the word "failure" appears within two words of "disclose" that appears within two words of any form of the word "asset" (such as "assets") or "stock"
terms of settlement	`settlement`	Cases where the word "settlement" appears

When these search commands are strung together, they form the following possible search query:

```
divorc! & settlement & failure /2 disclose /2
asset! or stock
```

EXERCISE 3 Finding cases

Suggest a possible Boolean query search that would find cases relevant to the following situations.

1. A Charter issue involving freedom of religion.

   _____

2. A constitutional question regarding property and civil rights.

   _____

3. A breach of trust in a takeover bid.

   _____

4. A custom official's power to seize obscene material at the border.

   _____

5. A case involving criminal negligence where a patient, with a transmittable disease, knowingly passes it on to another and causes death.

   _____

6. A public demonstration causing disruption of the peace.

   _____

EXERCISE 4 Searching news articles

Paragraph proximity connectors are very useful for searching newspapers and journals. A convention in journalistic reporting is to ensure that all the keywords and concepts of the story appear in the lead paragraph. Using the paragraph proximity connector (/p), suggest a possible Boolean search for news articles on the following situations.

1. The embezzlement of client trust accounts.

    _____

2. Lawyers' duty to disclose evidence and their duty of confidentiality to their clients.

    _____

3. The City of Toronto's bid for the Olympics.

    _____

4. The crisis in national health care and fiscal responsibility.

    _____

5. Corporate donations to political parties and conflict of interest.

    _____

6. Diplomatic immunity and drunk driving.

    _____

7. Non-insane automatism and unqualified acquittal (sleepwalking and murder).

    _____

8. Record snowfall for the Maritimes in 2001.

    _____

9. Earthquakes and nuclear testing.

    _____

10. Director's liability and environmental management.

    _____

EXERCISE 5 Searching with incomplete data (advanced Quicklaw skills)

Suggest a possible Boolean query search for the following situations and cite the relevant cases. Remember to select an appropriate database and that Quicklaw organizes searches according to jurisdiction and topics of law.

1. Two cases regarding the rights of same-sex couples to adopt a child in British Columbia.

   a. Construct a possible Boolean query search.

   _____

   b. Identify the cases from British Columbia.

   _____

   _____

   _____

   _____

   c. Do the British Columbia courts handle this situation in the same way as courts in Newfoundland and Manitoba?

   _____

   d. List the cases found in those jurisdictions.

   _____

   _____

   _____

   _____

2. Our client is a schoolteacher who was fired from her position for making hateful and racist remarks while teaching her history class. She maintains that her freedom of speech is protected under the *Canadian Charter of Rights and Freedoms*. Has the Supreme Court of Canada addressed this matter?

   a. Suggest a possible Boolean query search.

   _____

   b. Cite the relevant cases from the Supreme Court of Canada.

   _____

   _____

   _____

   _____

3. Our client had access to confidential information on Slide Steel Ltd., a publicly traded Canadian company. On the basis of that information, he knew that the price of the company's shares would appreciate substantially. He acted on this information when he agreed to participate in a takeover bid for Slide Steel. The law requires that, during a takeover bid, anyone having information that may affect the value of the shares must disclose that information. Afraid of being accused of industrial espionage, our client did not disclose his information. Have the Alberta courts dealt with this kind of problem before?

   a. Identify the most appropriate topical database to use.

   _____

   b. Suggest a possible Boolean query search.

   _____

   c. Use the "Commercial Law Topical, Global" database to find cases from other jurisdictions and general literature on this problem. List the number of cases or articles found from each jurisdiction.

   _____

   _____

   _____

   _____

4. How many cases can you find dealing with individuals who have come to Canada to escape political persecution and now seek refugee status?

   a. Identify the most appropriate topical database to use.

   _____

   b. Suggest a possible Boolean query search.

   _____

   c. List the jurisdictions in which relevant cases were found and the number of cases from each jurisdiction.

   _____

   _____

   _____

   _____

5. Our client is the development company, "Adventure Paradise Ltd." The company is about to purchase a large piece of land on which to construct a resort. Before it purchases the land, it wants to be absolutely sure it will be able to realize the development project. The company is concerned that there may be a restrictive convenant on the use of this land and wants to know what impact such a convenant would have on future development plans.

   a. Identify the most appropriate topical database to use.

   _____

   b. Suggest a possible Boolean query search.

   _____

   c. List the jurisdictions in which relevant cases were found and the number of cases from each jurisdiction.

   _____

   _____

   _____

   _____

6. Our client was driving his car and talking on the cell phone when he hit a pedestrian using a crosswalk. Use the motor vehicle topical database to find relevant cases.

a. Identify the most appropriate motor vehicle topical database to use.

_____

b. Suggest a possible Boolean query search.

_____

c. List the number of cases found from each jurisdiction.

_____

_____

_____

_____

EXERCISE 6   Search queries for chapter 1 problems

Reread the problems in chapter 1. Using the keywords and concepts raised in these problems, suggest at least three possible Boolean query searches for each problem.

1. Reread "Ms Ravji and the Ashtar Estate" on page 6. Use the keywords and facts that you identified for this problem to find the relevant case law.

   a. List the Quicklaw databases that might be used to research this problem.

   _____

   b. Suggest three possible Boolean query searches.

   1. _____

   2. _____

   3. _____

   c. Indicate the number of cases each query search found, using at least two databases.

   Database: _____

   Query search 1: _____

   Query search 2: _____

   Query search 3: _____

   Database: _____

   Query search 1: _____

   Query search 2: _____

   Query search 3: _____

   d. List the case(s) decided in 2000 that most resemble(s) the facts in the problem.

   _____

   _____

   _____

   _____

   e. If you had to refine the query search to find relevant cases, indicate which query search and which database you used.

   _____

   _____

2. Reread "Green Acres" on page 8. Use the keywords and facts that you identified for this problem to find the relevant case law.

   a. List the Quicklaw databases that might be used to research this problem.

   _____

   b. Suggest three possible Boolean query searches.

     1. _____

     2. _____

     3. _____

   c. Indicate the number of cases each query search found, using at least two databases.

     Database: _____

      Query search 1: _____

      Query search 2: _____

      Query search 3: _____

     Database: _____

      Query search 1: _____

      Query search 2: _____

      Query search 3: _____

   d. Find the case(s) decided between 1984 and 1987 that most resemble the facts in the problem. Circle the case that is most similar.

   _____

   _____

   _____

   _____

   e. If you had to refine the query search to find relevant cases, indicate which query search and which database you used.

   _____

   _____

   f. Which database produced the best results?

   _____

3. Reread "Mr. Kuresh" on page 20. Use the keywords and facts that you identified for this problem to find the relevant case law.

a. List the Quicklaw database that would be most effective in researching this problem.

_____

b. Suggest three possible Boolean query searches.

1. _____

2. _____

3. _____

c. Indicate the number of cases each query search found.

Database: _____

Query search 1: _____

Query search 2: _____

Query search 3: _____

d. Find the case(s) decided in 2000 that most resemble(s) the facts in the problem.

_____

_____

_____

_____

e. If you had to refine the query search to find relevant cases, indicate which query search and which database you used.

_____

_____

4. Reread "Rucz family" on page 26.

    a. List the Quicklaw database that would be most effective in researching this problem.

    _____

    b. Suggest three possible Boolean query searches.

        1. _____

        2. _____

        3. _____

    c. Indicate the number of cases each query search found.

        Database: _____

            Query search 1: _____

            Query search 2: _____

            Query search 3: _____

    d. List the Ontario cases decided since 1990 that most resemble the facts in the problem.

    _____

    _____

    _____

    _____

    _____

    _____

    _____

    e. If you had to refine the query search to find relevant cases, indicate which query search and which database you used.

    _____

    _____

f. List the advantages and disadvantages of using topical databases versus jurisdictional databases to research a problem.

_____

_____

_____

_____

_____

CHAPTER 4

Case-briefing skills: How to read a court case like a lawyer

INTRODUCTION

Lawyers read cases to understand how courts apply the law in similar situations. The skills used to read fact situations are also used to summarize the information from these cases. Since lawyers spend so much of their time reading, it is important to learn how to read quickly and take notes effectively.

Although there are various styles of briefing a case, certain information will always be relevant. It is helpful to read and take notes on a case with a series of questions in mind. This idea of briefing a case according to a series of questions was developed by the dean of Harvard Law School in 1870 in what was to be a major revision to the way law is taught. Dean Christopher Columbus Langdell believed that by applying the "scientific method" to legal analysis, the study of law would become as revered as the physical sciences. He argued that a lawyer could dissect a case to find out how the law works, just as a biologist might dissect an animal to discover the workings of its internal organs. Langdell's method is useful, but law is not biology. Sometimes the scientific method is inappropriate or simply breaks down when applied to legal reasoning: sometimes the internal workings of the law are not exposed so readily. For this reason, Langdell's method has as many critics as it does supporters.

The chapter introduces the questions used to brief cases and presents three different styles commonly used for note taking.

For further reading, see M. Moskovitz, "Beyond the Case Method: It's Time To Teach with Problems" (1992), 42 *Journal of Legal Education* 241; and P.F. Teich, "Research on American Law Teaching: Is There a Case Against the Case System?" (1986), 36 *Journal of Legal Education* 167.

QUESTIONS USED TO BRIEF A CASE

The name of the case, referred to as **style of cause**, answers questions about *who* is involved. For example:

Who?

> *Rowe v. Canning.*

Which court? A description of how the case moved through the court system, described as **procedural history**, answers questions about *which courts* heard the case. For example:

> This is an appeal to the Supreme Court of Canada from a decision of the Manitoba Court of Appeal, which allowed an appeal from Madam Justice Gwyer of the Court of Queen's Bench, who acquitted the accused at trial.

What happened? A summary of the most important facts of the case, referred to as **material facts**, answers questions about *what happened*. The summary highlights only those *actions*, *locations*, and *objects* that were important in the court's decision. It also identifies the people involved according to their role in the case. For example:

> Rowe and Furey, plaintiffs, struck off motorcycle by stray horse on highway.

> Boyd Canning, Defendant, owner of stray horse.

What legal questions? A statement of the *legal questions* the court was asked to decide, referred to as **issues**, answers questions about why the parties are in court. The issues are often stated in the form of a question about the law as it applies to a particular set of circumstances. For example:

> Are the Cannings liable in negligence for breach of a duty at common law?

Who won? A statement of a court's judgment, often referred to as its **decision** (or **holding**), answers questions about *who won*. For example:

> Defendants Boyd Canning and Renee Canning found liable for damages to Bryan Rowe and Wayne Furey

or in an appeal case

> Appeal dismissed; appellant's conviction by the Court of Appeal restored.

What message? A statement of the legal rule the court used to reach its decision, often referred to as **ratio** (*ratio decidendi* or **precedent**), identifies the court's answers to the legal questions and explains why the case is important. This statement answers questions about the *message* the case conveys, both for the people involved in the case (the immediate message), and for the future. The future message is for others not involved in the case at hand, but who may be affected by its example. Depending on who is reading the case and why, the message may be very specific or very general. To determine the ratio of a case, consider what the case says about the law and how the law applies to everyday life. For example:

> Animal owners are responsible for the damages caused when their animals stray.

What justification? An explanation of why the court reached its decision, referred to as its **reasons**, answers questions about the court's *justification* for a particular application of the law. For example:

> The court found that because it is reasonably foreseeable that animals roaming free will cause harm, animal owners are negligent when they fail to secure their animals properly.

**Case-briefing skills: *Rowe v. Canning*
(1994), 117 Nfld. & PEIR 353, 4 MVR (3d)
269 (Nfld. TD)**

L.D. BARRY J: — Prince the pony slipped its bridle and went exploring, on the first day Renée Canning brought it home as a present for his grandchildren. While Prince was at large, Rowe and Furey fell off their motorcycle, when a horse ran suddenly in front of them, near the Cannings' home. Rowe and Furey claim Prince was the perpetrator and now sue for damages.

Tip
J = judge
CJ = chief justice

THE FACTS

On June 27, 1990, Rowe and Furey were riding Rowe's motorcycle in a westerly direction along the Conception Bay Highway, in the Town of Conception Bay South. The driver, Rowe, heard a warning shouted by Furey, who was seated behind him, and almost simultaneously saw a horse running at full gallop from the side of the highway towards the motorcycle. Rowe and Furey said the left side of the motorcycle hit the horse's right front quarter and neck. The bike fell over, spilling Rowe and Furey to the roadway. The horse kept running across the highway and down Perrins Road, in Conception Bay South. After Rowe and Furey had picked themselves up and called the police, they saw Boyd Canning leading a horse along the highway and down Perrins Road. Rowe and Fury identified the horse as the one that had run across the road.

Boyd Canning testified that on June 27th his father, Renée Canning, brought home Prince, a small ten year old horse, about the size of a Newfoundland Pony, which Renée had purchased the previous Christmas for Boyd Canning's children. Prince had been stabled by its previous owner from Christmas until the day of the accident. Boyd Canning said he had earlier that day fastened the bridle, which was on Prince upon arrival, to a rope affixed to a steel peg in the ground. When Boyd Canning arrived home later, around the time of the accident, he found Prince's bridle still attached to the rope, but Prince had disappeared from the unfenced property. His father informed him Prince had slipped the bridle. Canning went looking for the horse and found Prince on a parking lot by a store on the Conception Bay Highway, not far from the intersection with Perrins Road where the accident occurred. Canning said he saw no indication on Prince of having been hit by a motorcycle.

Kimberly Greenslade, Steven Batten and Juanita Breen testified they had been walking together along the Conception Bay Highway towards St. John's, when they noticed a horse "dart" across the highway and run down Perrins Road. They all were of the opinion that the horse was a full-grown horse. When shown a photo of the pony owned by the Cannings, all three said the horse on the highway was larger.

> **Note:** The judgments in this workbook may have been edited for length or summarized for the purposes of the exercises.

The records of the Department of Municipal Affairs show that regulations prohibiting the roaming of animals were made by the Town of Conception Bay South and approved by the Minister on March 18, 1975. The Plaintiffs could not provide conclusive evidence, however, that these regulations had ever been posted for publication as required by the relevant legislation, because the minutes of Town Council meetings were not available for the period prior to 1977.

THE ISSUES

Three issues arise:

(1) Was Prince the horse involved in the accident?

(2) If the horse was Prince, are the Cannings liable in negligence either (a) for breach of a duty created by municipal regulations or (b) for breach of a duty at common law?

(3) Was Brian Furey keeping a proper lookout, while driving his motorcycle?

STATUTORY PROVISIONS AND REGULATIONS

The Livestock Act, RSN 1990, c. L-20, provides:

> 6. The minister may by order prohibit the running at large of a class of livestock within an area specified in the order.
>
> 7. An owner shall not permit ... a stallion over the age of 1 year ... to run at large without the written consent of the minister.
>
> 8. (1) The owner of livestock shall be liable for damages caused by that livestock to property.
>
> ...
>
> (3) Nothing in this section affects the liability of an owner of livestock where the livestock is involved in a collision with a motor vehicle.

The Town of Conception Bay South (Impounding of Animals) Regulations, 1975, approved by the Minister March 18, 1975, provided:

> 2. No person shall permit any animal of which he is the owner or guardian to roam at large in any street, road, or lane within the Town or in any open field or common from which free access can be had to such street, road, or lane. ...
>
> 4. All owners or guardians shall maintain a proper fence on their property so as to prohibit their animals from roaming at large.

The Local Government Act, Stats. Nfld. 1972, No. 32, provided:

> 99(1) Subject to the approval of the Minister, the council may make regulations ...
>
> > (e) Prohibiting ... the running at large ... of animals ... providing for the impounding of such animals ...
>
> (6) Regulations made under subsection (1) or (2) shall be made public by poster erected in such places as the council may direct and shall not have effect until they are so posted.

ANALYSIS

1. Identification of Horse

Rowe was certain that the horse he saw leaving the scene with Boyd Canning was the horse which ran across the road. He described the horse involved in the accident as a horse "a bit bigger than a pony, almost like a riding horse," and a mixture of light and dark brown in colour, with a dark mane. This accurately described Prince, shown in a photograph later tendered by Canning. One difference was the mane, which Rowe described as dark black, when it is in fact dark brown. Furey's description, while less precise than Rowe's, also adequately described Prince. I prefer the testimony of Rowe and Furey to that of Greenslade, Batten and Breen. Rowe and Furey were closer to the animal which ran across the road. Also, there was some uncertainty in the evidence of the three bystanders, who, like Rowe and Furey, only had seconds to view the horse. Greenslade estimated that she was 50 to 100 feet away from the animal but indicated she was not sure of the distance. Batten, who was with Greenslade and Breen, estimated the distance at 300 to 400 feet. Breen estimated the distance at 75 feet but admitted she was not good at judging distances. Neither Greenslade nor Batten were able to describe the colour of the horse. Breen said she thought it was brown but she wasn't sure. While each thought it was a full-grown horse they had seen, they had difficulty describing its height. Kimberly Greenslade stated she thought the horse was as tall as she was. Batten estimated that the back of the horse he saw would be about up to his chin. They both denied the horse shown on the photo was large enough to be the one they saw. But they could not estimate the height of the horse in the photo. Breen said merely that the horse she saw was not as tall as her.

Batten testified that the horse was galloping. Breen said it was moving between a slow walk and a run. Greenslade said it was running. These three witnesses also were of the opinion that the horse had not hit the motorcycle, because the horse kept going and did not make any sound. Counsel for the Cannings submits that, if the motorcycle hit the horse, as alleged by Rowe and Furey, there would have to be marks on the horse. He says that, since there were no marks on Prince, this supports the premise there was a second horse.

Juanita Breen testified that, in her twenty-three years in the area, this was the only time she had seen a horse roaming free along the Highway in Conception Bay South. Even without her testimony I believe I could take judicial notice this was an unusual occurrence on a busy highway. It would be an extraordinary and highly improbable coincidence for there to be another horse, in addition to Prince, roaming free at that exact time, in that same area, with that exact colour.

I am satisfied from the testimony of Rowe and Furey it was Prince which ran across the road. Rowe and Furey were closer to the animal than other witnesses and their evidence was more precise. I also accept the testimony of Rowe and Furey that their motorcycle hit the horse a glancing blow. I do not believe I should find that there was another horse running free at the time, merely because there were no signs of injury on Prince. This can be explained by the glancing blow. I find that Greenslade, Batten and Breen, who had discussed the incident amongst themselves, arrived at an erroneous conclusion as to the size of the horse they saw, probably because of the short time it was in view, their distance from the horse, and their lack of any references against which to measure the size from that distance.

2. Negligence of Cannings

(a) Statutory Duty

Although the Cannings' horse was named "Prince," not "Princess," I conclude this is insufficient evidence upon which to base a conclusion that Prince was a stallion. Neither was there any evidence of an order by the Minister under the *Livestock Act*, prohibiting the running at large of horses in the area. I am, therefore, unable to find that the *Livestock Act* is applicable.

There is, however, a statutory duty to prevent roaming animals, created by the Town of Conception Bay South (Impounding of Animals) Regulations, 1975. Section 2 of the Regulations is applicable. I do not accept the interpretation of Counsel for the Cannings that "permit" in that section should be interpreted as not applying to a person who has, as in the present case, attempted to keep an animal tied up. My interpretation of the section is that, if an owner improperly or inadequately ties up an animal so as to allow that animal to escape, then that owner has "permitted" the animal to roam at large. Also, in any event, the Cannings were also in breach of section 4 of the Regulations, which required that they maintain a proper fence on their property so as to prohibit Prince from roaming at large.

I am satisfied I should treat the 1975 Regulations as having been properly posted. The person who was Town Manager in 1975 set out in an affidavit that, while he has no specific recollection of the creation and implementation of the Regulations, the practice was to post regulations after they were returned with the Minister's approval. He deposed:

> ... given that the subject Regulations were prepared, passed by the Town Council of the Town of Conception Bay South, submitted to the Minister for his approval, I feel that they were posted in the Town Office in the same fashion as all other Regulations that had to be posted to give them force and effect, following their return from the office of the Minister of Municipal Affairs.

I conclude there is sufficient evidence in this affidavit of the former Town Manager to permit me to draw the inference that, on a balance of probabilities, all things concerning posting, required by the legislation, have been done. At the very least, this evidence shifted the evidentiary burden and required the Defendants to bring forward evidence, which would raise a doubt, as to whether the Town had properly posted the Regulations. This the Cannings have not done. There is no evidence at all that the Regulations were not properly posted and in effect. Even if there had been no evidence from which an inference of posting could have been drawn, there is authority supporting the proposition that, in circumstances such as the present, the initial onus is on the Defendants to prove that the Regulations were not properly posted. In *R v. Pay-N-Save Drugs Ltd.* (1960), 128 CCC 425 (Man. CA), the Court confirmed the decision of a Magistrate, who had held that the onus was on the accused to prove the Early Closing By-Law of the City of Winnipeg was invalid. The accused was questioning whether the By-Law had been advertised in accordance with the *Shops Regulation Act*, RSM 1954, c. 242. See also, Rogers, *The Law of Canadian Municipal Corporations* (2d ed., updated to 1994), at pp. 463-4.

(b) Duty at Common Law

In this case, even in the absence of applicable municipal regulations, one would have to consider whether there is a duty at common law on the owner of a horse to prevent that animal from roaming onto a busy highway and causing an accident. It should be foreseeable to an owner that, if a horse breaks loose, it is likely to cause such accidents. In those circumstances would it not be a breach of a common law duty for the owner of a horse to inadequately tie an animal and, thereby, allow the animal to get free?

In *Searle v. Wallbank*, [1947] AC 341 (HL), the House of Lords held that an owner of a field had no obligation to prevent his animals from straying upon an adjacent highway. The Supreme Court of Canada refused to follow this approach and held, in *Fleming v. Atkinson*, [1959] SCR 513, that the historical basis for the rule in *Searle*, dependent as it was on the peculiarities of highway dedication in England, where highways had come into being by adjoining owners giving only a right of passage to the public, had never existed in Ontario. The Court held that the ordinary rules of negligence applied to the case of straying animals and that regard should be had to all the circumstances, including the nature of the highway and the amount and nature of the traffic upon it. The development of Newfoundland highways may not have occurred in the same way as those in Ontario, where, for the most part, the fee was always in the Crown. However, in *Eales v. James* (1977), 17 Nfld. & PEIR 242 (Nfld. Dist. Ct.), McCarthy DCJ held that, since highways in this Province are vested in the Province or in municipalities, the law of Newfoundland can also be distinguished from the law of England. He applied *Fleming* and held the rule of *Searle* inapplicable in Newfoundland. I have been given no reason why I should not take the same approach.

I find that, even if the Regulations of the Town were not in effect, there was a common law duty upon the Cannings to prevent Prince from roaming upon the busy Conception Bay Highway, where the volume of traffic meant an accident would be likely.

(c) Breach of Duty

Boyd Canning says he merely tied Prince on by means of the bridle, which was already on the horse's head when his father brought Prince home. There is no evidence that his father was not involved in placing the bridle on the animal. Even if the previous owner had placed the bridle on Prince, the Cannings had a duty to ensure that the bridle was secure enough to hold, when Prince was tied on in the field. In the circumstances I must find that the Cannings were in breach of duty and negligent and are liable to Rowe and Furey for their damages in an amount to be assessed.

3. Contributory negligence

Counsel for the Cannings submits that, because Furey saw the horse on the side of the road, before it came upon the pavement, therefore Rowe could not have been keeping a proper lookout if he only saw the horse just at the moment of collision. I do not find this submission at all convincing. I accept the evidence of Rowe and Fury that they were traveling within the speed limit at the time. I also accept their evidence that Rowe was driving in a responsible and prudent fashion. Furey's evidence is that the horse was at full gallop when he first saw it proceeding from the side of the highway. The fact that Rowe saw the horse a second or so after Furey is no evidence that he was not keeping a proper lookout. As driver, Rowe had a responsibility to maintain a proper lookout on the road ahead, while also remaining reasonably alert for hazards entering from the side. Furey, as passenger, had the luxury of ignoring the road ahead, if he wished, and maintaining his gaze upon the side of the road. It is not strange, therefore, that he may have seen the horse a few seconds before Rowe. I find Rowe was keeping a proper lookout. There was no contributory negligence on his part.

SUMMARY AND DISPOSITION

1. Boyd Canning and Renee Canning are liable to Bryan Rowe (formerly known as Bryan Rowe Goodyear) and Wayne Furey for their damages in an amount to be assessed.

2. Rowe and Furey have leave to apply for an assessment of damages.

3. Rowe and Furey are entitled to their costs, to be taxed.

METHOD 1: USING A CHART SUMMARY

A lawyer needs certain information from each case. For this reason, a case is read with a series of general questions in mind. The chart summary in table 4.1 dissects the case into its component parts, extracting the relevant legal information in a question and answer format.

It is difficult to summarize lengthy decisions. The information included in a case brief depends on why the case is being read. If a case is being read to learn about the law in general, then the case brief is likely to include more detail than if the reader is interested in learning about how the courts have dealt with specific problems in the past. In general, however, a case brief will always include any information that relates directly to the legal significance or "future message" of the case. Table 4.2 presents a point-by-point explanation of what was included in the chart summary prepared for *Rowe v. Canning*.

TABLE 4.1 USING A CHART SUMMARY

Question	Answer	Legal term
a. Who?	(1) *Rowe v. Canning*	Style of cause
b. Which courts?	(2) Trial Level (Newfoundland)	Procedural history
c. What happened?	(3) Rowe and Furey, plaintiffs, struck off motorcycle by stray pony on highway.	Facts
	(4) The plaintiffs sue the defendant, Canning, claiming his pony, Prince, caused their accident.	
	(5) The defendant found his runaway pony, Prince, near the highway.	
	(6) Eyewitness statements inconsistent and cannot confirm that the animal they saw run across the highway was the pony Prince.	
	(7) The defendant argues that even if Prince did cause the accident, the plaintiffs were not driving carefully.	
	(8) For this reason, the defendant claims that the plaintiffs are partly responsible for their injuries, having contributed to the cause of the accident.	
d. Legal questions?	(9) A. Was Prince the horse involved in the accident?	Issues
	(10) B. Is there a common law or statutory duty to secure one's animals?	
	(11) C. If such a duty is owed, did the defendant breach the duty?	
	(12) D. Were the plaintiffs acting in a manner that contributed to the cause of the accident?	
e. Who won?	(13) The defendant is liable to the plaintiffs.	Decision (holding)
f. What message?	(14) A. Owners of animals have a responsibility to ensure that the animals do not cause injury to others.	Ratio
	(15) B. Because it is reasonably foreseeable that an animal roaming free will cause injury, the owners of such animals owe a duty of care to control their animals.	
g. Justification?	(16) A. The pony that caused the accident belonged to Canning.	Reasons
	(17) B. Under the *Livestock Act*, RSN 1990, c. L-20, an owner must not allow animals to run at large and shall be liable for any resulting damages.	
	(18) C. At common law, owners should anticipate responsibility for injuries resulting from animals roaming at large. In reaching this decision, the court rejected the ruling in the House of Lords decision in *Searle v. Wallbank*, [1947] AC 341 (HL), in which no duty for straying animals was found to exist. The court distinguished *Searle* as a British authority that had been replaced by the Supreme Court of Canada decisions in two Ontario cases, *Fleming v. Atkinson*, [1959] SCR 513, and *Eales v. James* (1977), 17 Nfld. & PEIR 242 (Nfld. Dist. Ct.) in which the court held that owners are responsible for damages caused by their straying animals.	
	(19) D. Drivers have a duty to keep a proper lookout. The court found that in this case, however, there was no contributory negligence regarding any of the plaintiffs' actions.	

TABLE 4.2   EXPLANATION OF TABLE 4.1

Reason for answer

(1)   This information is all that is required to index and identify the case. The case name is indexed as *Plaintiffs v. Defendant*.

(2)   This information tells us at what stage the case is in the court system. This case is a trial case; before relying on the case to support a legal argument, make sure that the case has not been appealed.

(3)   Identifies the main characters and summarizes what happened.

(4)   This case goes to court because the people involved in the motorcycle accident want the owner of the pony that caused the accident to take responsibility for what happened and bear the associated costs. Of course, the case is in court because the owner of the pony does not agree that his pony caused the accident or that he should take full responsibility for what happened.

(5) (6)   This information relates to the allegations that Prince was the pony that caused the accident.

(7) (8)   This information tells us more about the dispute between the parties and relates to the legal questions about "contributory negligence," in other words, whether the plaintiffs' negligent (or careless) actions contributed to what happened.

(9) (11)   Issues A, C, and D relate to the specific circumstances of this case. The court's answers to
(12)   these questions are important to the people involved in this case, but they may not be important in the future. We do not have to know the answer to these questions to appreciate what the law says about the responsibility of animal owners.

(10)   By contrast, the court's answers to issue B provide a concrete example of how a particular provision of statutory and common law is applied. In other words, the case teaches us lessons about the duty of animal owners in certain situations. The court's answers to issue B may be important to others who find themselves in similar circumstances in the future.

(12)   The answer to issue D is a finding of fact, but the facts also provide us with a concrete example of driving behaviour that constitutes "contributory negligence."

(13)   The decision is the short summary about what happened. It tells us who won. Depending on why a lawyer is reading the case, sometimes they might include information about what was won (for example, damages awarded).

(14) (15)   The ratio or "message" of the case is often difficult to extract. It is important to note that lawyers can and do argue about the significance of a case. It is clear that this case sends an important message to animal owners about their responsibilities for straying animals. But lawyers in the future might argue about whether the message applies only to pony owners, whether it applies to owners of all large animals or whether it applies to owners of all animals regardless of size.

(16) (17)   The reasons of a decision help us to understand why the court decided the way it did.

(18) (19)   Sometimes a court reaches a particular decision because it interpreted a statute in a particular way, or because it applied the case law in a particular way. In this case, there are conflicting court judgments on similar fact situations. The Newfoundland court's decision is noteworthy because it makes an important decision about which ruling it will follow. The law in *Searle* is left behind as the court affirms the decisions in the Ontario cases as the law or precedent to be followed in Canada.

Selecting the essential information

Summarizing the facts of a case and discerning the ratio or "future message" of a case can be difficult. This section explains why certain facts were left out, and outlines various techniques of extracting the ratio of a case.

WHAT IS THE RATIO?

To a certain extent, the ratio of a case is a matter of interpretation. The message of a case often depends on why or how the case is going to be used in the future. That said, the ratio extracted from a case should not twist or misrepresent the legal principles for which the case stands. In short, while it is possible to misconstrue the legal significance of a case, it is not possible to identify the definitive or exact phrasing of a case ratio. There are, however, a few tests that may be used to identify a satisfactory ratio.

The first is to test whether the court's answer to a particular issue may be used to decide another case in the future. In a review of the issues raised in *Rowe*, it becomes clear that the court's answers regarding the responsibilities of animal owners matters to other animal owners. Based on the decision in *Rowe*, other animal owners would probably be inspired to take extra precautions to ensure that their animals do not escape. Table 4.3 presents this review of the issues in chart form.

Just as a case may raise both specific and general legal issues, so too may the ratio extracted be specific or general. In table 4.4, the same legal issue is asked in four different ways, from very specific to very general. The chart illustrates that the ratio depends not only on how the legal issues are phrased and answered, but also the extent to which the ratio or message may be specific or general.

TABLE 4.3   ASSESSING THE FUTURE MESSAGE OF THE CASE

Issue	Court's answer	Does the court's answer send a message to any one facing similar circumstances in the future?
1. Was Prince the horse involved in the accident?	*Yes*	The court's answer is a finding of fact. The ownership of Prince the pony matters to the individuals involved in this case, but not to anyone in the future.
2. Is there a common law or statutory duty to secure one's animals?	*Yes* (According to the common law duty of care and the duties of animal owners under the *Livestock Act*, RSN 1990, c. L-20, owners of animals are responsible for damages caused when their animals roam free or stray).	The decision in *Rowe* sends a message to anyone owning a pony, or possibly any other animal, about the responsibilities of ownership.
3. If such a duty is owed, did the defendant breach the duty?	*Yes*	Even though Canning believed he had properly tethered his pony, the court found him responsible for the damages caused when the pony broke free. The court's answer helps animal owners understand the extent of their responsibilities.
4. Were the plaintiffs acting in a manner that contributed to the cause of the accident?	*No*	The court found that it was enough that Rowe was driving under the speed limit. The court's decision on this matter *may* be useful in the future, especially if someone is trying to determine the kind of driving behaviour that constitutes "keeping a proper lookout" under the law. Therefore, the decision to include this message as part of the case ratio depends entirely on why the case is being used.

TABLE 4.4   CONSTRUCTING A SPECIFIC OR GENERAL RULE

Specificity/ generality	Issue	Court's answer	Significance
Very specific	Is Canning liable to Rowe?	*Yes* or *No* The answer tells us who won = decision.	The decision matters to the parties to the case; it does not apply to anyone else. The answer is the decision.
Specific	Is the defendant liable to the plaintiff?	*Yes* or *No* The answer tells us who won = decision.	The decision matters to the parties to the case; it does not apply to anyone else. The answer is the decision.
General	Is the defendant owner of a pony liable to a plaintiff injured on a motorcycle hit by the pony?	*Yes* or *No* The answer tells us who won. The answer also tells us about the responsibilities of owners of ponies.	The answer matters to the parties to the case. It also sends a message to owners of ponies about their responsibilities. The message is the ratio. The ratio as stated applies specifically to pony owners.
Very general	Is the defendant owner of an animal liable to a plaintiff harmed by the animal?	*Yes* or *No* The answer tells us who won. The answer also tells us about the responsibilities of animal owners.	The answer matters to the parties to the case. It also sends a message to all owners of animals about their responsibilities. The message is the ratio. The ratio as stated is general and applies to all animal owners.

It is clear that the ratio extracted from the court's decision in *Rowe v. Canning* must say something about the responsibilities of owners for damages caused when their ponies or animals break free. Whether the message of the case is restricted to pony owners will depend on how someone in the future wants the case interpreted. For example, someone may argue that the message in *Rowe* was intended only for pony owners and should not be applied to animal owners in general. To test whether this interpretation of the case is correct, one would have to read similar cases of highway accidents involving other types of animals.

WHAT ARE THE IMPORTANT FACTS?

One way to identify the essential facts of a case is to describe the "how, when, where, and why" as if you were writing the notes for a television or video guide. If there is any question about whether a particular fact is relevant or not, test whether the absence or presence of that event, person or action would have altered the court's decision, changing the ratio or future message of the case.

For example, the ratio or future message of *Rowe v. Canning* is:

1. Owners of animals have a responsibility to ensure that their animals do not cause injury to others.

2. Because it is reasonably foreseeable that an animal roaming free will cause injury, the owners of such animals owe a duty of care to control the animals.

A decision was made to exclude the following four facts:

Fact	Test
1. The pony was travelling at a full gallop.	Whether the pony was standing still or galloping does not change the responsibility of the owner for the damage caused by allowing the animal to roam free.
2. Prince, the pony, had been stabled by its previous owner from Christmas until the day of the accident.	How or where the pony was stabled does not alter the owner's duty to control the animal and ensure that it does not roam free.
3. Prince had disappeared from the unfenced property.	Certainly, a fence might have prevented the pony from roaming free, but the precautions or an absence of precautions taken by the owner do not change the owner's responsibility at law.

Fact	Test
4. One of the witnesses testified that in her 23 years in the area, this was the only time she had seen a horse roaming free along the highway in Conception Bay South.	This evidence and the evidence given by Rowe and Furey persuaded the trial judge that the pony involved in the accident belonged to the Cannings. The ownership of this particular pony, however, does not change or alter the responsibilities of animal owners in general. It does, of course, matter to Mr. Canning. Would the absence of this information have changed the court's decision in this particular case? Probably not; there was still the evidence from Rowe and Furey. If one is reading the case to find out about the responsibilities of animal owners for damage caused by their animals, then this fact is unimportant. If one is reading the case to prepare for an appeal of the trial judge's application of the law to find fact, then this information is more important and could be included.

Arguably, if one were only interested in learning about the responsibilities of animal owners, then it would be sufficient to say "Rowe and Furey, plaintiffs, struck off motorcycle by stray pony belonging to defendant, Canning." Similarly, if one were only interested in learning about the responsibilities of drivers to keep a "proper lookout" while driving on highways, the facts used to determine contributory negligence on the part of the plaintiff are important. The point is that the summary of the facts should provide someone else with enough information about what happened in this specific instance to understand how the law would apply to similar situations in the future.

It is worth noting that not every case offers significant lessons about the law. Some cases reinforce existing lessons, simply repeating the application of a previously formulated rule or principle, in the same way as before. These cases are important in so far as they affirm what the law is and leave little doubt as to its application. Such cases are said to "uphold" the law.

EXERCISE 1 _Allied Plastering & Stucco Ltd. v. A. Visca Architect Inc._ (1999), 50 CLR (2d) 93 (Ont. SCJ)

MESBUR J: — This is an action for the recovery of $17,500.00 owed to the plaintiff for stuccowork, which was done on a residential property located at 101 Cameron Avenue in the City of North York. The plaintiff company, Allied Plastering & Stucco Ltd. (Allied), is co-owned by Aldo Chiarotto and another person. Aldo Chiarotto is the Vice-President of Allied. His wife, Orietta Chiarotto, handles Allied's purchase orders although her primary employment is elsewhere as a legal secretary. The defendant Tony Visca is an architect by trade. He is the primary shareholder of the defendant A. Visca Architect Inc. He also holds thirty three percent of the shares in the defendant company Antaj Inc., a general contractor. The defendant Roger Altobelli is the sole shareholder of 1012317 Ontario Limited, the company, which was the registered owner of the Cameron Avenue property. He is the primary shareholder of the general contractor, Antaj, as well as being a ten-percent shareholder in, and an officer of, A. Visca Architect Inc. He is also the President of 997785 Ontario Limited, the company which held the second mortgage on the Cameron Avenue property. Mr. Altobelli's young daughter is the sole shareholder of 997785 Ontario Limited.

THE FACTS AND THE LAW

In April of 1996 Mr. Altobelli's company 1012317 Ontario Limited ("101") purchased the Cameron Avenue property for $198,000.00 with a view to renovating it and selling it. To finance the purchase, Mr. Altobelli's lawyer, Mr. Walter Burych, provided a first mortgage of $140,000,00 through the estate of Annie Olech, of which he was sole estate trustee. The second mortgage of $60,192.04 came from 997785 Ontario Limited ("997") whose shares were owned by Mr. Altobelli's daughter and of which he was the president. Antaj was to be the general contractor on the job with the design work to be done by Tony Visca through his architectural firm, A. Visca Architect Inc.

In October 1996, Tony Visca spoke to Aldo Chiarotto regarding the possibility of Allied doing the stuccowork on the Cameron Avenue house. This was not the first time Mr. Chiarotto and Mr. Visca had done business. Mr. Visca had frequently recommended Allied to do stucco work for his clients and Allied had worked on some of Mr. Visca's projects. Allied had worked on another job in the same area on which Antaj was the general contractor.

Mr. Chiarotto, on behalf of Allied, surveyed the work, which needed to be done and provided Mr. Visca with a cost estimate in the form of a written contract between Allied and A. Visca Architect Inc. It described A. Visca Architect Inc. as owner of the property. Allied assembled its scaffolding at the job-site but refused to commence work until it received the completed contract. Rather than sign the contract, Mr. Visca sent Allied a purchase order for the work in the name of Antaj. The plaintiff complained about this because, as Mr. Chiarotto testified, it was his understanding that he was working for Tony Visca personally and he had been told the property was Mr. Visca's own home. I find this hard to believe considering the length of the professional relationship between Allied and Mr. Visca, Allied's experience in the business and the fact that Allied had done work for Antaj previously as a general contractor, including work on a neighbouring house and had been paid by Antaj. In light of subsequent events, I am not surprised that Mr. Chiarotto would later come to the conclusion he was dealing with Mr. Visca personally. However, at the time of the formation of the contract, it is clear to me that the contract was formed between Allied and Antaj.

Allied completed the work on the Cameron Avenue house on December 7, 1996. The work was done on time, on budget and completely satisfactorily. Allied rendered its first invoice on January 4, 1997. Under the provisions of section 31(2) of the *Construction Lien Act*, RSO 1990, c. C.30, any claim for a lien against the property for unpaid work had to be registered within 45 days of completion of the work, that is, by January 21, 1997. The original invoice provides for payment in 30 days, with interest to run on unpaid balances at the rate of 2% per month. These payment terms, however, did not alter the limitation period for Allied to register a construction lien.

By the middle of January 1997, Allied was still waiting to be paid. The lien period was about to expire. Allied was determined to get paid. Mr. Chiarotto spoke to Mr. Visca repeatedly about the unpaid account and about registering a lien on the property. According to Mr. Chiarotto's testimony, Mr. Visca asked him not to place a lien on the property because a lien would lead to problems with refinancing the property. Mr. Visca denies this conversation took place, stating that he told Aldo to do "whatever he needed to do." I find Mr. Chiarotto's evidence to be credible on this point. The evidence shows that the property was later refinanced to provide additional funding to finance the renovation. Mr. Chiarotto also testified that in this conversation Mr. Visca, relying on their history of business dealings in the past, reminded him that he had always paid Allied in the past and assured Mr. Chiarotto that it would be paid for this job. Mr. Chiarotto believed Mr. Visca and relied on these representations from him. I accept Mr. Chiarotto's evidence in this regard.

Mr. Chiarotto's wife testified that she was adamant about liens always being registered where invoices had not been paid, and that her husband knew this and agreed with her position. She was extremely forceful in her evidence and I believed her. There is no question in my mind that a lien would have been registered against the property but for the discussions between Mr. Visca and Mr. Chiarotto. I therefore find that Mr. Visca asked Allied to forbear putting a lien on the property in exchange for a promise to pay. Believing that Mr. Visca possessed some authority over the property, Mr. Chiarotto relied on these representations. Mr. Chiarotto testified that, because Mr. Visca had always honoured his trades in the past, he trusted him and took him at his word. They had enjoyed a good business relationship in the past and Mr. Chiarotto wanted to preserve it. He thus acquiesced and Allied lost its lien rights.

By April, 1997, the account had still not been paid, although it is clear from the documents produced at trial that Antaj continued to pay many of its other trades through this period, including many whose invoices were submitted later than Allied's. Mr. Chiarotto continued to press Mr. Visca for payment. Expecting the refinancing to be complete by early April, Mr. Visca promised to pay Allied by April 4, 1997. When the refinancing did not happen and Mr. Chiarotto pressed harder for payment, Mr. Visca approached his partner, Roger Altobelli, for assistance. Mr. Altobelli is a businessman with over thirty years of experience in the construction industry. Through his corporate holdings he was owner and general contractor of the property and he essentially controlled the second mortgagee. Tony Visca had been pressing Mr. Altobelli for payment for Antaj in order to allow Antaj to pay its trades. Mr. Altobelli testified that Mr. Visca asked if there was some way Mr. Altobelli could take care of the Allied account and asked him to speak to Mr. Chiarotto about it. Mr. Altobelli agreed. He called Mr. Chiarotto and told him that Antaj did not have the funds to pay the account but "we" would try to make arrangements to pay him. According to Mr. Chiarotto, Mr. Altobelli introduced himself as Mr. Visca's business partner. It is clear that he held himself out as someone with authority over both Antaj and the property. Mr. Chiarotto asked Mr. Altobelli to have all further discussions with his wife, who would have the authority to make decisions on behalf of Allied. Mr. Altobelli immediately called Mrs. Chiarotto and proposed a third mortgage on the property for the amount of the debt. In my view, Mr. Altobelli clearly made this offer on behalf of the owner (himself) in order to provide Allied with payment when the property was sold. Mrs. Chiarotto was happy with the proposal and asked Mr. Altobelli to have his lawyer draw the necessary papers.

At this point, Mr. Burych, the lawyer, entered the discussions. He was the lawyer for Antaj and had also incorporated the owner of the property, 101, of which he remained a director. He acted on the third mortgage on the property, as well as on the refinancing in September, 1997. He appears to have represented all of the individual defendants, as well as being the controlling mind behind the advance of the first mortgage funds from the estate of which he was the sole estate trustee. To Mrs. Chiarotto, Mr. Burych rejected the notion of a third mortgage. He confirmed that the invoice could not be paid until the sale of the property. He proposed a direction, which would direct payment of the invoice from the sale proceeds. He suggested a less onerous interest rate, one of 8% instead of 24%. He pointed out that a third mortgage would require the consent of both the owner and the first and second mortgagees or make these mortgages immediately due and payable, intimating that this would put payment of Allied's account in jeopardy. In his correspondence with Mrs. Chiarotto, Mr. Burych did not think to mention, however, that he controlled the first mortgagee, that the second mortgage was held through a company which Mr. Altobelli effectively managed or that the property was owned by a company Mr. Altobelli controlled. Allied was in agreement with any method which would have them paid when the property was sold. Allied agreed to the reduction in the interest rate. Allied had threatened litigation in April. Although Mr. Altobelli suggested in his testimony that it was of no importance to him if Allied sued or not, I do not believe him. It is clear to me that the proposal from Mr. Altobelli and the correspondence from Mr.

Burych were clearly designed to hold off any lawsuit from Allied with the promises Allied would be paid when the property was sold. It is clear that Allied agreed to forbear litigation in exchange for the promise and guarantee from Mr. Altobelli on behalf of 101 that the invoice would be paid when the property was sold, out of the proceeds of sale. It is settled law that a creditor's promise not to enforce a valid claim constitutes valid consideration for a promise given in return. See: *Callisher v. Bischoffsheim* (1870), LRS 449 (QB), *Miles v. New Zealand Alford Estate Company* (1886), 32 Ch. D 266, *Royal Bank of Canada v. Kiska*, [1967] 2 OR 379 (CA), *Stott v. Merit Investment Corp.* (1988), 63 OR (2d) 545 (CA). I find that there was an enforceable agreement between 101 and Allied that 101 would guarantee payment of the invoice and the invoice would be paid from the proceeds of sale. Having found an enforceable guarantee, I need not determine whether the conduct of the parties amounted to the granting of an equitable mortgage on the property or not.

Counsel for the defendants urged me to find that there was no agreement and the discussions of mortgages or directions were mere negotiations and point to the fact no agreement was reached. They suggest, as a result, that all of the correspondence discussing mortgages and directions is privileged as being aimed at settlement of the issue. I disagree. In my view, the agreement was a guarantee by 101 of payment of the invoice from the proceeds of sale. Whether this was effected by mortgage or direction was a matter of performance, not a question of the agreement itself.

Suffice it to say, Allied was not paid from the sale proceeds. In fact, in September of 1997, the property was refinanced with a new first mortgage providing an additional $100,000.00 of financing. This money was used, according to Mr. Altobelli, to finish the project. None of the money came to Allied. Mr. Altobelli stated that Antaj had not been able to finish the project as general contractor and 101 had taken over this role. Noting Mr. Altobelli's control of both corporations, I find his position somewhat disingenuous. In any case, both Antaj and 101 bound themselves to pay Allied's account and both failed to do so.

The plaintiff obtained a certificate of pending litigation against the property. When the property was sold, in order to lift the lien and close the transaction, the owner, 1012317 Ontario Limited was obliged to pay the sum of $25,000.00 from the proceeds of sale into court to the credit of this action. Counsel for the defendants advised that there is other litigation outstanding from other trades. They told me these are claims pursuant to the trust provisions of the *Construction Lien Act*. They did not advise me with any particularity of the actual claims advanced, the status of the actions, the defences or anything else pertaining to them. They suggested, however, that this action should be subsumed in them, and the money paid into court in this action be transferred to these other actions, about which I know nothing. I decline to do so. There was no evidentiary basis provided upon which I could make any such determination.

CONCLUSION

The plaintiff will have judgment in the amount of $17,500.00 against the defendants Antaj and 1012317 Ontario Limited. It is entitled to pre-judgment interest on that sum at the rate of 8% per annum from February 4, 1997, and post-judgment interest at the same rate. The monies paid into court to the credit of this action are from the sale of the property owned by 1012317 Ontario Limited. The plaintiff was to be paid from the proceeds of sale. I therefore order that the funds in court standing to the credit of this action will be paid out to the plaintiff to the extent required to pay this judgment. The action is dismissed against the other defendants. If the parties are unable to agree on the issue of costs, they may arrange an appointment for submissions on costs.

Case brief

Prepare a case brief for *Allied Plastering & Stucco Ltd. v. A. Visca Architect Inc.* (1999), 50 CLR (2d) 93 (Ont. SCJ). Use the chart below to identify the relevant information.

Question	Answer	Legal term
a. Who?	_____	Style of cause
b. Which courts?	_____ _____	Procedural history
c. What happened?	_____ _____ _____ _____ _____ _____ _____ _____	Facts
d. Legal questions?	_____ _____ _____ _____	Issues
e. Who won?	_____	Decision (holding)
f. What message?	_____ _____	Ratio
g. Justification?	_____ _____ _____ _____ _____	Reasons

EXERCISE 2 *Nguyen v. Canada (Minister of Citizenship and Immigration)*, [1998] IADD no. 1726

ORAL DECISION AND REASONS

These are the reasons for the decision in the appeal of Thi My Hanh NGUYEN, the appellant, pursuant to section 70 of the *Immigration Act*, RSC 1985, c. I-2, as amended (the "Act") from a departure order made by the adjudicator on March 5, 1997. The adjudicator found the appellant to be a person described in paragraph 27(1)(b), wherein she has failed to comply with the terms and conditions of landing by not marrying her former fiancé, Hoang Thanh Nguyen within 90 days. I shall refer to the appellant's former fiancé as the sponsor.

There being no challenge of the legal validity of the departure order and after review of the material before me, I found that the departure order is valid in law. As this appeal is based on the discretionary jurisdiction of the Appeal Division further to paragraph 70(1)(b) of the *Act*, the onus is on the appellant to satisfy me that having regard to all the circumstances of the case, she should not be removed from Canada.

The following is a chronological history of the events surrounding this appeal: the appellant and the sponsor were introduced to each other through the appellant's paternal uncle, who resides in Canada. Around January of 1993, the appellant and the sponsor began corresponding with other. In November 1993, they agreed to get engaged to each other. On December 10, 1993, the sponsor, together with the appellant's uncle, travelled to Vietnam. On this occasion, the appellant's uncle paid for the sponsor's airfare. One week after the sponsor's arrival in Vietnam, he and the appellant became engaged to each other after obtaining consent from their respective parents. The sponsor gave the appellant a ring and a pair of earrings as engagements presents. Thereafter, the sponsor remained in Vietnam until March 10, 1994. During this period of his stay in Vietnam, the sponsor alternated living with his parents and with the appellant at her aunt's residence.

On July 27, 1994 the Canadian Immigration authorities received the sponsor's undertaking of assistance to sponsor the appellant to come to Canada. On April 18, 1996, the appellant was landed in Canada with the condition that she was to marry her sponsor within 90 days of her landing, on or before July 17, 1996.

On May 3, 1996, the sponsor voluntarily reported to Canadian Immigration authorities. During an interview with an Immigration officer, Melinda Grantor, the sponsor related his difficulties in his relationship with the appellant. On January 7, 1997 the same Immigration officer interviewed the appellant with respect to her proposed marriage to the sponsor.

Around the same time, the appellant met her current husband, Dung Anh Tran. On February 27, 1997, the appellant started working at Cargill Foods, where Tran was also working. On March 5, 1997 a departure order was issued against the appellant. Around March 7 or 8, 1997 the appellant started dating Tran. At the end of March, the appellant and Tran began discussions of marriage. On April 6, 1997 the appellant married Tran in a civil ceremony. They did not live together or have any sexual relationship until their traditional marriage ceremony held on July 25, 1998.

The appellant testified that she was frustrated with the sponsor's repeated requests for sex before the marriage. She explained her reasons for not marrying the sponsor to be as follows: the sponsor did not ask her to marry him within 90 days of her landing in Canada, and thereafter he had a girlfriend. The sponsor testified that he was willing to wait until their marriage before they engaged in a sexual relationship and that he was never upset by the appellant's refusal in this regard. He further testified that he did ask the appellant to move into his house and suggested that she could stay in his niece's room should she feel uncomfortable staying in his room.

He explained his reasons for not marrying the appellant to be as follows: while the appellant made numerous requests to him to get a marriage certificate, she would not respond to the sponsor's discussions of wedding arrangements. He described her to be silent and disinterested whenever he raised a question of the wedding ceremony. On one occasion, the appellant told the sponsor that she could never marry anyone, including him. On another occasion the sponsor asked her if they were to live separate lives after obtaining the marriage certificate, whereas she would continue to live with her uncle and he would continue to live with his parents. The appellant replied "yes." The sponsor testified that deep in his heart he has always wanted a relationship with the appellant and that if she was free to marry, he would still marry her. He added that he was not in a committed relationship and he has no girlfriend.

Evidence adduced suggests that the sponsor was earnest in his pursuit of his marriage to the appellant. The appellant acknowledged receipt of a ring and a pair of earrings from the sponsor as engagement presents. She also testified that during his visit in Vietnam, they did sleep together in the same bed. However, they had no sexual relationship with each other since they had both agreed to wait until after their marriage. The sponsor testified that he had wanted to marry the appellant in Vietnam but he was prevented from doing so due to his lack of a certain document. Later the sponsor sponsored the appellant and paid for her airfare to Canada. The above evidence is not supportive of the appellant's proposition that the sponsor would refuse to marry her within the 90 days of her landing due to her refusal to move in with him and to have a sexual relationship with him prior to their marriage.

The appellant is a 24-year-old. She has been in Canada for only two and a half years. She testified that after her arrival in Canada, she participated in a 30-week course to learn English and in the evening she cleaned offices. Both the appellant's testimony and documentary evidence indicate that the appellant has been working at Cargill Food as a meat-cutter since February 24, 1997. The appellant testified that her father passed away in 1994 and that her relatives in Vietnam consist of her mother, stepfather, two younger brothers, her maternal grandparents and her maternal uncle and aunt. She also testified that her relatives in Canada consist of her paternal uncle, his family, some distant relatives from his father's side and her husband Tran. I note that Tran was the only witness who testified and that no other relatives or friends had come forward to express their support for the appellant's continued stay in Canada.

With respect to her marriage to Tran, the appellant testified that after they were married in the civil ceremony, they did not have any sexual relationship or live together as husband and wife. She explained that she did not believe that she and Tran should live together as man and wife until after their traditional wedding. She further explained that at the time they did not have sufficient financial means to have a traditional wedding, therefore their cohabitation needed to be delayed.

Tran confirmed the appellant's testimony that they did not have any sexual relationship or live together as husband and wife until after their traditional wedding, held on July 25, 1998. He explained that after their civil marriage on April 6, 1996, the appellant did not move into his home for the reason that they were both very busy and the appellant did not have any time to organize her belongings. Specifically, Tran testified that it was their plan to live together after their civil marriage and that on April 6, 1996 the appellant was at her own residence making preparations to move into his house on the following day. However, on April 7, 1996, his parents advised him that it was bad luck for him and the appellant to live together due to their age difference and that their cohabitation would best be delayed to a later date. Tran heeded to his parents' advice and in turn advised the appellant that she was unable to move in to live with him due to financial constraints on the part of his household. He described the appellant to have reacted with disappointment, sadness and surprise.

No evidence was adduced to explain why Tran testified that after their civil marriage, the appellant was willing and ready to move into his house, whereas the appellant testified that they had both agreed upon not living together until their traditional marriage ceremony which was to take place at a later date. Furthermore, no evidence was adduced to explain why Tran testified to refusing the appellant's desire and efforts to move into his residence due to financial constraints on the part of his household, whereas the appellant testified that they could not live together due to their inability to pay for a traditional marriage ceremony. Hence there is an absence of evidence to explain why the appellant and Tran did not live together as husband and wife for one year and three months after their civil marriage.

Furthermore, evidence adduced suggests that the appellant's civil marriage to Tran was done in a hasty manner. They started dating on March 7 or 8, 1996 and they were married on April 6, 1996. The appellant was asked why she and Tran would enter into a marriage contract when they were not intending to live together. She replied that Tran was aware that she was in trouble and wanted to help. She added that Tran took pity on her, since the sponsor did not marry her. Based on all the above evidence, I have given little weight to the alleged spousal relationship between the appellant and Tran.

The appellant gave two reasons for her inability to return to Vietnam. Firstly she explained that she would have no place to stay. She testified that since her father passed away, her mother remarried and she was fearful of her stepfather. Therefore, she moved to live with her aunt and since her aunt has now remarried she did not feel that she could live with either her mother or her aunt. I note that the appellant's two younger siblings are living with their mother. The appellant did not offer any further explanation as to why her aunt's marriage would prevent her from living there. I note that it was the appellant's testimony that from around July 16, 1996 to July 25, 1998 she was living with a married couple and their child in downtown Vancouver.

Secondly, the appellant explained that she would not be able to work in Vietnam because she will not have any ration coupons to get food. According to a report by Melinda Grantor dated January 14, 1997, the appellant stated that she had signed documents in Vietnam indicating that she would no longer be a citizen. The appellant was born in Vietnam and no evidence was adduced to indicate her residency status should she return to Vietnam. Furthermore, the appellant testified that while she was in Vietnam, she was financially independent, working as a seamstress and performing some additional part time work in a photographic shop. No evidence was adduced to indicate why the appellant could not return to her former profession should she return to Vietnam.

Based on the evidence before me, I find that the departure order is valid in law and I further find that having regard to all the circumstances of the case, the appellant has not satisfied me that she should not be removed from Canada. Therefore, pursuant to paragraph 73(1)(b) of the *Act*, I dismiss the appeal made under paragraph 70(1)(a) and 70(1)(b) of the *Act*.

ORDER

The Appeal Division orders that the appeal be dismissed. The removal order made the 5th day of March, 1997, is in accordance with the law, and the appellant has failed to show that, having regard to all the circumstances of the case, the appellant should not be removed from Canada.

Case brief

Prepare a case brief for *Nguyen v. Canada (Minister of Citizenship and Immigration)*, [1998] IADD no. 1726. Use the chart below to identify the relevant information.

Question	Answer	Legal term
a. Who?	_____	Style of cause
b. Which courts?	_____ _____	Procedural history
c. What happened?	_____ _____ _____ _____ _____ _____ _____ _____	Facts
d. Legal questions?	_____ _____ _____ _____	Issues
e. Who won?	_____	Decision (holding)
f. What message?	_____ _____	Ratio
g. Justification?	_____ _____ _____ _____ _____ _____ _____	Reasons

METHOD 2: PREPARING A WRITTEN SUMMARY

Often, people prefer a written summary of the important information in a case. The summary must be short, and sometimes, it may only be a few lines. A very short summary of the case resembles the synopsis of a play or a show in program notes. It sketches out the main characters and their relationship to the "plot" in only as much detail as is required to understand the message or ratio of the case. Other times, a full page is necessary to highlight potentially relevant details of the case for future use. Generally, a case brief should not exceed one page. Examples of the two different styles have been prepared for *Rowe v. Canning* below.

Demonstration examples *Rowe v. Canning* (1994), 117 Nfld. & PEIR 353, 4 MVR (3d) 269 (Nfld. TD)

EXAMPLE A: FULL PAGE SUMMARY

Procedural history
Trial case.

Facts
A pony running free on a provincial highway struck the motorcycle of the plaintiff, Rowe, causing the driver to lose control and crash. Rowe and his passenger, Furey, identified the pony as belonging to the defendant, Canning. They sued Canning for negligence. The defendant denied that his pony caused the accident. On the day of the accident, however, the defendant found his pony wandering free near the highway. It had broken free from where its owner had tied it up and run away from Canning's unfenced property. Statements from witnesses to the motorcycle accident were inconsistent and could not confirm that the animal they saw run across the highway was the pony Prince. The defendant argued that even if Prince did cause the accident, the plaintiffs were not driving carefully.

Issues

1. Was the pony Prince involved in the accident?

2. Do animal owners have a common law or statutory duty to secure their animals?

3. If animal owners have a common law or statutory duty to secure their animals, did the defendant, Canning, breach this duty?

4. Was the plaintiff, Rowe, driving in a manner that contributed to the cause of the accident?

Decision
The court found the defendant, Canning, liable for damages sustained by the plaintiffs.

Ratio
The owners of animals have a statutory and common law duty of care to control their animals. Because it is reasonably foreseeable that an animal roaming free may cause injury, an owner is responsible for the damage caused.

Reasons

1. The pony that caused the accident belonged to Canning.

2. Under the *Livestock Act*, RSN 1990, c. L-20, an owner must not allow animals to run at large and shall be liable for any resulting damages.

3. At common law, owners should anticipate responsibility for injuries resulting from animals roaming at large. In reaching this decision, the court rejected the ruling in the House of Lords decision in *Searle v. Wallbank*, [1947] AC 341 (HL), in which no duty for straying animals was found to exist. The court

distinguished *Searle* as a British authority that had been replaced by the Supreme Court of Canada decisions in two Ontario cases, *Fleming v. Atkinson*, [1959] SCR 513, and *Eales v. James* (1977), 17 Nfld. & PEIR 242 (Nfld. Dist. Ct.) in which the court held that owners are responsible for damages caused by their straying animals.

4. Drivers have a duty to keep a proper lookout. The court found that in this case, however, there was no contributory negligence regarding any of the plaintiff's actions.

EXAMPLE B: SHORT SUMMARY

1. The short summary can be organized according to headings:

Procedural history: Trial-level case.

Facts: Pony hit a motorcycle driven by plaintiffs, Rowe and Furey. Plaintiffs sue defendant, Canning, who owns a pony they allege hit them. Defendant owners claim contributory negligence on the part of plaintiffs.

Issues: 1. Liability of owners of a pony (animal) to control it.
2. Whether there was contributory negligence on part of plaintiffs.

Ratio: Owners of an animal have both common law and statutory duty to control their animal.

2. The short summary may even be reduced to a few brief lines:

Rowe v. Canning

Trial case. Vehicle struck by animal roaming free on highway. Court finds animal owners have a statutory and common law duty to control their animals, and are responsible for damages caused when such animals roam free.

This summary places the emphasis on the duty of animal owners. It does not include any information on how a court will assess contributory negligence. Primarily, the assessment of contributory negligence relies on the court's determination of factual circumstances. Unless one was looking to predict what constitutes "keeping a proper look out while driving," for example, the most important legal message of this case pertains to the responsibilities of animal owners.

EXERCISE 3 *Toronto (City) v. Ontario* (1999), 43 OR (3d) 281, 95 OTC 65 (SCJ)

APPLICATION for a determination whether the City of Toronto has the authority to change the number of elected members representing each city ward.

JURIANSZ J: — In this application, the court is asked to determine whether the City of Toronto has the authority to change the number of elected members representing each city ward on city council and to change the total number of elected members. The court's authority to determine the question, which depends solely on the interpretation of the *City of Toronto Act, 1997*, SO 1997, c. C.2 and the *Municipal Act*, RSO 1990, c. M.45, was not disputed.

The *City of Toronto Act, 1997* incorporated the inhabitants of the geographic area of the jurisdiction of the old Municipality of Metropolitan Toronto under the name "City of Toronto." Section 5(1) of the *Act* divided the city into 28 wards and s. 3(1) established a city council composed of the mayor elected by general vote and 56 other members, two to be elected for each ward. By amendment which came into force on June 26, 1998, the composition of city council was changed to provide for a third member for the ward of East York and 57 members in addition to the mayor.

At a special meeting held April 28 and May 1, 1998 the City council approved in principle the division of the existing wards to permit the election of a single councillor per ward in the next municipal election to take place in the year 2000.

At a subsequent meeting on December 16 and 17, 1998 the city council decided to seek a determination from the court of its authority to enact a by-law creating single member wards and changing the overall size of council's membership.

The City filed a factum setting out the basis upon which the authority of city council to pass a by-law changing the number of its elected members could be challenged.

The *Municipal Act* allows the council of a local municipality to pass by-laws dividing or re-dividing the municipality into wards or dissolving the existing wards, and to pass a by-law changing the number of its elected members. These general powers are set out in ss. 13(4) and 29(3). The basis of the City's concern is that the *City of Toronto Act, 1997* adopts by reference s. 13(4) of the *Municipal Act* but is silent as to s. 29(3) of the same Act. Section 5(2) of the *City of Toronto Act, 1997* provides "the wards may be changed or dissolved in accordance with the *Municipal Act.*"

The City first pointed out that every word in a statute is presumed to make sense and to have a specific role to play in advancing its legislative purpose. So, it was argued that s. 5(2) of the Act would be meaningless if the *Municipal Act* granted the city council the authority to change or dissolve wards. In order for s. 5(2) to have meaning, it must be understood that the *Municipal Act* did not bestow on the City of Toronto the general powers ordinarily bestowed on municipalities. The argument continued that, if this were not so, the June 1998 amendment to the Act to provide for a third member from East York would not have been necessary.

The City also submitted that the express provision in s. 5(2) of the *City of Toronto Act, 1997*, that wards may be changed or dissolved in accordance with the *Municipal Act*, implied that the omission of the legislature to provide that city council could change its size and composition was deliberate. The only reason, it was argued, that the legislature would expressly include the s. 13(4) power and omit the s. 29(3) power was that the legislature intended to exclude that power.

The City pointed to some additional provisions of the two statutes. Section 6 of *Municipal Act* provides:

> 6. Except where otherwise expressly provided, this Act does not affect the provisions of any special Act relating to a particular municipality.

Section 29(10) of the *Municipal Act* provides:

> 29(10) If there is a conflict between this section in any provision dealing with the size and composition of the council, the manner of election or the titles of members of council that is contained in a public or private Act this section prevails.

Section 27(1) of the *City of Toronto Act, 1997* provides:

> 27(1) This Act applies despite any general or special Act and despite any regulation made under another Act and in the event of a conflict between this Act and another Act or a regulation made under another Act, this Act prevails.

The City argues that the *City of Toronto Act, 1997* is more specific legislation than the *Municipal Act* because it focuses narrowly on the City of Toronto whereas the *Municipal Act* deals with municipalities generally. Therefore, matters that it specifically dealt with which are in conflict with the general powers under the *Municipal Act* should be treated as an exception to the general powers.

The City went further and argued that the two statutes were in irreconcilable conflict and that the *City of Toronto Act, 1997*, which was enacted after the *Municipal Act*, impliedly repeals the inconsistent provisions of the *Municipal Act*.

The intervenors, jointly, presented an argument that supported the City's position. In addition, the intervenors argued that an interpretation that accords with the larger social and legal context of the day is to be preferred over one that does not. They argued that the court could take judicial notice that there was an unprecedented referendum and political controversy associated with the legislative passage of the *City of Toronto Act, 1997*. The intervenors also argued that an earlier draft of the Act and a press release of the Ministry of Municipal Affairs and Housing announcing amendments to the Bill could be looked to assist in the interpretation of the Act. They argued that these items taken together demonstrated that the government did not intend to treat the new City of Toronto like any other local municipality, and that the powers generally granted to local municipalities by the *Municipal Act* were not available to the City of Toronto.

The Attorney General argued that the statutes should be interpreted so that the general powers granted by the *Municipal Act* were available to the City of Toronto unless there was some express reservation or exception. I find this is the correct approach.

Section 2 of the *Act* constitutes the City of Toronto as a body corporate and a "local municipality for all purposes."

Moreover, s. 2(5) stated that "the new city has every power and duty of an old municipality or old council under any public or private Act." The old municipalities possessed the general powers set out in the *Municipal Act*.

I find that the June 1998 amendment to add an additional member for East York to be irrelevant to the question before me. An amendment was required in that circumstance in order to give effect to the changes in mid term between general municipal elections held every three years. If the city council had made the change, it would not have taken effect until the election held in the year 2000.

I see no inconsistency between the *City of Toronto Act, 1997* and the *Municipal Act*. In my view, the interpretation put forward by the City is fraught with difficulty and leads to greater disharmony within the legislation. If the City could take action to dissolve wards without changing the number of members of council, i.e., the disputed authority under s. 29(3) of the *Municipal Act*, this would lead to conflict with the provisions that stipulate there are 57 members, two from each ward and three from East York.

As the City pointed out in reply the question remains why the legislature would expressly incorporate in the *City of Toronto Act* the power to change or dissolve wards but not the power to change the number of elected members. I agree with the intervenors' argument that I may take judicial notice that there was political controversy associated with the passage of the *Act*, though I do not consider the extrinsic evidence they put forward. I am prepared to surmise that where the legislature passes a statute amidst political controversy it may include provisions that speak to the electorate. I do not need to make a finding in this regard as I see no conflict between the two statutes.

Section 5(2) of the *Act* does have meaning. It confirms that wards may be changed or dissolved in accordance with the *Municipal Act*. However, I do not see anything in its words that convey the meaning that the general powers in s. 29(3) of the *Municipal Act* are withheld from city council. In my view, the stipulation in s. 3 of the *Act* of the size and structure of the new city council was simply to establish the governing body that could thereafter exercise the general powers it possessed under the *Municipal Act*.

Further, in my view, s. 29(10) of the *Municipal Act* deals specifically with the narrow subject of the size and composition of council, whereas s. 27(1) of the *City of Toronto Act, 1997* deals generally with conflict between the *City of Toronto Act* and another statute. Had I been persuaded that there was conflict between the two statutes, I would have been inclined to find, nevertheless, that the powers in s. 29(3) of the *Municipal Act* were available to city council.

For these reasons, the City of Toronto is entitled to a declaration that it possesses the jurisdiction under s. 13(4) and under s. 29(3) of the *Municipal Act* to change the number of elected members representing each city ward on city council and to change the total number of elected members.

The parties may write to me on costs if they wish.

Order accordingly.

TIP

Obiter dicta: When the court speaks beyond the matter at hand.

Often, judges will express judicial opinions on circumstances that "might have been or might be." Such statements are known as *obiter dicta*, or simply *obiter.* Statements made in *obiter* are not part of the binding decision, since they are opinions on hypothetical situations.

In *Toronto v. Ontario*, the court finds that there is no conflict between the two applicable statutes but indicates how it would have decided the case if such a conflict existed. In *obiter*, Judge Juriansz states: "Had I been persuaded that there was a conflict between the two statutes, I would have been inclined to find, nevertheless, that the powers in s. 29(3) of the *Municipal Act* were available to city council."

These "additional words" tell us something more about the powers of council that might be helpful in analysis of future cases dealing with council's powers. Comments made in *obiter* are certainly not *binding*, but they may foreshadow how the law will apply to the scenario described. For this reason, statements made in *obiter* may be considered *persuasive.*

THE LAW WORKBOOK: Developing skills for legal research and writing

Full-page summary

Write a page-long summary of the case under the following headings. This method prepares a detailed summary and is a useful record of a case to keep on file. In the space provided, prepare a case brief for *Toronto (City) v. Ontario* (1999), 43 OR (3d) 281, 95 OTC 65 (SCJ).

1. **Style of cause**

   _____

2. **Procedural history**

   _____

   _____

3. **Material facts**

   _____

   _____

   _____

   _____

   _____

   _____

   _____

   _____

4. **Issue(s)**

   _____

   _____

   _____

   _____

5. **Decision**

   _____

6. **Ratio**

   _____

   _____

7. **Reasons**

   _____

   _____

   _____

   _____

   _____

   _____

   _____

   _____

Short summary

When dealing with a number of cases, it can be more useful to prepare very short notes to summarize the important points of a case. In the space provided, prepare a more concise case brief for *Toronto (City) v. Ontario*.

1. **Style of cause**

   _____

2. **Procedural history**

   _____

3. **Material facts**

   _____

   _____

   _____

4. **Issue(s)**

   _____

   _____

5. **Decision**

   _____

6. **Ratio**

   _____

7. **Reasons**

   _____

   _____

   _____

EXERCISE 4 *Smart v. Law Society*: A matter of professional ethics

Application for judicial review of a decision of Convocation of the Law Society that the applicant was not of good character and not eligible for admission to the Bar.

By the Court: The Law Society determined that Louis Smart was not of good character and should not accordingly be enrolled as a solicitor in this province. This application for judicial review arises from that determination by Convocation.

THE FACTS

The applicant, Louis Smart, is a student member of the Law Society, having completed his articles in May 1989. In February 1990, the applicant successfully completed the Bar Admission Course.

Before entering law school, the applicant worked as a life insurance salesman. In the course of his work selling life insurance policies, he engaged in conduct which resulted in his guilty plea and conviction of two counts of fraud over $200. The applicant advised the Law Society that this had occurred prior to the time he was called to the Bar. As a result he was required to attend before an admissions committee, composed of three benchers, and bring forward sufficient evidence to show that he is of good character and therefore able to be called to the Bar pursuant to s. 27 of the *Law Society Act*, RSO 1980, c. 233.

The evidence before the court in the criminal proceedings and before the committee of benchers, who considered the applicant's application for admission to the Law Society, disclosed that, in furtherance of his fraud upon Montreal Life and Colonia Life, the applicant:

(1) Submitted 55 fraudulent policy applications after applying to law school, and a further 17 fraudulent policy applications after entering law school;

(2) "Sold" policies to persons whom he knew to have insufficient means to pay the premiums, and knowingly overstated the incomes of those persons on their policy applications;

(3) Sold policies to members of his immediate family and told them they would not have to pay the premiums;

(4) Represented to "applicants" who questioned the legality of the scheme that the activity in which he was engaged was not criminal though it was unethical;

(5) Made payments of $50 to persons who allowed their names to be used on policy applications or who introduced him to others who would allow their names to be used;

(6) Claimed these payments (which he described as "referral fees") as deductions on his income tax returns and falsely represented the amounts of the referral fees to be $200 each;

(7) Did not declare the income he received as a result of his scheme on his income tax returns, thereby evading the payment of

income tax on the fruits of his fraud, which amounted to well over $100,000 and at no time informed Revenue Canada that he had filed false income tax returns;

(8) Forged the names of "applicants" on policy applications;

(9) Made applications for and obtained policies from both Montreal Life and Colonia Life for the same impecunious persons, in result doubling up the commissions "earned" without disclosing to either company the application to the other;

(10) Did not inform either Montreal Life or Colonia Life that he was selling insurance for both companies contemporaneously.

During the police investigation, the applicant attempted to dissuade potential witnesses from co-operating with the police by telling them that they should not say anything to the police because the applicant was attempting to negotiate a settlement with the insurance companies and by urging them to tell "the truth," but furnishing a version of the truth that he knew to be false.

Judge Locke made a restitution order for immediate payment of $10,000, and a further compensation order in favour of Montreal Life in the amount of $90,000 and in favour of Colonia Life in the amount of $60,000.

It was the applicant's position before this court that, having persuaded a majority of a three-member committee that he is of good character, he is entitled to admission. In our view, the argument fails to properly consider the scheme of the Act.

Section 27 reads:

27(1) Every application for admission to the Society shall be on the prescribed form and be accompanied by the prescribed fees.

(2) An applicant for admission to the Society shall be of good character.

(3) No applicant for admission to the Society who has met all admission requirements shall be refused admission.

(4) No application for admission to the Society shall be refused until the applicant has been given an opportunity to appear in person before a committee of benchers.

(5) Where an applicant for admission to the society is refused admission, he is entitled to a statement of the reasons for refusal.

(6) Where an application for admission to the Society has been refused, another application based on new evidence may be made at any time.

The committee of benchers in the admission hearing is called upon to decide whether on the balance of probabilities the applicant is of good character at the time of his hearing. Both counsel made their respective submissions on the basis that s. 27 was applicable notwithstanding, apparently, that the applicant is seeking to be "called to the bar," as opposed to applying for "admission to the Society."

The requirement in s. 27(2) of the *Law Society Act*, that applicants for admission shall be of good character, finds expression also in rule 1 of the

Law Society's rules of professional conduct: "The lawyer must discharge with integrity all duties owed to clients, the court, the public and other members of the profession." Commentary 1 to rule 1 reads as follows:

> 1. Integrity is the fundamental quality of any person who seeks to practise as a member of the legal profession. If the client is in any doubt as to the lawyer's trustworthiness, the essential element in the true lawyer-client relationship will be missing. If personal integrity is lacking, the lawyer's usefulness to the client and reputation within the profession will be destroyed regardless of how competent the lawyer may be.

The purposes of the good character requirement include the protection of the public, the maintenance of high ethical standards, and the maintenance of public confidence in the legal profession.

Section 10 states:

> 10. [Government of the Society] The benchers shall govern the affairs of the Society, including the call of persons to practise at the bar of the courts of Ontario and their admission and enrolment to practise as solicitors in Ontario.

Rule 26 provides:

> 26. Except where a committee is expressly given power to act by Convocation and except in routine or inconsiderable matters, the exercise of any power by a committee is subject always to the approval of convocation.

The *Act* gives power to the Society to promulgate rules.

The committee heard evidence, including evidence from the applicant. Two members of the committee concluded that despite fraudulent conduct in the past, the applicant had reformed and was now of good character. The minority opinion concluded that, notwithstanding the present assertion of the applicant that he was now of good character, the post-fraud conduct of the applicant was such that he could not find the applicant had yet attained the state of being of good character.

Convocation held a hearing on whether to accept the majority or minority report. There is no real question that all relevant primary facts were contained in the two reports before Convocation. There was no issue of credibility at large before Convocation. The issue was whether the primary facts in themselves — the criminal conduct of the applicant, the measure of rehabilitation that the applicant had achieved, coupled with the character evidence he had called, in light of the solemn assurance of the applicant that he was now of good character and resolved to be honest in the future, established his present good character.

Convocation gave a fair hearing to the essential issue before it — whether the applicant was now of good character.

The applicant had every opportunity to present his best case to Convocation. Convocation had the responsibility to decide in accordance with its professional standards. As the watchdog of a self-governing profession, it was Convocation, and not the Committee, that had to make the ultimate decision in fulfilling its mandate to protect the public.

Convocation adopted the reasons given in the minority report and refused to admit the applicant to the Bar. It must be remembered that Convocation is exercising original, rather than appellate, jurisdiction.

We are satisfied that Convocation did not err in the exercise of its statutory power of decision.

Costs to the respondent if demanded. If costs are to be fixed, we may be faxed.

Application dismissed.

Case brief

In the space provided, prepare a case brief for *Smart v. Law Society*.

1. **Style of cause**

   _____

2. **Procedural history**

   _____

   _____

3. **Material facts**

   _____

   _____

   _____

   _____

   _____

   _____

   _____

   _____

   _____

4. **Issue(s)**

   _____

   _____

   _____

   _____

5. **Decision**

   _____

6. **Ratio**

   _____

   _____

7. **Reasons**

   _____

   _____

   _____

   _____

   _____

   _____

   _____

   _____

Concise case brief

In the space provided, prepare a more concise case brief for *Smart v. Law Society*.

1. **Style of cause**

   _____

2. **Procedural history**

   _____

3. **Material facts**

   _____

   _____

   _____

4. **Issue(s)**

   _____

   _____

5. **Decision**

   _____

6. **Ratio**

   _____

7. **Reasons**

   _____

   _____

   _____

METHOD 3: UNDERLINING AND MARGIN NOTES

Some people prefer to mark up a text, using a system of margin notes, highlighting and underlining to identify the important information in a case. The advantage of this method is that it may save time, and identifies the important information in the text. The disadvantage is that the relevant information is not readily available on a single page when it comes time to use the material. For this reason, it can be helpful to write the case *ratio* (or rule of law) in your own words at the beginning of the case, in plain view for future use.

Use the underline method to brief the cases that follow. You may develop your own method, or use the one we suggest. In either case, keep the method simple and easy to use. We suggest:

1. underlining all the relevant facts in pencil (indicated in the example that follows as a dashed underline);

2. number and mark the legal issues raised in the case with a line alongside the paragraph;

3. identify the ratio or future message of the case in a short statement on the front page of the decision and highlight or underline the specific sections of the decision directly relevant to the ratio of the case in red (indicated in the example that follows with a double underline);

4. underline all other important information in the case, such as reasons or other information in blue (indicated in the example that follows as a regular underline);

5. use a margin note summary and number system (R 1., R 2., R 3., etc.) to summarize the important reasons that correspond to a specific issue, such as issue "1," issue "2," or issue "3"; and

6. use an asterisk to add extra emphasize to information that is very important to the case.

Demonstration example *Rowe v. Canning*

Ratio: There is both a statutory and a common law duty on owners of animals to control such animals (i.e., to prevent such animals from roaming or straying free and from causing damage).

OR

Because it is reasonably foreseeable that an animal roaming free in public will cause damage; owners of such animals have a duty of care to control them.

L.D. BARRY J: — Prince the pony slipped its bridle and went exploring, on the first day Renee Canning brought it home as a present for his grandchildren. While Prince was at large, Rowe and Furey fell off their motorcycle, when a horse ran suddenly in front of them, near the Cannings' home. Rowe and Furey claim Prince was the perpetrator and now sue for damages.

THE FACTS

On June 27, 1990, Rowe and Furey were riding Rowe's motorcycle in a westerly direction along the Conception Bay Highway, in the Town of Conception Bay South. The driver, Rowe, heard a warning shouted by Furey, who was seated behind him, and almost simultaneously saw a pony or horse running at full gallop from the side of the highway towards the motorcycle. Rowe and Furey said the left side of the motorcycle hit the pony's right front quarter and neck. The bike fell over, spilling Rowe and Furey to the roadway. The pony kept running across the highway and down Perrins Road, in Conception Bay South. After Rowe and Furey had picked themselves up and called the police, they saw Boyd Canning leading a pony along the highway and down Perrins Road. Rowe and Fury identified the pony as the one that had run across the road.

Boyd Canning testified that on June 27th his father, Renee Canning, brought home Prince, a small ten year old pony, about the size of a Newfoundland Pony, which Renee had purchased the previous Christmas for Boyd Canning's children. Prince had been stabled by its previous owner from Christmas until the day of the accident. Boyd Canning said he had earlier that day fastened the bridle, which was on Prince upon arrival, to a rope affixed to a steel peg in the ground. When Boyd Canning arrived home later, around the time of the accident, he found Prince's bridle still attached to the rope, but Prince had disappeared from the unfenced property. His father informed him Prince had slipped the bridle. Canning went looking for the horse and found Prince on a parking lot by a store on the Conception Bay Highway, not far from the intersection with Perrins Road where the accident occurred. Canning said he saw no indication on Prince of having been hit by a motorcycle.

Kimberly Greenslade, Steven Batten and Juanita Breen testified they had been walking together along the Conception Bay Highway towards St. John's, when they noticed a horse "dart" across the highway and run down Perrins Road. They all were of the opinion that the horse was a full grown

Margin notes:

Might be impt fact

*

Owner ties animal

Pony escapes from unfenced property

Pony found near accident; no signs of injury

Witnesses cannot confirm that horse running free in area is the pony Prince horse. When shown a photo of the pony owned by the Cannings, all three said the horse on the highway was larger.

The records of the Department of Municipal Affairs show that regulations prohibiting the roaming of animals were made by the Town of Conception Bay South and approved by the Minister on March 18, 1975. The Plaintiffs could not provide conclusive evidence, however, that these regulations had ever been posted for publication as required by the relevant legislation, because the minutes of Town Council meetings were not available for the period prior to 1977.

Not clear if Town Regs prohibiting roaming animals posted as required

THE ISSUES

Three issues arise:

(1) Was Prince the horse involved in the accident?

1

(2) If the horse was Prince, are the Cannings liable in negligence either

    (a) for breach of a duty created by municipal regulations or

    (b) for breach of a duty at common law?

2: Owner, defendant: common law duty and or statutory duty for roaming animals?

(3) Was Brian Furey keeping a proper lookout, while driving his motorcycle?

3: Driver, plaintiff: contrib. negl. — proper lookout?

STATUTORY PROVISIONS AND REGULATIONS

The *Livestock Act*, RSN 1990, c. L-20, provides:

> 6. The minister may by order prohibit the running at large of a class of livestock within an area specified in the order.
>
> 7. An owner shall not permit ... a stallion over the age of 1 year ... to run at large without the written consent of the minister.
>
> 8. (1) The owner of livestock shall be liable for damages caused by that livestock to property.
>
> ...
>
> (3) Nothing in this section affects the liability of an owner of livestock where the livestock is involved in a collision with a motor vehicle.

* Owner liable for damages, except in vehicle accident

The Town of Conception Bay South (Impounding of Animals) Regulations, 1975, approved by the Minister March 18, 1975, provided:

> 2. No person shall permit any animal of which he is the owner or guardian to roam at large in any street, road, or lane within the Town or in any open field or common from which free access can be had to such street, road, or lane.
>
> 4. All owners or guardians shall maintain a proper fence on their property so as to prohibit their animals from roaming at large.

Owner must prevent animal from roaming

The Local Government Act, Stats. Nfld. 1972, No. 32, provided:

> 99. (1) Subject to the approval of the Minister, the council may make regulations
>
> (e) prohibiting ... the running at large ... of animals ... providing for the impounding of such animals ...
>
> (6) Regulations made under subsection (1) or (2) shall be made public by poster erected in such places as the council may direct and shall not have effect until they are so posted.

ANALYSIS

1. Identification of Horse

Rowe & Furey ID pony as Prince

Rowe was certain that the horse he saw leaving the scene with Boyd Canning was the horse which ran across the road. He described the horse involved in the accident as a horse "a bit bigger than a pony, almost like a riding horse," and a mixture of light and dark brown in colour, with a dark mane. This accurately described Prince, shown in a photograph later tendered by Canning. One difference was the mane, which Rowe described as dark black, when it is in fact dark brown. Furey's description, while less precise than Rowe's also adequately described Prince. I prefer the testimony of Rowe and Furey to that of Greenslade, Batten and Breen. Rowe

Court rejects witness evidence

and Furey were closer to the animal which ran across the road. Also, there was some uncertainty in the evidence of the three bystanders, who, like Rowe and Furey, only had seconds to view the horse. Greenslade estimated that she was 50 to 100 feet away from the animal but indicated she was not sure of the distance. Batten, who was with Greenslade and Breen, estimated the distance at 300 to 400 feet. Breen estimated the distance at 75 feet but admitted she was not good at judging distances. Neither Greenslade nor Batten was able to describe the colour of the horse. Breen said she thought it was brown but she wasn't sure. While each thought it was a full grown horse they had seen, they had difficulty describing its height. Kimberly Greenslade stated she thought the horse was as tall as she was. Batten estimated that the back of the horse he saw would be about up to his chin. They both denied the horse shown on the photo was large enough to be the one they saw. But they could not estimate the height of the horse in the photo. Breen said merely that the horse she saw was not as tall as her.

Batten testified that the horse was galloping. Breen said it was moving between a slow walk and a run. Greenslade said it was running. These three witnesses also were of the opinion that the horse had not hit the motorcycle, because the horse kept going and did not make any sound. Counsel for the Cannings submits that, if the motorcycle hit the horse, as alleged by Rowe and Furey, there would have to be marks on the horse.

Canning says no marks on Prince; there was a second horse in area

He says that, since there were no marks on Prince, this supports the premise there was a second horse.

Witness confirms roaming horses rare occurrence in C. Bay South

Juanita Breen testified that, in her twenty-three years in the area, this was the only time she had seen a horse roaming free along the Highway in Conception Bay South. Even without her testimony I believe I could take judicial notice this was an unusual occurrence on a busy highway. It would be an extraordinary and highly improbable coincidence for there to be another horse, in addition to Prince, roaming free at that exact time, in that same area, with that exact colour.

I am satisfied from the testimony of Rowe and Furey it was Prince which ran across the road. Rowe and Furey were closer to the animal than other witnesses and their evidence was more precise. I also accept the testimony of Rowe and Furey that their motorcycle hit the horse a glancing blow. I do not believe I should find that there was another horse running free at the time, merely because there were no signs of injury on Prince. This can be explained by the glancing blow. I find that Greenslade, Batten and Breen, who had discussed the incident amongst themselves, arrived at an erroneous conclusion as to the size of the horse they saw, probably because of the short time it was in view, their distance from the horse, and their lack of any references against which to measure the size from that distance.

2. Negligence of Cannings

(a) Statutory Duty

Although the Canning's horse was named "Prince," not "Princess," I conclude this is insufficient evidence upon which to base a conclusion that Prince was a stallion. Neither was there any evidence of an order by the Minister under the *Livestock Act*, prohibiting the running at large of horses in the area. I am, therefore, unable to find that the *Livestock Act* is applicable.

There is, however, a statutory duty to prevent roaming animals, created by the Town of Conception Bay South (Impounding of Animals) Regulations, 1975. Section 2 of the Regulations is applicable. I do not accept the interpretation of Counsel for the Cannings that "permit" in that section should be interpreted as not applying to a person who has, as in the present case, attempted to keep an animal tied up. My interpretation of the section is that, if an owner improperly or inadequately ties up an animal so as to allow that animal to escape, then that owner has "permitted" the animal to roam at large. Also, in any event, the Cannings were also in breach of section 4 of the Regulations, which required that they maintain a proper fence on their property so as to prohibit Prince from roaming at large.

I am satisfied I should treat the 1975 Regulations as having been properly posted. The person who was Town Manager in 1975 set out in an affidavit that, while he has no specific recollection of the creation and implementation of the Regulations, the practice was to post regulations after they were returned with the Minister's approval. He deposed:

> ... given that the subject Regulations were prepared, passed by the Town Council of the Town of Conception Bay South, submitted to the Minister for his approval, I feel that they were posted in the Town Office in the same fashion as all other Regulations that had to be posted to give them force and effect, following their return from the office of the Minister of Municipal Affairs.

R 1. Decision
Pony = Prince

R 1.

R 2. Livestock Act does not apply

R 2.a. Municipal statutory duty to prevent roaming animals

* R 2. Owner must not allow animal to roam free

I conclude there is sufficient evidence in this affidavit of the former Town Manager to permit me to draw the inference that, on a balance of probabilities, all things concerning posting, required by the legislation, have been done. At the very least, this evidence shifted the evidentiary burden and required the Defendants to bring forward evidence which would raise a doubt as to whether the Town had properly posted the Regulations. This the Cannings have not done. There is no evidence at all that the Regulations were not properly posted and in effect. Even if there had been no evidence from which an inference of posting could have been drawn, there is authority supporting the proposition that, in circumstances such as the present, the initial onus is on the Defendants to prove that the Regulations were not properly posted. In *R v. Pay-N-Save Drugs Ltd.* (1960), 128 CCC 425 (Man. CA), the Court confirmed the decision of a Magistrate, who had held that the onus was on the accused to prove the *Early Closing By-Law* of the City of Winnipeg was invalid. The accused was questioning whether the By-Law had been advertised in accordance with the *Shops Regulation Act*, RSM 1954, c. 242. See also, *Rogers, The Law of Canadian Municipal Corporations* (2d ed., updated to 1994), at pp. 463-4.

(b) Duty at Common Law

In this case, even in the absence of applicable municipal regulations, one would have to consider whether there is a duty at common law on the owner of a horse to prevent that animal from roaming onto a busy highway and causing an accident. It should be foreseeable to an owner that, if a horse breaks loose, it is likely to cause such accidents. In those circumstances would it not be a breach of a common law duty for the owner of a horse to inadequately tie an animal and, thereby, allow the animal to get free?

In *Searle v. Wallbank*, [1947] AC 341 (HL), the House of Lords held that an owner of a field had no obligation to prevent his animals from straying upon an adjacent highway. The Supreme Court of Canada refused to follow this approach and held, in *Fleming v. Atkinson*, [1959] SCR 513, that the historical basis for the rule in *Searle*, dependent as it was on the peculiarities of highway dedication in England, where highways had come into being by adjoining owners giving only a right of passage to the public, had never existed in Ontario. The Court held that the ordinary rules of negligence applied to the case of straying animals and that regard should be had to all the circumstances, including the nature of the highway and the amount and nature of the traffic upon it. The development of Newfoundland highways may not have occurred in the same way as those in Ontario, where, for the most part, the fee was always in the Crown. However, in *Eales v. James* (1977), 17 Nfld. & PEIR 242 (Nfld. Dist. Ct.), McCarthy DCJ held that, since highways in this Province are vested in the Province or in municipalities, the law of Newfoundland can also be distinguished from the law of England. He applied Fleming and held the rule of *Searle* inapplicable in Newfoundland. I have been given no reason why I should not take the same approach.

R 2.b.

R 2. *Court rejects decision in Searle & follows SCR decisions*

I find that, even if the Regulations of the Town were not in effect, there was a common law duty upon the Cannings to prevent Prince from roaming upon the busy Conception Bay Highway, where the volume of traffic meant an accident would be likely.

R 2.b. Common law duty to keep animals from roaming on busy hwy; foreseeable accident

(c) Breach of Duty

Boyd Canning says he merely tied Prince on by means of the bridle, which was already on the horse's head when his father brought Prince home. There is no evidence that his father was not involved in placing the bridle on the animal. Even if the previous owner had placed the bridle on Prince, the Cannings had a duty to ensure that the bridle was secure enough to hold, when Prince was tied on in the field. In the circumstances I must find that the Cannings were in breach of duty and negligent and are liable to Rowe and Furey for their damages in an amount to be assessed.

R 2. Decision

3. Contributory negligence

Counsel for the Cannings submits that, because Furey saw the horse on the side of the road, before it came upon the pavement, therefore Rowe could not have been keeping a proper lookout if he only saw the horse just at the moment of collision. I do not find this submission at all convincing. I accept the evidence of Rowe and Fury that they were traveling within the speed limit at the time. I also accept their evidence that Rowe was driving in a responsible and prudent fashion. Furey's evidence is that the horse was at full gallop when he first saw it proceeding from the side of the highway. The fact that Rowe saw the horse a second or so after Furey is no evidence that he was not keeping a proper lookout. As driver, Rowe had a responsibility to maintain a proper lookout on the road ahead, while also remaining reasonably alert for hazards entering from the side. Furey, as passenger, had the luxury of ignoring the road ahead, if he wished, and maintaining his gaze upon the side of the road. It is not strange, therefore, that he may have seen the horse a few seconds before Rowe. I find Rowe was keeping a proper lookout. There was no contributory negligence on his part.

R 3. Court rejects defendant claim that R negligent

R 3. Plaintiff travelling under speed limit & prudently

R 3. Decision

SUMMARY AND DISPOSITION

Decision summary

1. Boyd Canning and Renee Canning are liable to Bryan Rowe (formerly known as Bryan Rowe Goodyear) and Wayne Furey for their damages in an amount to be assessed.

2. Rowe and Furey have leave to apply for an assessment of damages.

3. Rowe and Furey are entitled to their costs, to be taxed.

EXERCISE 4 *Tutton et al. v. Corporation of the Town of Pickering et al.* (1996), 29 OR (3d) 539, 5 OTC 298 (Gen. Div.)

Use the underline method to brief this case. Complete the margin notes in the space provided, using key words to draw attention to the key facts and legal concepts that you have underlined. Remember to identify the relevant people, actions, and objects in summarizing the facts.

Margin notes

Ratio: _____

_____

_____

LOGAN J: — This is a motion brought by way of a special case for the opinion of the court, pursuant to Rule 22 of the Rules of Civil Procedure. The case stated involves a motor vehicle accident which occurred on June 19, 1991 at the intersection of Highway No. 2 and Brock Road in the Town of Pickering, Ontario.

The plaintiff Tracy Tutton was driving the plaintiff vehicle in a westerly direction along Highway No. 2 and collided with a vehicle operated by the defendant Tsuji who was travelling in a southerly direction along Brock Road. The action has been discontinued as against the defendant Kiyoshi Tsuji.

Tracy Tutton was injured in the accident. The remaining plaintiffs make claims pursuant to the *Family Law Act*, RSO 1990, c. F.3. The plaintiffs take the position that the injuries to Tracy Tutton may or may not satisfy the "threshold" in s. 266(1) of the *Insurance Act*, RSO 1990, c. I.8.

At the time of the accident a work crew employed by the defendant municipality was performing repairs on the control panel for the traffic signals governing the intersection. A Durham Region police constable directed traffic through the intersection. He ordered the Tsuji vehicle to move through the intersection.

The police constable, however, was not visible to the plaintiff because of other vehicles on the roadway. At the time the Tsuji vehicle moved through the intersection, the work crew re-activated the traffic signals for testing purposes, but did not notify the police constable. The plaintiff Tutton entered the intersection because she had a green light. She was unable to see the police constable. The defendant Tsuji entered the intersection, notwithstanding the red signal, because the police constable motioned her to proceed. The result was a collision between the two vehicles.

The defendant Regional Municipality of Durham has admitted negligence on the part of its work crew in their failure to advise the police constable of their activation of the traffic signals. The Region is vicariously liable in law for the negligence of its work crew.

The issues to be determined are:

1. Assuming that the plaintiff Tracy Tutton does not come within s. 266(1)(a) or (b) of the *Insurance Act*, is the defendant, the Regional Municipality of Durham, immune from liability with respect to any damages caused by the negligence of its work crew because of s. 266(5) of that Act?

2. If the answer to question 1 is yes, should the action be dismissed as against the Regional Municipality of Durham because there is no evidence of damages caused by negligence on its part and its only potential liability could be with respect to damages caused by its work crew?

3. Notwithstanding the answers to questions 1 or 2, should the action be dismissed as against the defendants other than the Regional Municipality of Durham because there is no evidence of any negligence on the part of any of them?

I find that s. 266(5) might give protection to the Regional Municipality of Durham if the evidence disclosed that its act along with that of its work crew or some other employee caused a single injury. In this case, however, it does not give immunity. The case law discloses that statutory immunity granted to one defendant does not cause the tort to disappear. Statutory immunity merely dictates the different forms of relief which may arise against the various defendants. In my view, it does not apply to the claim based on vicarious liability.

It is necessary at the outset to set out the relevant statutory provisions. These are:

> 266(1) In respect of loss or damage arising directly or indirectly from the use or operation, after the 21st day of June, 1990, of an automobile and despite any other *Act*, none of the owner of an automobile, the occupants of an automobile or any person present at the incident are liable in an action in Ontario for loss or damage from bodily injury arising from such use or operation ... involving the automobile unless, as a result of such use or operation, the injured person has died or has sustained (a) permanent serious disfigurement; or (b) permanent serious impairment of an important bodily function caused by continuing injury which is physical in nature.

(2) Subsection (1) does not relieve any person from liability other than the owner of the automobile, occupants of the automobile and persons present at the incident.

...

(5) In a proceeding involving a plaintiff who cannot recover against the owner of an automobile, the occupants of an automobile or a person present at the incident because of the operation of subsection (1), a defendant is not liable for damages caused by any person who is excluded from liability because of the operation of subsection (1) and is not liable to contribute or indemnify in respect of such damages.

The plaintiff's position is that s. 266(5) of the *Act* does not immunize the Region of Durham from its vicarious liability for damages. Rather the plaintiffs take the position that according to s. 266(2), the only persons who are excluded from liability under s. 266(1) are the owners, occupants or persons present at the incident. They argue that employers, who would be vicariously liable, are not persons expressly mentioned in s. 266(2) as being excluded from liability and therefore employers are not excluded from liability pursuant to s. 266(1). It therefore would follow that s. 266(5) does not apply with respect to the employer's vicarious liability.

The plaintiffs further argue that if there is any ambiguity in the interpretation of s. 266(5) of the *Act*, then because the *Act* is one which restricts the common law right to sue, the *Act* should be given a narrow and restrictive interpretation which least diminishes the plaintiffs' rights.

The defendants' position is that s. 266(2) cannot be considered in isolation. Rather, they argue that the section must be read in the context of the no-fault scheme as a whole and in particular it must be considered and interpreted in conjunction with the provisions of s. 266(5). The thrust of the defendant's argument is that the plain meaning of the phrase which relieves the defendant from liability for any "damages caused by any person who is excluded from liability because of the operation of subsection (1)" encompasses the defendant's potential vicarious as well as joint and several liability for damages. The defendants argue that such an interpretation results in a harmonious co-existence between the two subsections and gives each subsection a meaningful effect.

The defendants further argue that to interpret s. 266(5) in the manner suggested by the plaintiffs would amount to reading into the provision a limitation which is simply not there in the language used.

Their position is that if the legislature had intended for s. 266(2) to remain unqualified by s. 266(5) it would have employed clear language to do so. They submit that the court should not read qualifications into the language used in s. 266(5), which are not there.

With respect to the argument that the section should be interpreted in a manner which least diminishes the plaintiff's right to sue, the defendants argue that this principle does not apply, given that there is no ambiguity in the legislation. Furthermore, they point to the Ontario Court of Appeal decision *Meyer v. Bright* (1993), 15 OR (3d) 129, 110 DLR (4th) 354, where the court, in discussing the approach to the interpretation of s. 266, states at p. 134:

> [H]ere, the legislation has not completely taken away the right to sue but, and to the extent that right has been limited, there has been an attempt to compensate the accident victim by providing for increased no-fault benefits. Further, the court in *Berardinelli* found there was ambiguity in the wording of the section which gave rise to two distinct but equally reasonable interpretations. As we shall point out later, we do not find any ambiguity in the language of s. 266. In our opinion, the legislation here is essentially remedial and the words in s. 266 of the *Act* should be interpreted in their ordinary and natural sense, and in harmony with the object and scheme of the *Act*.

ANALYSIS REVIEW OF THE CASE-LAW

There is very little case law dealing with the issue of whether an action based on vicarious liability of an employer for an employee's negligence is statute-barred by s. 266. The earliest decision to deal with the issue is *Champagne v. Bell Canada* (1992), 16 CCLI (2d) 287, 41 MVR (2d) 154 (Ont. Gen. Div.). In that case, the plaintiff, a driver of a motorcycle, brought an action against Bell Canada and its employee to recover damages for personal injuries and property damage sustained when he was forced to take evasive action to avoid a telephone wire hanging across the road. Bell Canada moved before trial for a determination of whether the action was statute-barred on the grounds that the employee was a person present at the incident. Because there was some dispute as to whether the employee was actually present at the incident at the time of the accident, Brockenshire J. dismissed the motion and sent the matter on for trial. He stated however at p. 292:

> In view of the clear wording of s. 266(2), providing that s. 266(1) does not relieve any person from liability other than those named in s. 266(1), my provisional conclusion is that

even if this action should be found to be barred on the facts against Darcy Bell, it can still continue against Bell Canada.

More recently in *Musson v. Federal Express Canada Ltd.* (unreported decision dated February 15, 1996, with supplementary reasons released February 21, 1996 [now reported [1996] ILR 1-3326 (Ont. Gen. Div.)]) Daudlin J., in interpreting s. 267.1 of the *Insurance Act*, followed the reasoning *of Champagne v. Bell*, *supra*, and allowed the action against the employer to proceed to trial. In his supplementary reasons, Daudlin J. states [p. 4033]:

> Accordingly, I wish by these Supplementary Reasons to make it clear that in my view vicarious liability *qua* employer and *vis à vis* its driver and any direct liability for negligence in breach of its employer responsibilities are issues which are alive and ought to proceed to trial to be determined by the trial judge.

The issue of vicarious liability of an employer was also dealt with in *Bassie v. Brown* (unreported decision of Leitch J. dated April 6, 1993 [reported [1993] ILR 1-2945 (Ont. Gen. Div.)]). In that case which involved an interpretation of s. 263(5) of the *Act*, the court held that a claim against the employer based on vicarious liability was statute-barred. However, it must be noted that the legislative provision in question granted immunity to "any person involved in the incident."

Leitch J. held that this phrase could be given a broader interpretation than the s. 266 provision "any person present at the incident." She also noted that the provision regarding subrogation barred a claim against "any person." The plaintiff's claim was, therefore, dismissed. None of the above cases have dealt specifically with the issue of whether s. 266(5) operates as a further bar to a claim founded on vicarious liability.

THE NATURE OF VICARIOUS LIABILITY

In determining whether s. 266(5) of the Act operates as a bar to the vicarious liability of the employer, it is first necessary to examine the nature of vicarious liability. It is well established that vicarious liability is a distinct and separate liability. In *Munro v. Gibb*, [1981] 1 SCR 42, 117 DLR (3d) 513, the Supreme Court of Canada considered the issue of whether Schroeder, the owner of an automobile, who was by statute put into a master-servant relationship with a driver Munro, was liable for personal injuries sustained by the driver of another car, by reason of Munro's negligence, when both drivers and Munro's regular employer were under the *Workers' Compensation Act, 1968*, SBC 1968, c. 59. The court stated at p. 47:

The appellant seeks relief from this consequence by fastening on the immunity of the driver Munro from suit by the injured Patricia Gibb. The contention is that since both drivers are employees under the *Workers' Compensation Act*, compensation thereunder is the only relief. From this it is argued that the appellant's liability here is vicarious only and that she cannot, therefore, be sued when her deemed servant cannot be sued. The answer to this is clear enough. The tort committed by Munro does not disappear. Relief against it takes different forms. As against the negligent driver Munro, it lies in compensation; as against the appellant, it lies in court action.

More recently, in *Zago v. Davies* (1985), 50 OR (2d) 428, 18 DLR (4th) 272, the Ontario Court of Appeal dealt with the issue of whether a suit could proceed against the owner of a motor vehicle, despite the fact that the suit was statute-barred against the driver, who was protected by the limitation period in the *Public Authorities Protection Act*, RSO 1980, c. 406. The court stated at p. 431:

> If the driver of a motor vehicle falls within the ambit of s. 11 of the *Public Authorities Protection Act*, he will be shielded from liability if the action against him is not commenced within the six-month time limit. The protective shield, however, does not dissolve the negligence of that driver. There is no provision in the *Highway Traffic Act* to the effect that the passage of a special and unique limitation period exempting the Driver from liability also exempts the owner. In the absence of such a provision, there is no reason to exempt the owner from the clear liability imposed by the *Highway Traffic Act*.
>
> ...
>
> The owner's liability is distinct from that of the driver. That distinct liability arises as a result of the driver's negligence being imputed to the owner.

It is clear from the above authorities that vicarious liability is not derivative and its existence is not dependent on the negligent person being open to suit. In the case at bar, the liability of the employer, the Regional Municipality of Durham, is founded on responsibility for the employee work crew's breach of duty, not on responsibility for making good the employee's liability.

The defendant has indeed properly conceded this point. Paragraph 14 of the defendant's factum, which discusses *Zago v. Davies*, *supra*, states:

... one, however, is that the *Public Authorities Protection Act* contained no provision corresponding to s. 266(5) of the *Insurance Act*. Section 11 of the PAPA was the equivalent of s. 266(1), and were s. 266(1) to stand alone, *Zago* would be authority for the view that s. 266(1) should be interpreted so as not to afford protection to persons whose liability is vicarious. Unlike the provisions of the PAPA, however, s. 266(1) does not stand alone; s. 266(5) must also be considered and its plain meaning given effect. *Zago* is therefore distinguishable.

The next step then must be a determination of what, if any, limiting effect s. 266(5) has on the vicarious liability of the employer.

The defendant argues that the effect of s. 266(5) is to preclude any right of recovery from any other person for the damages attributable to the fault or negligence of those persons against whom the right of action is barred, and furthermore preclude any right to claim contribution or indemnity.

"Damage" is defined in *Black's Law Dictionary*, 6th ed. (St. Paul: West Publishing Co., 1990) as:

> Loss, injury, or deterioration, caused by the negligence, design or accident of one person to another, in respect of the latter's person or property. The definition goes on to state: The word is to be distinguished from its plural, "damages," which means a compensation in money for a loss or damage. "Damages" is correspondingly defined as: A pecuniary compensation or indemnity, which may be recovered in the courts by any person who has suffered loss, detriment, or injury, whether to his person, property or rights, through the unlawful act or omission or negligence of another.

In light of these definitions, it is readily apparent that "damage" and "damages" are not synonymous. The former refers to the injury while the latter refers to the compensation for that injury.

In interpreting s. 266(5), the question that must be asked, therefore, is whether the damages which flow from the vicarious liability are separate or independent from the damages flowing from the employees' negligence, although the ultimate quantum may be the same. If damages is accepted as referring to compensation for injury, then it follows that an independent injury gives rise to independent compensation.

If the defendant Regional Municipality of Durham's interpretation of s. 266(5) were to be accepted, the end result would be that the statute would preserve the plaintiff's right of action against the Regional Municipality, while barring any right of recovery in that same action.

This would amount to a denial of a claim based on vicarious liability, solely on the basis that the claim for indemnity is statute-barred. If this was the intent of the legislature, it would have been made clear in the legislation. Indeed such an interpretation runs counter to the principles of tort law. I adopt the statement of the Alberta Court of Appeal in *Wadsworth v. Hayes* (unreported decision dated January 16, 1996 [now reported 132 DLR (4th) 410, 36 Alta. LR (3d) 204]) where the court states at para. 29 [p. 420 DLR]:

> It would be an unusual torts scheme which made the main claim depend upon the existence of the claim for contribution or indemnity. Still less does our torts law say that. The common law is to the opposite effect. There was no contribution or indemnity at all among joint tortfeasors at common law. Such legislation was first passed in the 1930s …
>
> In my view, the effect of s. 266(5) is simply to modify the common law rule regarding the liability of joint and/or several tortfeasors for the entire amount of the plaintiff's damages.

The defendant, in making its argument, stated that s. 266(5) of the Act was analogous to s. 10(11) of the *Workers' Compensation Act*, RSO 1990, c. W.11. In my opinion the cases cited did not advance the defendant's argument. In all of the cases cited, the issue was the liability for and apportionment of damages between joint tortfeasors who were granted statutory immunity and those who were not. None of the cases dealt with the issue of whether the contribution and indemnity provision barred vicarious liability. Indeed the issue of vicarious liability did not arise in those cases because the employers were also granted statutory immunity from suit under the provisions of the *Workers' Compensation Act*.

Indeed the reasoning of the Supreme Court in *Munro, supra,* is in my view more applicable to the case at bar. As was already noted, the court, in that case, recognized that the statutory immunity granted one defendant does not cause the tort to disappear. Rather, the statutory immunity merely dictates the different forms of relief which may arise against the various defendants.

The Relief Sought on the Determination of the Questions Stated is:

1. If the answer to question 1 is yes, an order declaring that the defendant, the Regional Municipality of Durham, is immune from liability

with respect to any damages caused by the negligence of its work crew. If the answer is no, an order declaring that the defendant, the Regional Municipality of Durham, is liable with respect to the damages caused by the negligence of its work crews.

2. If question 2 is answered, and the answer is yes, an order dismissing the action as against the defendant, the Regional Municipality of Durham. If it is answered, and the answer is no, an order declaring that the action may continue against the defendant, the Regional Municipality of Durham, subject to the declaration in para. 1 of the order.

3. If the answer to question 3 is yes, an order dismissing the action as against the defendants other than the defendant, the Regional Municipality of Durham. If the answer is no, an order declaring that the action may continue as against the defendants other than the Regional Municipality of Durham.

Therefore I find that the suit against the defendant the Regional Municipality of Durham can proceed on the basis that the Regional Municipality is vicariously liable for the negligence of its work crew. The answer to question 1 is no. Order to go that the Regional Municipality is liable with respect to damages caused by the negligence of its work crew. The answer to the second question is no, and the action of the plaintiff may continue against the Regional Municipality of Durham subject to the declaration in para. 1 of the order. The answer to question 3 is no and the action may continue against the parties.

Order accordingly.

The court's decision in the above case set out the legal issues clearly. In the next example, the presentation of the court's decision requires the reader to identify the legal issues raised in the case.

EXERCISE 5 *Peinet Inc. v. O'Brien (c.o.b. Island Services Network (ISN)) (1995), 130 Nfld. & PEIR 313, 40 CPC (3d) 58 (PEI TD)*

Use the underline method to brief this case. Complete the margin notes in the space provided, using key words to draw attention to the key facts and legal concepts that you have underlined. Remember to identify the relevant people, actions, and objects in summarizing the facts.

Margin notes

Ratio: _____

_____

_____

MacDonald CJ: — The plaintiff seeks an interlocutory injunction preventing the defendants from using the name PEI.NET or any similar name or address, which may be confused by the public with the corporate name of the plaintiff. The action is one of "passing off." Throughout this decision I shall refer to the two named defendants as "the defendant."

Undoubtedly, there was some confusion by the plaintiff as to the domain name being used by the defendant as the plaintiff kept referring to upper case letters while the defendant stated the name was registered in lower case letters. The final correspondence was from the defendant's attorney on January 13, when he stated the defendant would not de-list because the domain name was assigned to him by the Internet network and was governed by the conventions of Internet.

The defendant, in referring to his efforts to satisfy the plaintiff, filed an affidavit from Peter Richards, Managing Editor of the Buzz magazine. Mr. Richards states that on January 8th his company was contacted to change the name pei.net to isn.net in advertising for Island Services Network. The defendant also filed an affidavit from Curtis Duckworth, of Graphic Communications Inc., who states he prepared communication materials for the defendant containing the name pei.net when Internet addresses were being used. However, he states that "about January 5th" this was suspended and about two weeks later Island Services Network requested the name pei.net be changed to isn.net on all communication material.

A further affidavit filed by the defendant is from Peter Rukavina who stated his company, Digital Island, assisted Island Services Network in registering the domain name isn.net with Internet on January 6, 1995. He stated that after January 6, no technical reference to the domain name pei.net existed in Island Services Network Internet host computer. Finally, the defendant filed a fax from the InterNIC Domain Register, Duane Stone, who states he was contacted on January 6, 1995 and asked to register that day the name ISN.NET, which he did, despite their usual time being two to three weeks to change a listing. The correspondence from Mr. Stone used upper case letters further adding to the confusion.

The plaintiff asks for an injunction restraining the defendant from using the domain name of PEI.NET. The plaintiff uses upper case letters. There is no evidence that the defendant used such a domain name, rather the name pei.net was used. The plaintiff also states that the defendant by using the domain name PEI.NET confused the public as to the identity of the plaintiff and defendant, however, it is to be noted that the plaintiff's name is PEINET INC. and the plaintiff does not use a period to separate PEI and NET.

The defendant states that anyone using the Internet network would not confuse the plaintiff and the defendant. The defendant states anyone intending to contact the plaintiff using its domain name would not be able to contact the defendant and vice versa. The plaintiff did not answer that allegation.

The whole area of the use of the Internet network and its conventions is new to the Court. I find that the plaintiff has only made superficial submissions without explaining the Internet system. The plaintiff merely filed a short affidavit of its president, which leaves much to be desired insofar as an explanation of Internet is concerned. The plaintiff's president did not give *viva voce* evidence to further expand on his affidavit. The defendant, Kevin O'Brien, did give direct evidence. He raised sufficient concerns to cast doubt on the plaintiff's case. It must be remembered that the burden is upon the plaintiff to prove its case.

Even if the plaintiff had proven that the defendant's use of the domain name pei.net was an infringement of the plaintiff's use of the name PEINET Inc., I am of the opinion that the plaintiff has not established all of the elements of a passing-off action. The Supreme Court of Canada in *Ciba-Giegy Canada Ltd. v. Apotex Inc.*, [1992] 3 SCR 120, 95 DLR (4th) 385 has recently stated that the three components of a passing off action are; (1) the existence of goodwill; (2) deception of the public due to a misrepresentation; and (3) actual or potential damage to the plaintiff.

The plaintiff has failed to establish that the defendants had misrepresented the public. I do not consider the limited use the defendants had of pei.net to be sufficient to meet the component of deception of the public due to misrepresentation. It must be remembered that the defendants did not operate or use the plaintiff's company name of PEINET. Basically all the defendants did was, for a very short period of time, use a "telephone" number that was the same as the plaintiff's name. This use of the same name consisted of a reference to it in a newspaper article, not an advertisement, and a listing on Internet, also for a very short period of time.

The misrepresentation must lead or likely lead the public to believe that the goods or services offered by the defendant are the goods and services of the plaintiff. That has not been established.

The plaintiff has shown no actual damage loss. Neither will there be a potential loss to the plaintiff as the defendant has agreed to delist the domain name pei.net from its Internet server.

Neither am I satisfied that the plaintiff has established himself in business under its trade name for such a reasonable time and to such a reasonable extent that it has acquired a reputation under that trade name that would prevent the defendants from using a similar name: *Remedies in Tort*, Klar, Linden, Cherniak, Kryworuk, pp. 19-21.

In the circumstances I would dismiss the application. There shall be no order for costs.

EXERCISE 6 Prepare a case brief for *Peinet Inc. v. O'Brien*

Using the categories below, prepare a concise, written case brief for *Peinet Inc. v. O'Brien*.

1. **Style of cause**

   _____

2. **Procedural history**

   _____
   _____

3. **Material facts**

   _____
   _____
   _____
   _____
   _____
   _____
   _____
   _____
   _____

4. **Issue(s)**

   _____
   _____
   _____
   _____
   _____

5. **Decision**

   _____

6. **Ratio**

   _____
   _____

7. **Reasons**

   _____
   _____
   _____
   _____
   _____
   _____
   _____
   _____
   _____

CASES

Allied Plastering & Stucco Ltd. v. A. Visca Architect Inc. (1999), 50 CLR (2d) 93 1999 (Ont. SCJ).

Nguyen v. Canada (Minister of Citizenship and Immigration), [1998] IADD no. 1726 [unreported].

Peinet Inc. v. O'Brien (c.o.b. Island Services Network (ISN)) (1995), 130 Nfld. & PEIR 313, 40 CPC (3d) 58 (PEI TD).

Rowe v. Canning (1994), 117 Nfld. & PEIR 353, 4 MVR (3d) 269 (Nfld. TD).

Toronto (City) v. Ontario (1999), 43 OR (3d) 281, 95 OTC 65 (SCJ).

Tutton v. Pickering (Town) (1996), 29 OR (3d) 539, 5 OTC 298 (Gen. Div.).

Skills of legal analysis: How to use the law to solve problems and predict outcomes

INTRODUCTION

Legal analysis is based on the premise that like cases should be treated alike. In other words, the reasons given by a court to support its decision in one case justify a similar ruling on similar situations in future cases. The lawyer analyzes the case law by:

- evaluating the similarities and differences between each case and the problem,
- identifying any inconsistencies in the courts' application of the law in prior cases, and
- observing any patterns or trends developing in the law.

There are four analytical tools used to analyze the case law in this manner.

Analogy

First, the lawyer identifies the cases that are *analogous*. These are the cases in which the facts or issues closely resemble those in the problem at hand. Analogous cases are used to predict how the courts will apply the law to a particular problem. When a court applies the ruling in one case to determine the outcome of another, the court is said to "follow" precedent.

Distinction

Second, the lawyer identifies the cases that are *distinguishable* from the problem at hand. These are the cases in which there is an important difference between facts or issues addressed in the case and those raised in the problem at hand. Distinguishable cases are used to predict or explain why the courts should not apply a particular legal principle to another, similar situation. Similarly, when a court does not follow the ruling in one case to determine the outcome of another or to support its reasoning, the court is said to "distinguish" the cases.

Synthesis

Third, the lawyer identifies any trends or developments in the law, *synthesizing* the law from all the cases pertaining to a similar legal matter. Sometimes the law on a particular matter develops over a number of cases, each case adding definition and clarity to the legal principle and its application. Other times, the law on a particular matter is not developed fully. Writing a coherent statement about the law not only assembles the precedents from a number of cases over a period of time, but also identifies gaps in the law and highlights legal uncertainties.

Reconciliation

Finally, the lawyer must *reconcile* or explain apparent inconsistencies in the governing law. Effective *reconciliation* of the governing case law explains why a court may rule differently on similar issues and fact situations. Sometimes, the explanation is that the law may have changed from one time to the next, or from one jurisdiction to another. In the former case, the lawyer must develop a temporal theory about how the law will develop in the future in order to predict which precedent is likely to be followed. In the latter case, the lawyer must decide which ruling is most binding and most relevant to the problem at hand.

The exercises in this chapter provide practice in developing these four analytical techniques, as well as applying these techniques to predictive writing. The techniques are demonstrated in the analysis of the following problem.

DEMONSTRATION: LEGAL ANALYSIS SKILLS

The motorcycle accident: *Romeo and Juliet v. Dean Pelletier*

Romeo and Juliet fell in love in spite of the horrible feud between their families. Determined to live their lives together, they decided to elope to avoid objections to their marriage. On Friday July 13, 2000, they packed their bags, loaded Romeo's motorcycle and set off at about 6 a.m. to be married by a justice of the peace in a neighbouring town, two hours away. It was a clear morning and the couple took their time along the winding country roads, enjoying the sunrise over lush pastures.

At 7:30 a.m. the sun was fully risen; already, it was a swelteringly hot day. Juliet complained to Romeo that wearing full-face helmets and leather motorcycling suits on such a day was unbearable. Even though the state laws would have allowed it, Romeo would not let her ride on the back of his bike without the protection of her full-face helmet and motorcycle suit. As Juliet admired the beautiful, open fields, something dark moved in the side ditch. She cried out to Romeo when she saw a large dog about to leap out in front of the bike. The dog seemed to spring out from the ditch, running directly into the path of the bike. Romeo responded quickly, swerving sharply to miss the dog. As he did so, Juliet was thrown from the back of the motorcycle. Her body skidded across the road. When Romeo went to her, he found her body lying like a rag doll in the ditch on the other side of the road. She was barely conscious. The frightened dog continued running, leaping over a fence and disappearing into the next field. Out of the corner of his eye Romeo observed that the dog had a leash trailing behind it.

Earlier that same morning, Dean Pelletier awoke as usual to begin training and grooming the show dogs boarded at his kennels. When he was done at about 7:15 a.m., he prepared to take his own Doberman, "Shadow," on a morning walk. Shadow was highly excitable and had never been a well-disciplined dog in spite of Dean's best efforts. A client drove up to the kennel gates just as Dean had finished attaching Shadow's leash. Dean dropped Shadow's leash for a moment while he opened the gates to let in the car. Shadow took off in a flash. Dean immediately called the local police and set out to find his dog.

Constable Chekim found Shadow at 9 a.m., playing in a field nearby. By that time, Chekim was also aware of the motorcycle accident. But Shadow showed nothing that would indicate that he had been hit by a motorcycle. There was, however, one eyewitness to the accident. A retired commercial flight pilot was out early that same morning in his ultralight aircraft. He had been flying low over Pelletier's kennels just as Pelletier was preparing to take Shadow on his morning walk. He saw the dog flee and followed its path. From his plane, he saw the dog shoot out from the ditch and across the path of Romeo's motorcycle. The pilot could not be certain, however, whether the bike had actually hit the dog.

The doctors who set Juliet's broken hands and wrists and tended to her broken ribs said that it was the leather gear and full-face helmet that saved her from the most gruesome of motorcycle injuries. Judging by the way she fell face first, the helmet had saved Juliet from severe facial injuries. Even so, she must take six months off work and may never be able to use her hands with ease again. As a self-employed writer, she stands to lose the career of her dreams. Moreover, to meet her mortgage payments and therapeutics needs, Juliet estimates she needs $20,000 in the short term.

Analysis of case law

The following section illustrates how a lawyer would read and categorize the case law to determine legal trends or patterns, and assess how the case law may apply to the problem at hand. A step-by-step analysis of the first case, *Rowe v. Canning*, shows how to determine the applicability of similar, subsequent cases. The full-page case brief prepared earlier for *Rowe* is reproduced on the following page.

Rowe v. Canning (1994), 117 Nfld. & PEIR 353, 4 MVR (3d) 269 (Nfld. TD)

Procedural history

Trial case.

Facts

A pony running free on a provincial highway struck the motorcycle of the plaintiff, Rowe, causing the driver to lose control and crash. Rowe and his passenger, Furey, identified the pony as belonging to the defendant, Canning. They sued Canning for negligence. The defendant denied that his pony caused the accident. On the day of the accident, however, the defendant found his pony wandering free near the highway. It had broken free from where its owner had tied it up and run away from Canning's unfenced property. Statements from witnesses were inconsistent and did not confirm that the animal they saw run across the highway was the pony Prince. The defendant argued that even if Prince did cause the accident, the plaintiffs were not driving carefully.

Issues

1. Was the pony Prince involved in the accident?

2. Do animal owners have a common law or statutory duty to secure their animals?

3. If animal owners have a common law or statutory duty to secure their animals, did the defendant, Canning, breach this duty?

4. Was the plaintiff, Rowe, driving in a manner that contributed to the cause of the accident?

Decision

The court found the defendant, Canning, liable for damages sustained by the plaintiffs.

Ratio

The owners of animals have a statutory and common law duty of care to control their animals because it is reasonably foreseeable that an animal roaming free may cause injury.

Reasons

1. The pony that caused the accident belonged to Canning.

2. Under the *Livestock Act*, RSN 1990, c. L-20, an owner must not allow animals to run at large and shall be liable for any resulting damages.

3. At common law, owners should anticipate responsibility for injuries resulting from animals roaming at large. In reaching this decision, the court rejected the ruling in the House of Lords decision in *Searle v. Wallbank*, [1947] AC 341 (HL), in which no duty for straying animals was found to exist. The court distinguished *Searle* as a British authority that had been replaced by the Supreme Court of Canada decisions in two Ontario cases, *Fleming v. Atkinson*, [1959] SCR 513, and *Eales v. James* (1977), 17 Nfld. & PEIR 242 (Nfld. Dist. Ct.), in which the court held that owners are responsible for damages caused by their straying animals.

4. Drivers have a duty to keep a proper lookout. The court found that in this case, however, there was no contributory negligence regarding any of the plaintiff's actions.

GENERAL COMPARISON OF MAIN FEATURES (FACTS AND LAW)

The first step in predicting how the ruling in a case applies to the problem at hand is to identify the similarities and differences between the problem and the case. In this example, the point of comparison between the case and the problem are striking. In each case,

1. An animal escapes and strays onto a highway causing the driver of a vehicle to lose control.

2. There is some question about who owns the stray animal.

3. Concerns are raised about whether the drivers of the vehicles were driving carefully when the accident occurred.

Below is a comparison of the facts and legal issues of Romeo and Juliet's motorcycle accident and the similar accident in *Rowe v. Canning*. This comparison shows how a lawyer may read a precedent case in order to answer specific legal questions.

SPECIFIC COMPARISON OF MAIN FEATURES (FACTS AND ISSUES)

Fact comparison

A fact comparison shows strong similarities between the problem and the case. For this reason, any court ruling on Romeo and Juliet's motorcycle accident must use the precedent in *Rowe* to answer any similar legal questions in Romeo and Juliet's case. Table 5.1 compares the facts in the two cases.

TABLE 5.1 FACT COMPARISON

Facts of the cases

Romeo and Juliet v. Dean Pelletier	*Rowe v. Canning*
A <u>Doberman ran out across the highway, striking Romeo's motorcycle</u>, causing him to lose control. The passenger on the motorcycle, Juliet, suffered serious <u>injuries</u> when she was thrown from the bike and landed in the highway ditch. <u>Juliet saw the dog approaching</u> the highway <u>and alerted Romeo</u> to the danger. As the dog ran away from the accident, <u>Romeo observed that the dog</u> had a leash and collar. An eyewitness could not confirm if the motorcycle hit the dog.	Rowe wins lawsuit against Canning for damages suffered when a <u>stray pony</u> belonging to Canning <u>hit Rowe's motorcycle</u>. Rowe and his passenger, Brian Furey, both suffered <u>injuries</u> when a pony ran out onto the highway and knocked them off Rowe's motorcycle. <u>Furey saw the pony approaching and alerted Rowe</u> to the danger. As they got back on their bike, <u>the two men saw Canning</u> leading away the pony that had hit them.

Differences between the cases

Romeo and Juliet v. Dean Pelletier	*Rowe v. Canning*
• Romeo lost control of his motorcycle when <u>he swerved</u> to avoid hitting a <u>dog</u> running free on the highway.	• Rowe lost control of his motorcycle when a <u>pony</u> running free on the highway <u>struck</u> his motorcycle.
• Romeo's passenger, Juliet, suffered <u>serious injuries</u> and was taken to the hospital. Her injuries may prevent her from pursuing her career as a writer.	• Rowe and his passenger suffered <u>minor injuries</u>. They were able to walk away from the accident.
• <u>An eyewitness confirmed</u> that a dog, which escaped from Dean Pelletier's kennels, ran out in front of Romeo's motorcycle.	• <u>Witnesses could not confirm</u> that a pony running free at the time of the accident belonged to Canning.

Legal comparison

The next step is to identify the similarities and differences between the legal issues raised in the problem and the court's treatment of similar legal issues in the precedent case. This comparison is done by testing whether the court's "answers" in the precedent case resolve the legal issues in the problem at hand. Table 5.2 compares the legal issues of the two cases.

TABLE 5.2   LEGAL COMPARISON

Legal questions or issues	Answers to similar legal questions or issues
• Is Dean Pelletier's dog, Shadow, the dog that ran out onto the highway and caused Romeo to lose control of his motorcycle?*	• Although the motorcycle accident in *Rowe* raised a similar question about a pony, the court's answer is a finding of fact and cannot be used to determine the ownership of a dog in another case. The court dealing with Romeo's case will have to decide if the dog in that case belonged to Dean Pelletier.
• Is an owner of a stray animal responsible for damage caused by that animal?	• According to the common law duty of care and the duties of animal owners under the *Livestock Act*, RSN 1990, c. L-20, owners of animals are responsible for damages caused when their animals roam free or stray.
• Does the driver of a vehicle have a duty to keep a proper look out while driving?	• Yes, at common law, the driver of a vehicle has the duty to keep a proper lookout.
• If so, was Romeo driving in a manner that contributed to the cause of the accident?*	• Although the motorcycle accident in *Rowe* raised a similar question about Rowe's responsibility for his accident, the court's answer constitutes a finding of fact about specific incidents in the Rowe case and cannot be used to determine whether or not Romeo was driving carefully at the time of his accident.
	• Decision: Defendant 100% negligent and liable for plaintiff's damages.
	• Ratio/applicable legal principle: Animal owners have a statutory and common law duty to prevent their animals from roaming free and causing harm to others.

*   Note: Beware of "factual issues." The determination of identities, dates, times, and other questions of fact do not have the same legal significance as issues that clarify or resolve points of law. Generally, the court's answers to factual issues are not as helpful as its answers to purely legal issues in resolving similar legal problems in the future.

APPLICATION OF THE CASE TO THE PROBLEM

Given the strong similarities between the problem and the *Rowe* case, a court will likely apply the ruling in *Rowe* to determine the respective responsibilities of Romeo and Dean Pelletier. It is possible, however, that a court might draw a distinction between an accident caused when a driver swerves to avoid hitting an animal roaming free and an accident caused when an animal strikes a vehicle. In such a situation, a court will characterize this difference in facts as being so "material" as to strike out the helpfulness of a precedent case.

PREDICTION: SYNOPSIS OF RELEVANT LEGAL PRINCIPLE

Formulate a specific message to the immediate parties

If the legal outcome in *Rowe* is applied to Romeo's case, then Dean Pelletier will be held responsible for the damages caused when his dog strayed across the highway.

Formulate a broader message

For the problem at hand, it may be summarized as: The owner of an animal has a duty under statutory law and at common law to ensure the animal is tied up safely.

The research on Romeo and Juliet's case uncovered other cases of potential significance. These cases should also be examined for the factual and legal similarities they have with the Romeo case. We have prepared case briefs for each of these cases.

Canadian General Insurance Co. v. Rowsell (1996), 140 Nfld. & PEIR 329, 438 APR 329 (Nfld. TD)

Procedural history
Trial Court, Newfoundland.

Facts
Two Newfoundland ponies owned by the second defendant, Rowsell, were killed when they broke free from their tether, wandered onto the provincial highway, and were struck by the plaintiff, a truck driver. Rowsell was rounding up his ponies when the accident occurred. He was following the ponies in his truck and was flashing his high-beam headlights as a warning to oncoming traffic. The plaintiff driver slowed down but was blinded by the headlights. Since he could not see the ponies on the road, he hit them. The accident occurred on a clear night and at a straight section of the road.

Issues

1. Is an owner of a stray animal responsible for damage caused by that animal?

2. Is the driver of a vehicle responsible for damage caused as a result of hitting a stray animal on a highway?

Decision
Defendant 80% negligent and liable for damages; plaintiff 20% contributorily negligent.

Ratio
Animal owners have a statutory and common law duty to prevent their animals from roaming free and are responsible for damages caused when their animals stray.

Reasons
The court applied the ruling in *Rowe* to support its finding of the defendant's negligence. In finding contributory negligence on the part of the plaintiff, the court ruled that in certain circumstances, it is reasonable to expect that an experienced driver take additional precautions other than slowing down when reacting to unusual or dangerous circumstances.

COMPARISON OF FACTS AND ISSUES

Fact comparison

SIMILARITIES

- Both cases involve a vehicle accident that occurred when animals broke away from their owners' property and roamed onto the highway.

- In both cases, the driver of the vehicle received some kind of warning about the potentially dangerous situation developing on the highway.

Note that when the facts are generalized, the similarities between the two cases are highlighted.

DIFFERENCES

Romeo's case	*Rowsell*
• Accident involved a dog.	• Accident involved two ponies.
• Romeo's passenger warned him about the danger.	• The owner of the ponies tried to round them up and warn oncoming traffic of the dangerous situation.
• The accident occurred in daylight; Romeo's vision was not obstructed.	• The accident occurred at night; headlights blinded the driver.

Legal comparison

Legal issues raised in Romeo's case	*Answers to legal issues in Rowsell*
• Is Dean Pelletier's dog, Shadow, the dog that ran out onto the highway and caused Romeo to lose control of his motorcycle?*	• No similar factual issue raised, no answer.
• Is an owner of a stray animal responsible for damage caused by that animal?	• According to the common law duty of care and the duties of animal owners under the *Livestock Act*, RSN 1990, c. L-20, owners of animals are responsible for damages caused when their animals roam free or stray.
• Does the driver of a vehicle have a duty to keep a proper look out while driving?	• Drivers of vehicles have a duty to keep a proper lookout.
• If so, was Romeo driving in a manner that contributed to the cause of the accident?*	• A person is driving carefully if they are following the speed limit. In this case, however, the court found that as an experienced driver, the plaintiff should have anticipated danger and should have taken extra precaution when the defendant swung his truck around and began flashing his headlights to oncoming traffic.

---

* Note that this issue is more of a "factual" issue than a "legal" one.

APPLICATION OF THE CASE TO THE PROBLEM

Given the strong similarities between the problem and the *Rowsell* case, it is highly likely that a court will follow the ruling in *Rowsell* to determine the respective responsibilities of Romeo and the dog owner, Dean Pelletier.

It is possible, however, that a court might draw a distinction between an accident caused when a driver swerves to avoid hitting an animal roaming free and an accident caused when an animal strikes a vehicle. In such a situation, a court will characterize this difference in facts as being so "material" as to strike out the helpfulness of a precedent case.

PREDICTION: SYNOPSIS OF RELEVANT LEGAL PRINCIPLE

Formulate a specific message to the immediate parties

If the legal outcome in *Rowsell* is applied to Romeo's case, then Dean Pelletier will be held responsible for the damages caused when his dog strayed across the highway. Even though Romeo was driving at or below the speed limit, he may bear some responsibility for the accident since Juliet warned him of approaching danger.

Formulate a broader message

The owner of an animal has a duty under statutory law and at common law to ensure the animal is tied up safely.

THE LAW WORKBOOK: Developing skills for legal research and writing

Ruckheim v. Robinson, [1995] 4 WWR 284, 1 BCLR (3d) 46 (CA)

Procedural history
Court of Appeal, British Columbia.

Facts
The defendant's dog jumped out of its pen and escaped onto the highway. The dog ran unexpectedly into the path of the plaintiff, who was driving his motorcycle. The plaintiff suffered a serious ankle injury when the collision caused the motorcycle to topple onto him. The plaintiff's injuries disabled him for a year and prevented him from earning his living as a carpenter for a year and a half. Even after full recovery, it was unlikely that the plaintiff would ever be able to take on large jobs.

Issues

1. Did the owners of the escaped dog have a duty to keep the dog on the property to avoid foreseeable risk?

2. Did the owners meet that duty?

Decision
For the plaintiff. The trial judge awarded the plaintiff $40,000 for non-monetary damages for the plaintiff's injuries, $63,000 for past wage loss, and $130,000 for future income loss. On appeal, the court found that the trial judge had miscalculated past wages and future income, and reduced these awards to $37,000 and $35,000, respectively.

Ratio
Animal owners have a duty to ensure their animals are under control and cannot injure other persons, since it is reasonably foreseeable that an escaped animal may cause damage.

Reasons
The trial judge rejected the defendant's evidence that the dog could not jump out of its fenced area.

The judge applied the test of reasonable foreseeability correctly to find the defendant negligent in failing to provide an area from which the dog could not escape.

COMPARISON OF FACTS AND ISSUES

Fact comparison

SIMILARITIES

- Both cases involve a highway motorcycle accident that occurred when a dog broke away from its owner's property and ran unexpectedly into the path of the driver.

- In both cases, people involved in the accident sustained serious injuries that will impede their work and career.

Note that when the facts are generalized, the similarities between the two cases are highlighted.

Romeo's case	*Ruckheim*
• Romeo's passenger warned him about the danger.	• Driver received no warning of the approaching dog.
• Accident occurred because Romeo swerved to avoid hitting the dog. It is not clear whether the motorcycle actually struck the dog.	• The accident occurred when the dog ran on the highway and struck the motorcycle.

Legal comparison

Legal issues raised in Romeo's case	*Answers to legal issues in Ruckheim*
• Is Dean Pelletier's dog, Shadow, the dog that ran out onto the highway and caused Romeo to lose control of his motorcycle?*	• No similar factual issue raised. It was conceded that the dog in the accident belonged to the defendant. The answer is a finding of fact and cannot apply to another case.
• Is an owner of a stray animal (or stray dog) responsible for damage caused by that animal?	• According to the common law duty of care, owners of animals (or stray dogs) are responsible for damages caused when their animals roam free.
• Does the driver of a vehicle have a duty to keep a proper lookout while driving?	• Drivers of vehicles have a duty to keep a proper lookout.
• If so, was Romeo driving in a manner that contributed to the cause of the accident?	• No issue was raised regarding contributory negligence.

---

* Note that this issue is more of a "factual" issue than a "legal" one.

APPLICATION OF THE CASE TO THE PROBLEM

Given the strong similarities between the problem and the *Ruckheim* case, it is highly likely that a court will follow the ruling in *Ruckheim* to determine the respective responsibilities of Romeo and the dog owner.

It is possible, however, that a court might draw a distinction between an accident caused when a driver swerves to avoid hitting an animal roaming free and an accident caused when an animal strikes a vehicle. In such a situation, a court will characterize this difference in facts as being so "material" as to strike out the helpfulness of a precedent case.

PREDICTION: SYNOPSIS OF RELEVANT LEGAL PRINCIPLE

Formulate a specific message to the immediate parties

If the legal outcome in *Ruckheim* is applied to Romeo's case, then Dean Pelletier will be held responsible for the damages caused when his dog strayed across the highway. Even though Romeo was driving at or below the speed limit, he may bear some responsibility for the accident since Juliet warned him of approaching danger.

Formulate a broader message

The owner of an animal has a duty under statutory law and at common law to ensure that the animal is tied up safely.

Bujold v. Dempsey (1996), 181 NBR (2d) 111 (QB)

Procedural history
Trial case, New Brunswick.

Facts
The plaintiffs, Bujold and Dobson, were walking their dogs without a leash along a rural highway. The defendant, Dempsey, lost control of her car and struck the plaintiffs when she swerved to avoid hitting the dogs. The plaintiffs sued for damages.

Issues

1. Did the dogs cause the accident?

2. If the dogs caused the accident, are their owners negligent in failing to restrain their dogs while walking them on the highway?

3. Was the defendant keeping a proper look out and driving safely?

Decision
The plaintiffs won the action for negligence.

Ratio
Animal owners have a duty to control their animals and prevent their animals from causing harm. Drivers have a duty to keep a proper look out.

Reasons
The judge found that the defendant, Dempsey, was driving carelessly and was responsible to the plaintiffs for their injuries. The defendant could have avoided hitting the dogs and remained on the road. The fact that the dogs were roaming free does not alone explain or justify the extent to which Dempsey lost control of her car.

The judge found the plaintiffs were contributorily negligent because they failed to control their animals and permitted them to roam free on a highway.

COMPARISON OF THE FACTS AND ISSUES

Fact comparison

SIMILARITIES

Both cases involve a highway vehicle accident that occurred when a driver swerved to avoid hitting dogs that were running free on the highway.

Note: The similarities between the two cases are described in a manner that draws attention to the identical facts, but other details are described in a general manner to de-emphasize the differences:

In both cases, the drivers *swerved* to avoid hitting the *dogs*.

But: One accident involved a motorcycle; the other accident involved a car. The word "vehicle" is used to draw attention to the similarities rather than the differences. The inference is that for the purposes of understanding the application of the law, the type of vehicle is not important.

DIFFERENCES

Romeo's case	*Bujold*
• Romeo's passenger warned him about the danger.	• Driver received no warning of the approaching dog.
• Accident involved a motorcycle.	• Accident involved a car.
• The driver is suing the animal owner for the injuries sustained by his passenger.	• The animal owners were pedestrians injured in the accident and are suing the driver.

Legal issues

Issues raised in Romeo's case	*Answers to legal issues in Bujold*
• Is Dean Pelletier's dog, Shadow, the dog that ran out onto the highway and caused Romeo to lose control of his motorcycle?*	• No similar factual issue raised. It was conceded that the dog in the accident belonged to the Plaintiffs. The answer is a finding of fact and cannot apply to another case.
• Is an owner of a stray animal (or stray dog) responsible for damage caused by that animal?	• According to the common law duty of care, owners of animals (or stray dogs) are responsible for damages caused when their animals roam free or stray.
• Does the driver of a vehicle have a duty to keep a proper lookout while driving?	• Drivers of vehicles have a duty to keep a proper lookout.
• If so, was Romeo driving in a manner that contributed to the accident?*	• A finding of fact specific to the circumstances of *Bujold*'s case cannot be applied to another case. In *Bujold*, however, the court found that the driver lost control because she was driving too fast to swerve safely to miss the dogs.

---

* Note that this issue is more of a "factual" issue than a "legal" one.

APPLICATION OF THE CASE TO THE PROBLEM

Given the strong similarities between the problem and the *Bujold* case, it is highly likely that a court will apply the ruling in *Bujold* to determine the respective responsibilities of Romeo and the dog owner.

PREDICTION: SYNOPSIS OF RELEVANT LEGAL PRINCIPLE

Formulate a specific message to the immediate parties

If the legal outcome in *Bujold* is applied to Romeo's case, then the court will find that Romeo was driving safely, and swerved safely to avoid a collision. Dean Pelletier will be held responsible for the damages caused when his dog strayed across the highway.

If the court finds that Romeo lost control of his motorcycle when he swerved because he was not driving safely, then the court will find that (1) Dean Pelletier was responsible for the damages caused when his dog strayed across the highway, but that (2) Romeo was contributorily negligent.

Formulate a broader message

The owner of an animal has a duty under statutory law and at common law to ensure the animal is tied up safely.

The following overview illustrates how a case may predict the court's decision in Romeo's case. Note that the cases are organized in chronological order and indicate the jurisdiction. Had the Supreme Court or an appeal court heard any of these cases, it would have been useful to note this as well.

Overview of legal analysis

The overview chart (see the following page) serves four important purposes:

1. First, the legal implications of the case law for Romeo's case are better appreciated after reviewing all the answers to the legal issues from each case. The chart shows what message a particular case sends to Romeo.

2. Second, the chart identifies whether the case in point is *analogous* or *distinguishable* from the problem at hand.

3. Third, in comparing the case ratios, a *synthesis* of the law as it applies to Romeo's case may be constructed. The comparison allows patterns and trends developing in the law to be readily visible.

4. Fourth, the apparent discrepancies among court decisions can be explained or *reconciled* through an overview of any legal inconsistencies, and differences between the case law and the problem.

   To illustrate how this may be constructed, synthesis and reconciliation of the law are provided below.

SYNTHESIS OF LAW

The easiest way to synthesize the applicable law is to enumerate the main legal findings of the various cases on point.

1. Owners of animals have a statutory and common law duty for damages caused when their animals run free.

2. Owners of animals must ensure that their animals are safely tied up.

3. Animal owners are responsible for damages arising from traffic accidents caused when their animals roam free.

4. The driver's contributory negligence will be assessed on the facts to determine whether the driver was keeping a proper lookout or ought to have anticipated the dangerous situation developing.

RECONCILIATION

At first, it appears that the finding in favour of the animal owners and against the driver in *Bujold* goes against the case law. Upon review, it is clear that the court in *Bujold* found that the law would apply differently when a driver loses control as a result of swerving to miss hitting an animal. In *Bujold*, the court found that the driver was already driving "out of control" when she swerved to miss the dogs. Recall that the court said that the presence of the dogs on the road was not sufficient to explain the extent to which the driver lost control of her car.

TABLE 5.3 OVERVIEW TABLE

Case	Issue	Answer	Applicability of answer	Legal significance of case (i.e., ratio)	How to apply case	Result of application	Reason for not applying
Ruckheim v. Robinson 1993 BC	1. Did the owners of the escaped dog have a duty to keep the dog on the property to avoid foreseeable risk? 2. Did the owners meet that duty?	Yes No	✓ ✗	Animal owners have a duty to prevent their animals from roaming free and causing harm.	Analogous facts and issues	Romeo will win his suit against Dean Pelletier.	Distinguishable facts: Romeo lost control when he swerved to miss the animal; in *Ruckheim*, the dog struck the motorcycle.
Rowe v. Canning 1994 Nfld.	1. Was the pony Prince involved in the accident? 2. Do animal owners have a common law or statutory duty to secure their animals? 3. If yes, did the defendant, Canning, breach this duty? 4. Was the plaintiff, Rowe, contributorily negligent?	Yes Yes Yes No	✗ ✓ ✗ ✗	Animal owners have a duty to prevent their animals from roaming free and causing harm.	Analogous facts and issues	Romeo will win his suit against Dean Pelletier.	Distinguishable facts: Romeo lost control when he swerved to miss the animal; in *Rowe*, the animals struck the vehicle.
Canadian General Insurance Co. v. Rowsell 1996 Nfld.	1. Is an owner of a stray animal responsible for damage caused by that animal? 2. Is the driver of a vehicle responsible for damage caused as a result of hitting a stray animal on a highway?	Yes Yes, under certain circumstances	✓ Depends on circumstances	Animal owners have a duty to prevent their animals from roaming free and causing harm.	Analogous facts and issues	Romeo will win his suit against Dean Pelletier. Possible finding of contributory negligence on the part of Romeo.	Distinguishable facts: Romeo lost control when he swerved to miss the animal; in *Rowsell*, the animals struck the vehicle.
Bujold v. Dempsey 1996 NB	1. Did the dogs cause the accident? 2. If yes, are their owners negligent in failing to restrain their dogs? 3. Was the defendant keeping a proper lookout and driving safely?	Yes Yes No	✗ ✓ Possible ✓	Animal owners have a duty to prevent their animals from roaming free and causing harm. Drivers are contributorily negligent for accidents caused when they fail to take precautions against losing control of their vehicles.	Analogous facts and issues	Romeo will win his suit against Dean Pelletier. Possible finding of contributory negligence on the part of Romeo.	Distinguishable facts: Romeo was a cautious driver and was driving under the speed limit when he swerved to miss the animal; in *Bujold*, the court found that the defendant was driving too fast.

DEMONSTRATION: PREDICTIVE WRITING SKILLS

Having completed the analysis of the case law, the task is to report the findings in a prediction of how the law is likely to apply in Romeo's case. It is helpful to organize the findings according to the following outline:

1. Usually, the first sentence states the answer to the particular or general legal question, predicting how the courts are most likely to rule.

2. A supporting statement of the general legal rule that will apply to the facts of the problem at hand follows this prediction. Usually, this statement is the *synthesis* of the relevant law.

3. Next, specific examples from *analogous* and *distinguishable* cases demonstrate how the courts have applied the law in question to similar situations in the past.

4. Any discrepancies in the case law are explained in a statement of *reconciliation.*

5. A final concluding statement summarizes the applicable law and the likely outcome when it is applied to the problem at hand.

Thus, predictive legal writing organizes the analysis of the law according to the following general pattern: the answer to the question is first; the explanation and reasons for that answer are second. The same outline is used to organize the analysis of a single case or a number of cases.

Below is an illustration of how this predictive writing pattern may be used to predict the court's answer to two of the legal issues in Romeo's case — namely, whether animal owners are responsible for damages caused when their animals roam free, and whether Romeo is contributorily negligent. Note how the subheadings used to introduce the prediction summarize the applicable law (just like a newspaper headline). Effective use of headings and subheadings allows the reader to see the primary legal conclusion immediately.

Predict how the law applies to Romeo's case

Explanatory notes

Prediction: Result when legal rule is applied

General legal rule

Result when rule applied

Proof: Use ratios from analogous cases

If appropriate, explain why a case is significant

On the strength of similarities and differences, show how case law applies to problem

Prediction

1. Animal owners are responsible for damages caused when animals roam free

The defendant in this case, Dean Pelletier, acted negligently when he allowed his dog to escape onto the highway, causing Romeo to lose control of his motorcycle. Courts have repeatedly found that animal owners have a duty to prevent their animals from roaming free and are responsible for the damages caused when they fail to secure their animals. In _Ruckheim v. Robinson_ and in _Rowe v. Canning_, the court found that the owners of animals have a statutory and common law duty of care to control their animals because it is reasonably foreseeable that an animal roaming free may cause injury. In reaching its decision in _Rowe_, the court rejected definitively the ruling in the House of Lords decision in _Searle v. Wallbank_ in which no duty for straying animals was found to exist. Courts have followed the precedent established in _Rowe_ to support similar findings in cases with facts similar to the case at bar, such as _Canadian General Insurance Co. v. Rowsell_ and _Bujold v. Dempsey_. In _Rowsell_, the court held the animal owner responsible for the accident caused when a truck struck his escaped ponies. As in Romeo's case, the defendant driver in _Bujold_ swerved to avoid hitting unleashed dogs on the highway. In that case, the court ruled that even though the animals were not hit, the owners were still liable for damages when the driver swerved to avoid hitting the dogs. Applying the rulings in these cases to the case at bar, Dean Pelletier is liable for the damages suffered when his dog ran out onto the highway.

2. Court unlikely to find driver negligent

Drivers have a duty to keep a "proper lookout" while driving and are liable for damages incurred in the event that they have acted negligently. Generally, the courts have found that drivers fulfill this duty as long as they drive in an alert manner and do not exceed the speed limit. A finding of contributory negligence against Romeo is unlikely. In _Ruckheim_ and _Rowe_, the courts found no contributory negligence on the part of drivers who were struck by animals wandering free on the highway. As in the case at bar, the courts found that the drivers were driving with reasonable caution, at or under the speed limit, and that there were no unusual circumstances that would have alerted the drivers to foreseeable danger. There was no evidence to support a finding of contributory negligence.

In _Rowsell_ and _Bujold_, however, the courts found the drivers partially responsible for the accident. In _Rowsell_, the court found that given the driver's experience and in light of the defendant's extraordinary efforts to warn oncoming traffic of the danger, the driver ought to have taken extra precautions to avoid the accident. In _Bujold_, the court determined that the reason the driver lost control of her vehicle was because she was driving too fast when she swerved to avoid hitting the animals running free on the highway.

At this point, there are two possible predictions to be made. The choices are:

1. The court may support a finding of contributory negligence on the part of Romeo. Romeo was driving too fast or failed to take extra precaution when Juliet warned him of approaching danger on the road.

   Possible prediction 1   No effort is made to distinguish the facts in Romeo from the facts in the precedent cases.

2. Romeo's accident may be distinguished from the facts in these cases. Although Romeo lost control of his motorcycle when he swerved to avoid hitting the unleashed dog on the highway, unlike the defendant driver in *Bujold*, Romeo was keeping a proper lookout at the time of the accident. The facts show that Romeo was an especially cautious driver (he was "taking his time" and took extra precautions to ensure that he and Juliet were wearing appropriate clothing for motorcycling). Furthermore, unlike the accident in *Rowsell* where the plaintiff was blinded by the defendant's headlight warnings, there were no unusual developments on the highway to warn Romeo of any approaching danger.

   Possible prediction 2   The statement distinguishes the case law against Romeo in order to demonstrate why the rulings should not apply. Note how a reference to factual differences is used to explain and justify why the law does not apply to the circumstances of the case at bar. The prediction outlines how an argument can be made in Romeo's favour.

The writer needs to identify either that both possibilities exist or that one possibility is preferable, and provide supporting reasons.

Conclusion

Dean Pelletier is liable for damages caused when Romeo swerved to avoid hitting Pelletier's dog, which had escaped onto the highway. If a court finds that Romeo was keeping a proper lookout and driving cautiously, the court is unlikely to assess contributory negligence on Romeo's part.

Concluding paragraph states the outcome when the applicable and distinguishable legal principles are applied to the case at bar.

> **Tip:** A court never "argues" a point of law. Only the parties to the case "argue." A court gives "reasons" to support its "finding," "holding," "ruling," or "decision" on a point of law.

PRACTISING THE TOOLS OF LEGAL ANALYSIS: ANALOGY, DISTINCTION, SYNTHESIS, AND RECONCILIATION

Problem A: The town of Glenmore

The exercises that correspond to problem A provide a step-by-step introduction to the tools of legal analysis and their application.

Consider the similarities between the positions taken by the town of Glenmore and the North American Union of Drivers and Technicians in the problem below, and the positions taken by the town of Ajax and CAW, Local 222 in the case that follows. Choose one of the methods of briefing a case to facilitate the legal analysis of the problem.

FACT SITUATION

Town of Glenmore v. North American Union of Drivers and Technicians

From 1982 to 1993, the garbage disposal company Enviro-Clean contracted with the town of Glenmore regarding the operation of the town's municipal garbage disposal system. The town owned and supplied the garbage trucks and all other tangible assets used to operate the system. It also controlled dump sites, pick-up schedules, and the recycling program and set the rates for collection. Enviro-Clean provided and coordinated the schedules for the drivers, mechanics, and cleaners whom Enviro-Clean employed to operate the town's system. The North American Union of Drivers and Technicians represented Enviro-Clean's employees as the certified bargaining agent for the garbage truck drivers, mechanics, and cleaners employed by the company in these garbage operations.

At the beginning of 1993, the town council voted to terminate its contract with the company and to commence the operation of the system on its own. Consequently, Enviro-Clean laid off all of the drivers, mechanics, and cleaners involved in the garbage operations of Glenmore. The town placed advertisements for qualified drivers, mechanics, and cleaners in the local papers. Although the town did not hire back all the former employees of Enviro-Clean, it did hire a number of Enviro-Clean's former employees, who formed a substantial proportion of the town's new garbage staff.

The union argued that a sale of a business within the meaning of section 64 of the *Ontario Labour Relations Act*, RSO 1990, c. L.2, that relates to the obligations of successor employers had occurred. Section 64 of the Act states:

> (2) Where an employer who is bound by or is a party to a collective agreement with a trade union or council of trade unions sells his, her or its business, the person to whom the business has been sold is, until the Board otherwise declares, bound by the collective agreement as if the person had been a party thereto and, where an employer sells his, her or its business while an application for certification or termination of bargaining rights to which the employer is a party is before the Board, the person to whom the business has been sold is, until the Board otherwise declares, the employer for the purposes of the application as if the person were named as the employer in the application.

Consequently, the union maintained that the town was bound by the terms of the union's collective agreement with Enviro-Clean. On the contrary, the town argued that s. 64 of *the Ontario Labour Relations Act* was not applicable since there had been no change in ownership. The town maintained that the cancellation of a commercial contract does not implicate a transfer of ownership, as implied by successorship under the Act. The dispute was taken to the Ontario Labour Relations Board (OLRB). The OLRB found in favour of the union, ruling that the sale of a business within the meaning of s. 64 of the *Ontario Labour Relations Act* concerning successor employers had occurred.

The town now appeals this decision on the grounds that the board's decision was patently unreasonable. The town argues that the board interpreted the statute unreasonably to support its finding. The town argues that the cancellation of a contract for the supply of services cannot be construed as either the acquisition of a business or the transfer of ownership of one business to another within the meaning of the Act. The North American Union of Drivers and Technicians argues that the OLRB acted within its jurisdiction, and that its ruling was reasonable and appropriate to the circumstances of the case. Accordingly, the union argues that because the standard for reviewing the board's decision cannot be met, there are no grounds for an appeal.

EXERCISE A1   Identify the key words, facts, and legal concepts raised by the problem

1. Who is taking whom to court and why?

_____

_____

_____

_____

_____

_____

_____

_____

2. What is the legal problem (or issues)?

_____

_____

_____

_____

_____

_____

_____

_____

3. What are the material facts?

_____

_____

_____

_____

_____

_____

_____

_____

4. Are there any background or remedial facts important to this case?

_____

_____

_____

_____

_____

STEP 2   RESEARCH THE LEGAL PROBLEM

Normally, at this stage, the lawyer follows the research methodology developed in chapters two and three to find the relevant legislation and case law. The research has been provided here. It will, however, be helpful to brief the governing case law.

STEP 3   READ AND ANALYZE THE APPLICABLE LAW

Ajax (Town) v. CAW, Local 222, [2000] 1 SCR 538

The Supreme Court upheld the findings of the Ontario Labour Relations Board which found that the nexus between the termination of a contract with a transportation company and the hiring of many of that company's employees to work in the new municipal transit system was sufficiently strong as to trigger successorship under section 64 of *the Ontario Labour Relations Act*, RSO 1990, c. L.2.

The appellant town and a transportation company entered into a contract regarding the operation of the town's municipal transit system. The town owned and supplied the buses and tangible assets used to operate the system as well as controlled the routes, schedules, rates and fare collection. The company provided and co-coordinated the drivers, mechanics and cleaners who operated the system. The respondent union was the certified bargaining agent for the bus drivers, mechanics and cleaners employed by the company in the transit operations. As a result of a vote by town council to cancel the contract at the end of 1992, the company laid off all of the drivers, mechanics and cleaners involved in the transit operations. A number of the employees were hired by the town and formed a substantial portion of the new transit staff. The union maintained that the town had in effect taken over the business provided by the bus company. As a result, the town was bound by the collective agreement that had governed the bus company's dealings with its employees. The Ontario Labour Relations Board held that the sale of a business within the meaning of section 64 of the *Ontario Labour Relations Act* concerning successor employers, had occurred. The divisional court quashed the board's decision but the court of appeal allowed the union's appeal.

Held: Appeal dismissed.

The Court of Appeal's reasons were substantially agreed with. The function of the reviewing court in this case is not to test the correctness of the Board's decision, but rather to decide whether the decision was patently unreasonable. It was not patently unreasonable for the Board to find a nexus between the transportation company and the town, as required for successorship. Since the historical and functional connection between the company and the town constitutes evidence upon which the Board would rationally have based its conclusion of successorship, that conclusion was not "clearly irrational."

EXERCISE A2 Is the case analogous to the problem at hand?

Test the similarities:

1. List the facts in the problem facing the town of Glenmore that closely resemble the important facts in the reported court case, *Ajax (Town) v. CAW, Local 222*.

_____

_____

_____

_____

_____

_____

_____

_____

2. What reasons does the North American Union of Drivers and Technicians use to support its argument that the town of Glenmore cannot appeal the Labour Board's decision?

_____

_____

_____

_____

_____

_____

_____

_____

3. How are these reasons similar to the argument made by *CAW, Local 222* in the reported case *Ajax (Town) v. CAW, Local 222*?

_____

_____

_____

_____

_____

_____

_____

_____

THE LAW WORKBOOK: Developing skills for legal research and writing

Testing the analogous case

THE IMPORTANCE OF SIMILARITIES

When a reported case such as *Ajax (Town) v. CAW, Local 222* shares important similarities with the problem at hand or another reported case, the cases are said to be *analogous.*

In the example here, the town of Glenmore faces a situation that is remarkably similar to the situation in *Ajax (Town) v. CAW, Local 222*. The cases are "factually analogous" because the facts of the two cases here are similar. The legal questions raised in the *Glenmore* problem also mirror those dealt with by the court in the *Ajax* case. The legal researcher should keep in mind that sometimes there are important analogies to be drawn between cases with very different fact situations but similar legal questions.

THE IMPORTANCE OF DIFFERENCES

It is equally important to determine the differences between the problem at hand and an applicable case. Use the following exercise to identify the important differences between the situations dealt with in the reported case, *Ajax (Town) v. CAW, Local 222*, and the situation developing between the town of Glenmore and the North American Union of Drivers and Technicians.

EXERCISE A3   Is the case distinguishable from the problem at hand?

Test the differences:

1. Identify the differences between the important facts in the problem facing the town of Glenmore and the facts as reported in the case *Ajax (Town) v. CAW, Local 222.*

_____

_____

_____

_____

_____

_____

_____

2. Identify the differences in the legal question(s) or issue(s) between the problem at hand and the case *Ajax (Town) v. CAW, Local 222.*

_____

_____

_____

_____

_____

_____

_____

3. Consider the significance of these differences. Do the factual differences between these two cases change the legal issue in any way? Explain why or why not.

_____

_____

_____

_____

_____

_____

_____

_____

Applying the analogous case

Lawyers use analogous cases to predict the outcome of a particular legal problem. In the example used here, it is clear that both the facts and the legal questions raised in the *Glenmore* problem closely resemble the facts and issues raised in the *Ajax* case. Therefore, the precedent or ruling in the *Ajax* case may be used to predict how the court will deal with the situation developing in the town of Glenmore. The idea is simple: under similar circumstances, the reasons given by the court for the ruling in one case will be *followed* to support a similar ruling in the future. The stronger the similarities between cases, the stronger the argument is that the prior ruling should be applied. There are few significant differences between the *Ajax* case and the problem in *Glenmore*. Based on the strong similarity between the cases, the argument that a court's treatment of the problem in *Glenmore* should follow the ruling in *Ajax* is both strong and persuasive.

Because both the facts and issues raised in the case of *Ajax (Town) v. CAW, Local 222* closely resemble the situation confronting the town of Glenmore, the ruling in *Ajax (Town) v. CAW, Local 222* may be used to predict the outcome of an appeal launched by the town of Glenmore. Generally, a statement of prediction follows a certain pattern. Follow the steps in the following exercise to predict the outcome of *Glenmore* based on the ruling in *Ajax*.

EXERCISE A4   Applying the law: Using analogous cases

1. Referring to the ruling in *Ajax (Town) v. CAW, Local 222*, state the general principle of law regarding the judicial review of the Ontario Labour Relations Board's decisions.

_____

_____

_____

_____

_____

_____

2. Based on the ruling and general principle of law stated in *Ajax (Town) v. CAW, Local 222*, how is a court likely to decide the *Glenmore* case?

_____

_____

_____

_____

_____

_____

3. List the reasons why a court should use the decision in *Ajax (Town) v. CAW, Local 222* to resolve the dispute between the town of Glenmore and the North American Union of Drivers and Technicians. Make references to specific examples of the factual and legal similarities between the two cases to support your reasons.

_____

_____

_____

_____

_____

_____

_____

_____

_____

_____

_____

_____

4. Test the strength of your analogy again: Consider the differences between the two cases. Are the circumstances of the two cases sufficiently different to justify treating the situation in *Glenmore* differently from the situation in *Ajax*? Explain.

_____

_____

_____

_____

_____

Predicting the outcome from the analogous case

Lawyers must consider both the similarities and differences between each case and the problem at hand. It is clear from the analysis of the similarities and differences between the problem in *Glenmore* and the decision in *Ajax* that if a court follows the ruling in *Ajax* to decide the *Glenmore* case, the North American Union of Drivers and Technicians will win. According to the reasons used to support the ruling in *Ajax*, the town of Glenmore cannot appeal the Ontario Labour Relations Board's decision.

The ruling in *Ajax* presents a problem for the town of Glenmore. It is expected that the lawyers representing Glenmore will review the differences between *Ajax* and *Glenmore* carefully in an attempt to *distinguish* the situation in *Ajax* from the problem in *Glenmore*. Distinguishing or proving the differences between cases is the technique lawyers use to demonstrate that the situations or legal issues in two cases are sufficiently different that the ruling in one should not be used to decide the outcome of the other. In the example here, however, there are few significant differences between *Ajax* and *Glenmore*. Glenmore's lawyers will have to search for analogous cases that, if applied to the *Glenmore* problem, would support the town's position. Consider the similarities and differences between the *Glenmore* problem and the following cases.

W.W. Lester (1978) Ltd. v. United Assn. of Journeymen and Apprentices of the Plumbing and Pipefitting Industry, Local 740, [1990] 3 SCR 644

W.W. Lester Ltd. is a construction company that carries on business subject to a union contract. In accordance with a practice known as "double breasting," Lester set up a second parallel company, called Planet, which operates without a union. The respondent construction companies possessed similar share structures and principals and operated side by side. They shared the same office, secretary, telephone number, and office expenses but had separate employees. While they shared a minor amount of equipment by renting the equipment to each other, each owned or leased its own equipment. The finances of the companies were separate. One of the principals prepared bids on construction projects on behalf of either company, depending on whether the job in question was a union or non-union construction site in accordance with the practice of "double breasting."

The appellant union, which represented Lester's employees, attempted to organize the non-unionized employees of Planet but withdrew its application for certification before the hearing. In its place, the union deposed an application alleging unfair labour practices on the part of the companies and sought a declaration of successorship pursuant to section 89 of *The Labour Relations Act, 1977*, SN 1977, c. 64, s. 89(1).

At the same time, the respondent companies laid a complaint alleging unfair labour practices on the part of the union. The Labour Relations Board granted the successorship declaration but found it unnecessary to make findings on the allegations of unfair labour practices. The respondent companies applied unsuccessfully to the Trial Division of the Newfoundland Supreme Court for an order of *certiorari* to quash the Board's order. The Court of Appeal held the Board's decision to be patently unreasonable and remitted the matter of the unfair labour practices to the Board.

The issues raised in this appeal are: (1) whether the Board had the jurisdiction to enter into the inquiry as to whether or not successorship had occurred; and (2) if so, whether the exercise of its jurisdiction was patently unreasonable.

Held: The appeal should be dismissed.

Section 18 of the *Act* limits judicial review of the Board's decisions concerning an error in interpreting the jurisdictional provisions or excess of jurisdiction by reason of a patently unreasonable error in the performance of its function. It is not enough that a mere transfer of assets occurs because a business is not a mere collection of assets. A finding of successorship under section 89(1) could not be based on common shareholdings and a common business enterprise or on the fact that the same people owned or worked for both companies. Corporate interrelationship, without some evidence of disposition, would not be enough to trigger the successorship provisions. The absence of evidence establishing a disposition under section 89 rendered the Board's decision patently unreasonable and, therefore, subject to judicial review. The Board's action in construing the successorship provisions as if they were common employer provisions was contrary to precedent.

EXERCISE A5　Applying the law: Using distinguishable cases

Identify the similarities and differences between *W.W. Lester (1978) Ltd. v. United Assn. of Journeymen and Apprentices of the Plumbing and Pipefitting Industry, Local 740* and the problem at hand, *Glenmore (Town) v. The North American Union of Drivers and Technicians, Local 306.*

FIRST　Weigh the similarities between the case and the problem at hand.

1. Explain how the significant facts in *W.W. Lester (1978) Ltd.* resemble the problem in *Glenmore (Town).*

_____

_____

_____

_____

_____

_____

2. The town of Glenmore wants to appeal the decision of the Ontario Labour Relations Board. How are the reasons for Glenmore's appeal similar to the complaint made by W.W. Lester (1978) Ltd. against Local 740?

_____

_____

_____

_____

_____

_____

3. What would be the outcome if a court applied the ruling in *W.W. Lester (1978)* to the appeal launched by the town of Glenmore?

_____

_____

_____

_____

_____

_____

SECOND Weigh the differences between the case and the problem at hand.

4. Identify the important differences between the significant facts in *W.W. Lester (1978) Ltd.* and the significant facts in *Glenmore (Town)*.

_____

_____

_____

_____

_____

_____

5. What reasons did the court in *W.W. Lester (1978) Ltd.* give to support its finding that the Labour Relations Board made "patently unreasonable errors in the performance of its function"?

_____

_____

_____

_____

_____

_____

6. Why would a court use or not use these reasons to support a similar finding in the town of Glenmore's appeal of the board's decision?

_____

_____

_____

_____

_____

_____

Predicting the outcome from the distinguishable case

As in *Lester*, the question before the court in the appeal launched by the town of Glenmore is whether the Ontario Labour Relations Board made unreasonable errors in its application of the law. At first glance, it looks like a court would follow the decision in *Lester* to decide the outcome in *Glenmore*. The key facts in *Lester*, however, are significantly different from the key facts in *Glenmore*. For this reason, it should be anticipated that the union in the town of Glenmore would distinguish the situation in *Lester* from that in *Glenmore* to support its argument that the Appeal Court should not apply the ruling in *Lester* to decide *Glenmore*.

Cases are distinguished from each other on the basis of key factual differences, or by making the argument that the two cases raise significantly different legal questions or key concepts. In an explanation of why a court should not follow a particular ruling, it is important to identify the differences between the two cases.

EXERCISE A6   Reconcile the differences in the case law

1. Identify the most authoritative case. Rank the cases by order of judicial importance:

   a. _____

   b. _____

2. What would be the result if a court applied the decision in the most important case "a" to decide the *Glenmore* case?

   _____

3. Under what circumstances would a court be persuaded to follow the ruling in case "b"?

   _____

   _____

   _____

Deciding which law applies

Different courts often apply similar law to different fact situations (and different law to similar fact situations). When a lawyer explains why different courts reach different decisions when faced with similar fact situations, the lawyer is reconciling the law. *Reconciliation* is just as important to legal analysis as the identification of analogous and distinguishable cases. The ability to explain differences within the law provides a court with reasons why one ruling should be followed over another.

In the example here, the *Ajax* case and the *Lester* case were decided differently, yet both bear important similarities to the problem in *Glenmore*. It would seem that the rulings in these cases produce conflicting results when applied to the problem in *Glenmore*. In arguing for the most favourable interpretation, a lawyer must explain why the law appears inconsistent. The search for an explanation requires a few steps. To review:

1. *Rank authority*   First, the lawyer must check which case is most authoritative. The apparent inconsistency may result from a change in the law. Similarly, a higher court may have decided one of the cases, or a court from another jurisdiction. Generally, the most persuasive and authoritative case is the most recent, analogous case from the highest court in the relevant jurisdiction.

2. *Distinguish cases*   Second, if the decision in this case is unfavourable, the lawyer must work to distinguish this case from the situation at hand, or find other reasons why the decision should not be followed.

3. *Support the favoured interpretation*   Third, if there are really different interpretations of the law, the lawyer explains the differences between the cases in a manner that provides sound reasons why a court should follow the interpretation most favourable to the client. In this instance, a lawyer may explain that applying the ruling in one case over the other makes for good policy. In other words, the application of one interpretation of the law achieves the aims and objectives of the law, is in keeping with the spirit of the law, or supports Parliament's legislative intentions better than another interpretation.

Synthesizing the applicable law

The ability to extract the legal principle established or supported by several cases is called *synthesis*. A synthesis of the law allows the writer to identify trends and patterns in the law. Read the following cases and use them to develop a synthesis of the law as it applies to *Glenmore*'s appeal.

UES, Local 298 v. Bibeault, [1988] 2 SCR 1048

At issue is the dismissal from an appeal from a decision that allowed a writ of evocation concerning succession rights under section 45 of the Québec *Labour Code* (*Labour Code*, RSQ, c. C-27, ss. 45, 46), MBD and Netco handled janitorial services in six CSRO schools under contracts for janitorial services awarded annually through calls for tenders. At the time, the appellant was certified to represent the Netco and MBD employees assigned to the cleaning of the schools. Following a strike by MBD and Netco employees, the CSRO legally terminated the contracts for janitorial services and, after calls for tenders, assigned the janitorial services of the six schools by contract to Services Ménagers. The appellant filed applications with the labour commissioner general citing sections 45 and 46 of the *Labour Code*, seeking to have the transfer of the rights and obligations of MBD and Netco to Services Ménagers recorded and so defeat respondent's application for certification in respect of the Services Ménagers employees. The labour commissioner granted the appellant's applications. He recorded the transfer of the rights and obligations of MBD and Netco to Services Ménagers and declared that the latter was bound by the certification of MBD and Netco. On the same day he dismissed the respondent's application for certification. In a majority judgment, the Labour Court upheld the decisions of the labour commissioner. The respondent then applied to the Superior Court for a writ of evocation against the decisions of the Labour Court and the commissioner. The Superior Court allowed the motion for evocation ruling that the labour commissioner and the court erred as to jurisdiction and in their application of section 45 of the Code. The Court of Appeal affirmed the judgment.

Held: The appeal should be dismissed.

The chief problem in a case of judicial review is determining the jurisdiction of the tribunal whose decision is impugned. In the absence of any coherent test for distinguishing what is in fact preliminary, the prerequisite concept does not assist in the inquiry. It diverts the courts from the only question they should ask, "Did the legislator intend such a matter to be within the jurisdiction conferred on the tribunal?" By limiting the concept of the preliminary or collateral question and by introducing the doctrine of a patently unreasonable interpretation, this Court is giving notice of the development of a new approach to determining jurisdictional questions. Henceforth, the formalistic analysis of the preliminary or collateral question must give way to a pragmatic and functional analysis. This analysis, hitherto associated with cases of patently unreasonable error on a matter within the Court's jurisdiction, is just as suited to a case in which an error is alleged in the interpretation of a provision limiting that jurisdiction. In both cases, the first stage of the analysis involves determining the tribunal's jurisdiction. To do this, the Court examines not only the wording of the enactment conferring jurisdiction on the administrative tribunal, but the purpose of the statute creating the tribunal, the reason for its existence, the area of expertise of its members and the nature of the problem before the tribunal.

In deciding whether there was a transfer of rights and obligations under section 45 of the *Labour Code*, the labour commissioner and the Labour Court did not perform an act within their jurisdiction *stricto sensu*. The labour commissioner only records the transfer of rights and obligations guaranteed in section 45. The powers conferred on the commissioner in section 46 of the *Code* are thus limited to resolving administrative difficulties that may arise out of an alienation or operation by another of an undertaking. In the *Labour Code* context, the legislator intended that the bargaining and the resulting collective agreement take place within the following three-part framework: an employer, his undertaking and the association of employees connected with that employer's undertaking. When an undertaking is alienated or operated by another in whole or in part, the essential components of this three-part framework must continue to exist if the certification or collective agreement is to remain relevant. For the purposes of section 45, the undertaking is the most important component. The test of continuity in an undertaking requires identification of the essential elements of the undertaking, which must be found to exist to a sufficient degree in the new employer's operations. Each component must be weighed according to its respective importance.

In the case at bar, section 45 did not bring about a transfer of rights and obligations from Netco and MBD to Services Ménagers. The three subcontractors are competitors in the janitorial services industry. CSRO is a client that dealt first with Netco and MBD and then with Services Ménagers. Section 45 does not support the conclusion that rights and obligations have been transferred from one employer to another solely because each of them hires employees engaged in similar activities. Only an alienation or agreement to operate made by Netco or MBD in favour of Services Ménagers of that part of their undertaking concerned with janitorial services in the CSRO schools would have caused a transfer of rights and obligations to be effected between Netco and MBD on the one hand and Services Ménagers on the other. By rejecting the need for a legal relation between successive employers and adopting a "functional" definition of the undertaking, the labour commissioner is giving section 45 an interpretation that does not recognize the existence of the three-part context in which the collective bargaining must necessarily take place and which also disregards the basis of that section. Because of their desire to protect the certification and collective agreement despite all the vicissitudes of the undertaking, the labour commissioner and the majority of the Labour Court have taken a position inconsistent with the purpose of the *Labour Code*: to promote collective bargaining as a better means of guaranteeing industrial peace and to establish equitable relations between employer and employees.

Canadian Broadcasting Corp. v. Canada (Labour Relations Board), [1995] 1 SCR 157

The respondent G was the host of a current affairs radio program on CBC and the president of the union that represents writers, journalists and performers. Under the union's by-laws, the president is also its official spokesperson. In the midst of an election campaign in which free trade was a central issue, G wrote an article against free trade in the union newspaper. The CBC was concerned that his article and his public involvement as president of the union violated the CBC's journalistic policy requiring impartiality of journalists. It was agreed that, as an interim measure, G would cease hosting his program until after Election Day. After the election, G offered to relinquish his duties as the union's spokesperson, while remaining its president, in order to accommodate the CBC's concerns. The CBC rejected the offer and forced him to choose between his job as host of a radio program and his role as the president of the union. G resigned as union president and resumed hosting his radio program. The union filed a complaint with the Canada Labour Relations Board, alleging that the CBC had interfered with the activities of a trade union, contrary to section 94(1)(a) of the *Canada Labour Code*. A majority of the Board upheld the complaint. The majority found that G's article was a union activity protected by section 94(1)(a) and concluded that the CBC committed an unfair labour practice in forcing him to choose between the two positions and that the CBC's journalistic policy did not justify its action. The Federal Court of Appeal dismissed the CBC's application for judicial review.

Held (McLachlin J dissenting): The appeal should be dismissed.

Per Lamer CJ and Cory, Iacobucci and Major JJ: The proper standard of judicial review to be applied to the Board's decision that the CBC had committed an unfair labour practice is one of patent unreasonableness.

The tribunal may have to be correct in an isolated interpretation of external legislation, but the standard of review of the decision as a whole, if that decision is otherwise within its jurisdiction, will be one of patent unreasonableness. The Board's decision that the CBC had interfered with the administration of a trade union or the representation of employees by that union was not patently unreasonable. The Board, while recognizing that section 94(1)(a) has its limits, found that the publication by a union and its officer of an article in a union newsletter expressing an opinion that a government economic policy constituted a threat or a benefit to its members was protected by section 94(1)(a). Given the context, the extension of the content protection was not wholly unwarranted. The substance of the article was not aimed at the employer, but rather at gathering support from members for the union's official position. Further, the decision of the majority was arrived at in a principled manner and was not irrational. The Board was entitled to apply the law as found in existing decisions to new and analogous facts. It is not unreasonable to find a connection between the collective bargaining relationship and the activities of unions as they relate to external social issues affecting their members. Alternatively, the Board also found that the CBC's action in refusing to accept G's offer that he retain his position as union president while no longer serving as its spokesperson had the effect of preventing any broadcast journalist from being the president of the union, and thus affected the right of the union to choose its president from among its entire membership. This act alone amounted to a violation of the *Code*. Finally, the Board's conclusion that the CBC had failed to show a valid and compelling business justification for its interference is not unreasonable.

Canada (Attorney General) v. Public Service Alliance of Canada (PSAC), [1993] 1 SCR 941

In April 1985 the federal government approved a Work Force Adjustment Policy, which was subsequently incorporated as part of the master collective agreement between Treasury Board and the respondent PSAC. The Policy was designed to minimize the impact of a lack of work or the discontinuance of government functions on indeterminate employees, and requires departments to review their use of contracted services and to "terminate them where such action would facilitate the redeployment of affected employees, surplus employees or laid-off persons." In May 1985 the Minister of Finance called for the reduction of 15,000 person-years from the public service over a five-year period. In order to reduce person-years the Department of National Revenue, Customs and Excise, contracted out the work performed by 270 data processors. PSAC filed a reference pursuant to what is now s. 99 of the *Public Service Staff Relations Act* (*PSSRA*) alleging that this contracting out was contrary to the Policy and thus to the master collective agreement between the parties. Section 99 allows an employer or bargaining agent to refer a matter to the Public Service Staff Relations Board where the obligation at issue is not one that could be enforced through an employee grievance. The Board found that it had jurisdiction to hear the reference and ruled in PSAC's favour. The Federal Court of Appeal upheld that decision. This appeal is to determine whether the Board had jurisdiction to determine the reference submitted to it, and, if so, whether it made a patently unreasonable decision in finding that the appellant contravened its collective agreement with PSAC in contracting out data-capture activities.

Held: The appeal should be dismissed.

Per Lamer CJ and Sopinka, Cory and Iacobucci JJ: When an administrative tribunal is acting within its jurisdiction, it will lose jurisdiction only if it acts in a patently unreasonable manner. If the question at issue concerns a legislative provision limiting the tribunal's powers, however, a mere error will cause it to lose jurisdiction. When considering whether a tribunal has made a simple error on the issue of its own jurisdiction, the court should adopt the pragmatic and functional approach.

The Board's decision that it had jurisdiction to entertain PSAC's reference under section 99 *PSSRA* was correct. The Board's ruling that the employer breached its obligation under the policy is not patently unreasonable interpretation of the Policy was not patently unreasonable. The intent of the Policy is that indeterminate employees can rely on the termination of contracting out in order to protect their jobs. While contracting out is not prohibited, the employer had an obligation under the Policy to review and when possible terminate contracting-out arrangements in order to ensure the continued employment of indeterminate employees within the public service. Rather than attempting to safeguard jobs of indeterminate employees, the employer set out to reduce the number of such employees by contracting out the identical tasks that they were employed to do, contrary to the obligation set out in the Policy. The Board's finding that the employer failed to carry out this obligation cannot be characterized as patently unreasonable, and the Court should not interfere in it.

Per L'Heureux-Dubé, Gonthier and McLachlin JJ: Cory J's conclusion that the Board did not make a patently unreasonable decision in finding that the appellant contravened the terms of its collective agreement with PSAC was agreed with. However, the standard of review for the Board's decision as to whether or not a matter is properly brought under section 99 *PSSRA* is not one of correctness. This is a question within the Board's jurisdiction to which the patently unreasonable standard will apply. Since the section itself does not provide a definitive answer as to whether the legislator intended the question to be within the tribunal's jurisdiction, the Court must consider the other factors that inform the pragmatic and functional approach articulated in *Bibeault*. The Board's empowering legislation gives it broad and extensive powers, and by according the Board's decisions the protection of a broadly worded privative clause, Parliament made express its intention that these decisions be accorded a great deal of deference. The expertise of the Board and its members also supports the proposition that the grant of jurisdiction in section 99 was intended to be broad rather than narrow. Further, the question to be answered is one which lies at the centre of the Board's specialized expertise. The question being within jurisdiction, the Board was not patently unreasonable in concluding that the obligation was the type which could properly form the basis of a section 99 reference, and the Court should therefore defer to its decision.

EXERCISE A7 Based on the case law, synthesize the applicable law

1. Based on a reading of the three preceding cases, write a short statement summarizing the circumstances under which a court may interfere with the decision of a labour board.

_____

_____

_____

_____

_____

A synopsis of case law, such as you have just prepared, focuses attention on similar legal themes or issues, rather than the specific details of individual cases. A synthesis of the law allows the writer to predict legal outcomes more effectively, even in areas where courts are not in agreement or where the law has not been decided definitively. Generally, there are two components to an effective synthesis of the law: first, a concise summary of the law or general legal principles and, second, a few key examples from previous decisions that provide reasons or proof to illustrate how courts employ the principle.

2. On the basis of all the cases you have just read, provide specific examples of when a court may interfere with the decision of a labour board.

_____

_____

_____

_____

_____

_____

_____

_____

_____

3. Provide specific examples of occasions when courts may not interfere with the decision of a labour board.

_____

_____

_____

_____

_____

_____

_____

_____

4. Based on these examples, state the reasons why the appeal launched by the town of Glenmore is likely to fail.

_____

_____

_____

_____

_____

_____

_____

_____

Problem B: Hats & Ts Ltd.

The exercises in problem B present the tools of legal analysis in the order in which they are used in predictive legal writing. The steps of legal analysis and predictive writing developed in this book follow a pattern, summarized in the following outline:

Step 1   Analyze the problem — chapter 1

Step 2   Research the legal problem — chapters 2 and 3

Step 3   Read and analyze the applicable law — chapters 4 and 5

        a. Brief the relevant case law — chapter 4

        b. Synthesize the applicable law — chapter 5

        c. Identify binding authorities — chapter 5

        d. Analyze analogous and distinguishable cases — chapter 5

        e. Reconcile discrepancies in case law — chapter 5

Step 4   Report the analytical results — chapter 5

        a. Predict how the law applies to the problem

        b. Identify applicable principle(s)

        c. Show how the law applies to the problem

        d. Deal with potential trouble spots

        e. Summarize the results of the legal analysis

HATS & Ts LTD.

Tanja Jones started up Hats & Ts Ltd. when she graduated from university. At the time, baseball caps and logo T-shirts were becoming very popular, and her basement business grew quickly into a retail chain. By 1985, Hats & Ts Ltd. operated 10 retail stores throughout Ontario. Tanja expanded her business rapidly in a manner that eventually overextended her line of credit at her bank, Community Credit Union. Consequently, Hats & Ts used up all its operating funds.

On January 5, 1989, an unpaid supplier petitioned Hats & Ts into bankruptcy. Two days later, a receiving order was issued against the company's assets. Tanja had little choice but to consent to the order. The order resulted in the termination of the employment of the company's employees.

According to the terms of the receiving order issued on January 7, 1989, Smith, Carter & Associates became trustee of Hats & Ts Ltd., and in that role, they had control of all of the company's assets. Hats & Ts' banker, Community Credit Union, appointed Rubinovich Ltd. as Hats & Ts' receiver and manager. Between March 3, 1989 and May 5, 1989 Rubinovich Ltd. liquidated all of the company's assets and closed all 10 outlets. In its capacity as asset manager, Rubinovich Ltd. paid employees all of the wages, commissions, and deductions they had earned up to January 7, 1989.

In October 1989, the Employment Standards Branch of the Ministry of Labour for Ontario conducted a routine audit of Hats & Ts records. Their purpose was to determine if there was any outstanding termination or severance pay owing to former employees under the *Employment Standards Act* (ESA), RSO 1980, c. 137, ss. 7(5), 40(7), 40a, as amended.

On April 23, 1990, the ministry auditor filed a claim with the respondent trustee, Smith, Carter & Associates, on behalf of the former employees of Hats & Ts. The claim was for termination pay and vacation pay in the amount of approximately $1.3 million and for severance pay totalling $7,108. The trustee rejected the claim and issued a notice of disallowance on September 28, 1991. In disallowing the claim, the trustee argued that loss of employment due to the bankruptcy of Hats & Ts did not constitute a dismissal from employment. Consequently, the employees were not entitled to severance, termination, or vacation pay under the ESA.

The Employment Standards Branch appealed the decision of the trustee to the Ontario Court (General Division). At trial, the court rejected the trustee's argument and allowed the employees to file their claims as unsecured creditors of Hats & Ts.

The trustee appealed the decision of the General Division to the Ontario Court of Appeal, which reversed the trial court's ruling and restored the decision of the trustee. The Court of Appeal handed down its decision on May 17, 1993, and 60 days later the trustee paid a dividend to Hats & Ts' creditors, effectively using up all of the funds in the estate.

Sonny Rollins, Hannah Barthez, and Samantha Liptkin are former employees of Hats & Ts Ltd. They retained you to act on their behalf. On December 10, 1996, the General Division granted your application to have your clients become a party to these proceedings. As a result, your clients now have the legal status to appeal the decision of the trustee to the Supreme Court of Canada.

STEP 1   ANALYZE THE PROBLEM

EXERCISE B1   Identify the key words, facts, and legal concepts raised by the problem

1. Who is taking whom to court and why?

_____

_____

_____

_____

_____

_____

_____

_____

2. What is the legal problem (or issues)?

_____

_____

_____

_____

_____

_____

_____

_____

3. What are the material facts?

_____

_____

_____

_____

_____

_____

_____

_____

4. Are there any background or remedial facts important to this case?

_____

_____

_____

_____

_____

_____

STEP 2 RESEARCH THE LEGAL PROBLEM

Normally, at this stage, the lawyer follows the research methodology developed in chapters 2 and 3 to find the legislation and case law that will govern the problem. The research has been provided. You may wish to brief the cases, however.

Step 3: Read and analyze
the applicable law
(chapters 2 and 4)

STEP 3   READ AND ANALYZE THE APPLICABLE LAW

Relevant legislation

- *Bankruptcy Act*, RSC 1985, c. B-3 [now *the Bankruptcy and Insolvency Act*], s. 121(1):

Claims provable

121(1) All debts and liabilities, present or future, to which the bankrupt is subject on the day on which the bankrupt becomes bankrupt or to which the bankrupt may become subject before the bankrupt's discharge by reason of any obligation incurred before the day on which the bankrupt becomes bankrupt shall be deemed to be claims provable in proceedings under this Act.

- *Employment Standards Act*, RSO 1980, c. 137, ss. 7(5), 40(7), 40a, as amended:

7(5) Every contract of employment shall be deemed to include the following provision:

All severance pay and termination pay become payable and shall be paid by the employer to the employee in two weekly instalments beginning with the first full week following termination of employment and shall be allocated to such weeks accordingly. This provision does not apply to severance pay if the employee has elected to maintain a right of recall as provided in subsection 40a (7) of the *Employment Standards Act*.

40(7) Where the employment of an employee is terminated contrary to this section,

(a) the employer shall pay termination pay in an amount equal to the wages that the employee would have been entitled to receive at his regular rate for a regular non-overtime work week for the period of notice prescribed by subsection (1) or (2), and any wages to which he is entitled;

40a(1a) Where,

(a) fifty or more employees have their employment terminated by an employer in a period of six months or less and the terminations are caused by the permanent discontinuance of all or part of the business of the employer at an establishment; or

(b) one or more employees have their employment terminated by an employer with a payroll of $2.5 million or more,

the employer shall pay severance pay to each employee whose employment has been terminated and who has been employed by the employer for five or more years.

CHAPTER 5   Skills of legal analysis: How to use the law to solve problems and predict outcomes   241

- *Employment Standards Amendment Act, 1981*, SO 1981, c. 22:

2(1) Part XII of the said Act is amended by adding thereto the following section: ...

(3) Section 40a of the said Act does not apply to an employer who became a bankrupt or an insolvent person within the meaning of the *Bankruptcy Act* (Canada) and whose assets have been distributed among his creditors or to an employer whose proposal within the meaning of the *Bankruptcy Act* (Canada) has been accepted by his creditors in the period from and including the 1st day of January, 1981, to and including the day immediately before the day this Act receives Royal Assent.

- *Interpretation Act*, RSO 1990, c. I.11:

10. Every Act shall be deemed to be remedial, whether its immediate purport is to direct the doing of anything that the Legislature deems to be for the public good or to prevent or punish the doing of any thing that it deems to be contrary to the public good, and shall accordingly receive such fair, large and liberal construction and interpretation as will best ensure the attainment of the object of the Act according to its true intent, meaning and spirit.

...

17. The repeal or amendment of an Act shall be deemed not to be or to involve any declaration as to the previous state of the law.

EXERCISE B2 Brief the relevant case law

Step 3a: Brief the relevant case law (chapter 4)

Use the "underline-and-margin-note method" to brief the cases as you read them. Remember to state the ratio briefly at the top of the first page.

Re Malone Lynch Securities Ltd., [1972] 3 OR 725 (SC)

Ratio: _____

_____

Houlden J (orally): This is an appeal from the order of the Registrar allowing an appeal from the trustee's disallowance of the claim of G. Gray for severance pay pursuant to the *Employment Standards Act*, RSO 1970, c. 147. A number of points were argued before me, but I do not propose to deal with them as, in my opinion, the application can be disposed of on one of the grounds advanced by counsel for the appellant. I may say that this point was either not argued or was not adequately argued before the learned Registrar, as it was not referred to in his reasons for judgment.

The claim is made pursuant to section 13(2) of *the Employment Standards Act*, which reads as follows:

> 13(2) Notwithstanding subsection 1, the notice required by an employer to terminate the employment of fifty or more persons in any period of four weeks or less shall be given in the manner and for the period prescribed in the regulations, and until the expiry of such notice the terminations shall not take effect.

Held: Appeal allowed.

The requirements of the notice of termination and the requisite period of time have been spelled out in *Regulation 251*, RRO 1970. In view of the number of employees of the bankrupt company, it was conceded by all counsel that, if the *Act* was applicable, the claimant was entitled under the Regulations to eight weeks' notice.

Counsel for the appellant submitted that, when the *Employment Standards Act* is examined, it is obvious that it can have no application to a bankrupt employer.

Under section 13(2) of the *Act*, if an employer wishes to terminate the employment of 50 or more persons in a period of four weeks or less, he must give the notice in the manner and for the period prescribed in the Regulations. Until such notice is given, the terminations do not take effect. If it is assumed that the receiving order in bankruptcy brought the employment of the claimant to an end, as no notice was given as required by section 13(2), the termination of the employment of the claimant has not taken effect. The requirement for eight weeks' notice only applies if notice has been given in accordance with the section.

When the other provisions of section 13 are examined, they substantiate the position of counsel for the appellant that section 13 was not designed to apply to a bankrupt employer. For instance, section 13(4) provides that an employer who is required to give the notice required by section 13(2) shall co-operate with the Minister of Labour during the period of the notice in any action or program intended to facilitate the re-establishment in employment of the persons whose employment is to be terminated. Again, section 13(5) provides that, where notice has been given under section 13(2), the employer shall not alter the wages or the terms or conditions of employment of any person to whom notice has been given, and upon the expiry of the notice, the employer shall pay to the employee the wages and vacation pay to which he is entitled. As counsel for the appellant put it, the section contemplates an on-going employer not a bankrupt one.

In the case of a non-bankrupt employer, section 13(2) is a very effective section. If such an employer attempts to terminate employment without complying with its terms, the terminations do not take effect until the section is complied with. In other words, the employees continue to be entitled to collect their wages until the employer observes the provisions of section 13(2). In the case of a bankrupt employer, this is, of course, meaningless. It is trite law that a proof of claim can only be filed against a bankrupt estate for claims that were in existence at the date of bankruptcy; hence, the fact that by reason of the *Employment Standards Act* the employment of the claimant was not terminated is of no assistance to the claimant.

In the present case, apart from the provisions of the *Employment Standards Act*, there is no right to damages for termination of employment. The trustee employed the claimant for a considerable period of time immediately upon the bankruptcy occurring so that he suffered no damages by reason of the insolvency.

For the above reasons, it is my opinion that the claim does not come within the provisions of section 13(2) of the *Employment Standards Act* and the appeal must, therefore, be allowed. I express no opinion on the constitutionality of the *Employment Standards Act* or on the other issues that were argued before me.

With reference to costs, the trustee will be entitled to its costs out of the assets of the bankrupt estate. As this was in the nature of a test case, I direct that the costs of the claimant which I propose to fix shall also be paid out of the assets of the estate. There will be no order as to the costs of the Attorney-General.

Mills-Hughes et al. v. Raynor et al. (1988), 63 OR (2d) 343, 25 OAC 248, 47 DLR (4th) 381 (CA)

Ratio:

Under section 114 of the *Canada Business Corporations Act*, SC 1974-75-76, c. 33, the directors of a corporation are personally "liable to employees of the corporation for all debts ... for services performed for the corporation." The corporation having been petitioned into bankruptcy, 19 middle and senior management employees brought an action under section 114, claiming entitlement to bonus payments, vacation pay and severance pay. The trial judge dismissed the action.

Held: The appeal should be allowed in part.

A guaranteed bonus is not dependent on profit and therefore was to be regarded as an increase in salary, and payable by the directors as a debt for services performed for the corporation.

Vacation pay, upon termination, is a debt due to the employees for services performed. The corporation was obliged under section 15 of the *Employment Standards Act*, RSO 1980, c. 137, to accumulate vacation pay as it was earned and hold it in trust for employees to be paid on termination of employment. The directors were liable for vacation pay payable.

Under the employment contract, severance payments were not compensation for past services. Under sections 40(7)(a) and 40a of the *Employment Standards Act*, termination and severance payments are claims arising from termination of employment (measured by years of service) and not debts due to employees for services performed. Therefore, the directors were not liable for those payments.

Rizzo & Rizzo Shoes Ltd. (Re), [1998] 1 SCR 27

Ratio:

A bankrupt firm's employees lost their jobs when a receiving order was made with respect to the firm's property. All wages, salaries, commissions and vacation pay were paid to the date of the receiving order. The province's Ministry of Labour audited the firm's records to determine if any outstanding termination or severance pay was owing to former employees under the *Employment Standards Act* ("*ESA*"), RSO 1980, c. 137, and delivered a proof of claim to the Trustee. The Trustee disallowed the claims on the ground that the bankruptcy of an employer does not constitute dismissal from employment and accordingly creates no entitlement to severance, termination or vacation pay under the *ESA*. The Ministry successfully appealed to the Ontario Court (General Division) but the Ontario Court of Appeal overturned that court's ruling and restored the Trustee's decision. The Ministry sought leave to appeal from the Court of Appeal judgment but discontinued its application. Following the discontinuance of the appeal, the Trustee paid a dividend to Rizzo's creditors, thereby leaving significantly less funds in the estate. Subsequently, the appellants, five former employees of Rizzo, moved to set aside the discontinuance, add themselves as parties to the proceedings, and requested and were granted an order granting them leave to appeal. At issue here is whether the termination of employment caused by the bankruptcy of an employer give rise to a claim provable in bankruptcy for termination pay and severance pay in accordance with the provisions of the *ESA*.

Held: The appeal should be allowed.

At the heart of this conflict is an issue of statutory interpretation. Although the plain language of sections 40 and 40a of the *ESA* suggests that termination pay and severance pay are payable only when the employer terminates the employment, statutory interpretation cannot be founded on the wording of the legislation alone. The objects of the *ESA* and of the termination and severance pay provisions themselves are broadly premised upon the need to protect employees. Finding sections 40 and 40a to be inapplicable in bankruptcy situations is incompatible with both the object of the *ESA* and the termination and severance pay provisions. The legislature does not intend to produce absurd consequences and such a consequence would result if employees dismissed before the bankruptcy were to be entitled to these benefits while those dismissed after a bankruptcy would not be so entitled. A distinction would be made between employees merely on the basis of the timing of their dismissal and such a result would arbitrarily deprive some of a means to cope with economic dislocation. Finally, since the *ESA* is benefits-conferring legislation, it ought to be interpreted in a broad and generous manner. Any doubt arising from difficulties of language should be resolved in favour of the claimant.

When the express words of sections 40 and 40a are examined in their entire context, the words "terminated by an employer" must be interpreted to include termination resulting from the bankruptcy of the employer. The impetus behind the termination of employment has no bearing upon the ability of the dismissed employee to cope with the sudden economic dislocation caused by unemployment. As all dismissed employees are equally in need of the protections provided by the *ESA*, any distinction between employees whose termination resulted from the bankruptcy of their employer and those who have been terminated for some other reason would be arbitrary and inequitable. Such an interpretation would defeat the true meaning, intent and spirit of the *ESA*. Termination as a result of an employer's bankruptcy therefore does give rise to an unsecured claim provable in bankruptcy pursuant to section 121 of the *Bankruptcy Act* for termination and severance pay in accordance with sections 40 and 40a of the *ESA*. It was not necessary to address the applicability of section 7(5) of the *ESA*.

Eland Distributors Ltd. (Trustee of) v. British Columbia (Director of Employment Standards), [1996] 7 WWR 652, 21 BCLR (3d) 91 (SC)

Ratio: _____

_____

_____

Toys and Wheels, a partnership composed of Eland Distributors Ltd. and Eland Distributors (Eastern) Ltd., made an assignment in bankruptcy. The Director of Employment Standards claimed in the bankruptcy for severance pay for the employees of Toys and Wheels. The trustee disallowed the claim. The director appealed the trustee's decision. Sinclair Prowse J held that the employees were entitled to severance pay and that the severance pay claim was valid and subsisting. The trustee raised an issue regarding the constitutionality of a severance pay claim under section 42 of the *Employment Standards Act* in these circumstances.

Held: Constitutional challenge dismissed.

The Director of Employment Standards may prove a claim for employees' severance pay under section 42 of the *Employment Standards Act* in the bankruptcy of an employer who enters bankruptcy voluntarily by making an assignment.

The trustee argued that section 42 of the *Employment Standards Act* was inoperative to support a claim provable in bankruptcy for employees' severance pay where the bankruptcy resulted from a voluntary assignment. The first stage in analyzing whether paramountcy applies is to determine if the laws were valid provincial and federal legislation. The validity of the *Bankruptcy and Insolvency Act* is unchallenged. Section 42 is also valid provincial legislation. Its pith and substance, the setting of minimum standards that employers must meet in terminating employees, is property and civil rights. The interaction of the two laws must therefore be considered to determine if they are in conflict.

The trustee argued that section 42 purported to create a provable claim on the basis that the employer made a voluntary assignment into bankruptcy. This was said to conflict with section 121 of the *Bankruptcy and Insolvency Act*, as section 121 did not distinguish between provable and non-provable claims on this basis. The claim was not considered a debt to which the employer was subject on the date of bankruptcy. The severance pay claim was therefore provable by operation not of section 42, but by section 121 of the *Bankruptcy and Insolvency Act*. Furthermore, the *Bankruptcy and Insolvency Act* contains no prohibition on claims for severance pay resulting from an employer's assignment in bankruptcy. Silence in a federal statute is insufficient to render a provincial enactment inoperative.

UFCW, Local 617P v. Royal Dressed Meats Inc. (Trustee of) (1989), 70 OR (2d) 455, 63 DLR (4th) 603 (HCJ)

Ratio: _____

_____

This is an appeal from a decision of a deputy registrar who upheld the disallowance of a claim by the appellant union on behalf of the unionized former employees of the bankrupt company. The Minister of Labour intervened on behalf of the non-unionized employees. The issue is whether the liability of an employer for termination pay and severance pay under sections 40 and 40a respectively of the *Employment Standards Act*, RSO 1980, c. 137, as amended (the "*ESA*"), is provable as a claim in the bankruptcy of the employer.

An employer terminated the employment of its employees, and subsequently became bankrupt. The question arose whether the employer's liability under the *Employment Standards Act*, RSO 1980, c. 137, for termination and severance pay was provable as a claim in the bankruptcy. By section 121(1) of the *Bankruptcy Act*, RSC 1985, c. B-3, "all debts and liabilities ... to which the bankrupt is subject at the date of the bankruptcy ... shall be deemed to be claims provable in proceedings under this Act." The deputy registrar held that the employees' claims were not provable.

It is not disputed that there was a termination of employment on or about July 15, 1987. It is also not disputed that the termination gave rise to a statutory obligation for termination pay and severance pay under the *ESA*, subject to consideration of the effect on that obligation of the subsequent bankruptcy and the then current receivership.

Held: Appeal should be allowed.

The obligation in question arose before the date of the bankruptcy, and was, therefore, according to section 121(1), a claim provable in the bankruptcy. By reason of section 7(5) of the *ESA*, the termination pay and severance pay became payable before the assignment in bankruptcy on August 27, 1987. In this case the liability of the employer was clear and undisputed. The issue then becomes whether the liability is a claim provable in bankruptcy. In my view, the claim in this case falls under the previously quoted section 121(1) of the *Bankruptcy Act*. While the point does not have to be decided on this appeal, it seems to me an inescapable inference that the legislature intended liability for severance payments to arise on a bankruptcy. That intention would, in my opinion, extend to termination payments that are similar in character. Whether those liabilities would be provable as a claim in bankruptcy can be left for another day.

It follows that the appeal should be allowed and the claim of the union for termination and severance pay should be allowed. It is agreed that as a result the claim for vacation pay is also allowable. The union and the trustee should have their costs out of the estate. Those of the trustee on a solicitor-and-client basis. The Minister does not ask for costs.

ANALYZE THE CASE LAW

Use the following exercises to analyze the case law. The exercises present the tools of legal analysis (synthesis, analogy, distinction, and reconciliation), according to the general outline used to present the results of legal analysis in predictive writing.

EXERCISE B3   Synthesize the applicable law

Purpose: To provide a general statement of the law applicable to a legal question or issue. Patterns and trends in law are important to note.

1. What legal issue is raised in problem B?

    _____

    _____

2. Consider the trend or pattern in the law. How did the law change between 1972 and 1998?

    _____

    _____

3. Summarize the law on point. Briefly state the law regarding the wages, payments, and other benefits owed to employees of bankrupt companies in accordance with the provisions of the *Employment Standards Act*.

    _____

    _____

    _____

    _____

    _____

EXERCISE B4   Identify binding authorities

A thorough analysis of the case law requires an examination of each case and an assessment of how each one affects the problem at hand. It is important to have a clear idea about which cases are the most important. Begin by identifying the most recent case from the highest court, and assessing the relevance of that case to the problem. The most relevant (i.e., similar) and most recent case from the highest court of the most binding jurisdiction is the case that is the most binding, regardless of whether that case is for or against the client.

The cases here have been ranked according to their court level, jurisdiction, and date. Complete the following chart for a helpful summary of the relevance of each case to the problem at Hats and Ts.

Rank	Legal issue	Facts
Re Rizzo & Rizzo Shoes Ltd., [1998] 1 SCR 27		
British Columbia (Director of Employment Standards) v. Eland Distributors Ltd. (c.o.b. Toys & Wheels) (Trustee of), [1996] 7 WWR 652 (BC SC)		
United Food and Commercial Workers International Union, Local 617P v. Royal Dressed Meats Inc. (Trustee of) (1989), 70 OR (2d) 455 (HCJ)		
Mills-Hughes et al. v. Raynor et al. (1988), 63 OR (2d) 343 (CA)		
Re Malone Lynch Securities Ltd., [1972] 3 OR 725 (SC)		

1. Study the results of this chart. Which one of these cases most resembles the legal issue raised in problem B?

_____

This case is analogous to the problem at hand.

2. Of the remaining cases, which cases raise legal issues that are analogous to the case just identified?

_____

_____

3. Which cases raise legal issues that are somewhat different from the analogous case?

_____

_____

_____

_____

It may be possible to distinguish some of these cases from the problem at hand. In preparing legal research material, it is important to note the similarities as well as the differences between cases and the problem. The following exercise works through the process of analogy and distinction for each case.

EXERCISE B5   Analyze analogous and distinguishable cases

Purpose: To understand and demonstrate how the general law applies to specific circumstances and legal issues.

Re Rizzo & Rizzo Shoes Ltd., [1998] 1 SCR 27

PART 1   Identify the grounds for drawing an analogy between this case and the problem at hand.

1. Beginning with *Rizzo*, identify the legal and factual similarities between *Rizzo* and the problem.

   _____

   _____

   _____

   _____

   _____

   _____

2. If the facts or legal issues in *Rizzo* are analogous to the problem, what is the result if a court applies the ruling in *Rizzo* to the situation in problem B?

   _____

   _____

   _____

   _____

   _____

   _____

3. Is the result favourable to your clients? Circle "yes" or "no."

YES	NO
If yes, proceed to part 2	If no, proceed to part 3

PART 2 Test the strength of the analogy.

4. Identify the differences between *Rizzo* and the problem.

_____

_____

_____

_____

_____

_____

5. Are these differences more important than the similarities between *Rizzo* and the problem? If the answer is "yes," proceed to part 3 to test whether *Rizzo* can be distinguished from the problem.

PART 3 Identify the grounds for distinguishing this case from the problem at hand.

6. Consider the significant differences between *Rizzo* and the problem. List specific legal and factual differences.

_____

_____

_____

_____

_____

_____

7. Based on these differences, explain why it may be an incorrect application of the law if a court used the reasons in *Rizzo* to support a similar ruling in the problem.

_____

_____

_____

_____

_____

_____

_____

Eland Distributors Ltd. (Trustee of) v. British Columbia (Director of Employment Standards), [1996] 7 WWR 652, 21 BCLR (3d) 91 (SC)

PART 1   Identify the grounds for drawing an analogy between this case and the problem at hand.

1. Identify the legal and factual similarities between *Eland* and the problem.

_____

_____

_____

_____

_____

_____

2. If the facts or legal issues in *Eland* are analogous to the problem, what is the result if a court applies the ruling in *Eland* to the situation in problem B?

_____

_____

_____

_____

_____

_____

3. Is the result favourable to your clients? Circle "yes" or "no."

               YES   NO

         If yes, proceed to part 2   If no, proceed to part 3

PART 2   Test the strength of the analogy.

4. Identify the differences between *Eland* and the problem.

_____

_____

_____

_____

_____

5. Are these differences more important than the similarities between *Eland* and the problem? If the answer is "yes," proceed to part 3 to test whether *Eland* can be distinguished from the problem.

PART 3   Identify the grounds for distinguishing this case from the problem at hand.

6. Consider the significant differences between *Eland* and the problem. List specific legal and factual differences.

_____

_____

_____

_____

_____

7. Based on these differences, explain why it may be an incorrect application of the law if a court used the reasons in *Eland* to support a similar ruling in the problem.

_____

_____

_____

_____

_____

_____

UFCW, Local 617P v. Royal Dressed Meats Inc. (Trustee of) (1989), 70 OR (2d) 455, 63 DLR (4th) 603 (HCJ)

PART 1 Identify the grounds for drawing an analogy between this case and the problem at hand.

1. Identify the legal and factual similarities between *Royal Dressed Meats* and the problem.

_____

_____

_____

_____

_____

_____

2. If the facts or legal issues in *Royal Dressed Meats* are analogous to the problem, what is the result if a court applies the ruling in *Royal Dressed Meats* to the situation in problem B?

_____

_____

_____

_____

_____

_____

3. Is the result favourable to your clients? Circle "yes" or "no."

              YES   NO

    If yes, proceed to part 2   If no, proceed to part 3

PART 2 Test the strength of the analogy.

4. Identify the differences between *Royal Dressed Meats* and the problem.

_____

_____

_____

_____

_____

_____

5. Are these differences more important than the similarities between *Royal Dressed Meats* and the problem? If the answer is "yes," proceed to part 3 to test whether *Royal Dressed Meats* can be distinguished from the problem.

PART 3 Identify the grounds for distinguishing this case from the problem at hand.

6. Consider the significant differences between *Royal Dressed Meats* and the problem. List specific legal and factual differences.

_____

_____

_____

_____

_____

_____

7. Based on these differences, explain why it may be an incorrect application of the law if a court used the reasons in *Royal Dressed Meats* to support a similar ruling in the problem.

_____

_____

_____

_____

_____

_____

Mills-Hughes et al. v. Raynor et al. (1988), 63 OR (2d) 343, 25 OAC 248, 47 DLR (4th) 381 (CA)

PART 1   Identify the grounds for drawing an analogy between this case and the problem at hand.

1. Identify the legal and factual similarities between *Mills-Hughes* and the problem.

   _____

   _____

   _____

   _____

   _____

   _____

   _____

2. If the facts and issues in *Mills-Hughes* are analogous to the problem, what is the result if a court applies the ruling in *Mills-Hughes* to the situation in problem B?

   _____

   _____

   _____

   _____

   _____

   _____

3. Is the result favourable to your clients? Circle "yes" or "no."

   YES   NO

   If yes, proceed to part 2   If no, proceed to part 3

PART 2 Test the strength of the analogy.

4. Identify the differences between *Mills-Hughes* and the problem.

_____

_____

_____

_____

_____

_____

5. Are these differences more important than the similarities between *Mills-Hughes* and the problem? If the answer is "yes," proceed to part 3 to test whether *Mills-Hughes* can be distinguished from the problem.

PART 3 Identify the grounds for distinguishing this case from the problem at hand.

6. Consider the significant differences between *Mills-Hughes* and the problem. List specific legal and factual differences.

_____

_____

_____

_____

_____

_____

7. Based on these differences, explain why it may be an incorrect application of the law if a court used the reasons in *Mills-Hughes* to support a similar ruling in the problem.

_____

_____

_____

_____

_____

_____

_____

Re Malone Lynch Securities Ltd., [1972] 3 OR 725 (SC)

STEP 1 Identify the grounds for drawing an analogy between this case and the problem at hand.

1. Identify the legal and factual similarities between *Malone* and the problem.

_____

_____

_____

_____

_____

_____

2. If the facts and legal issues in *Malone* are analogous to the problem, what is the result if a court applies the ruling in *Malone* to the situation in problem B?

_____

_____

_____

_____

_____

_____

_____

3. Is the result favourable to your clients? Circle "yes" or "no."

| YES | NO |
| If yes, proceed to part 2 | If no, proceed to part 3 |

PART 2 Test the strength of the analogy.

4. Identify the differences between *Malone* and the problem.

_____

_____

_____

_____

_____

_____

5. Are these differences more important than the similarities between *Malone* and the problem? If the answer is "yes," proceed to part 3 to test whether *Malone* can be distinguished from the problem.

PART 3 Identify the grounds for distinguishing this case from the problem at hand.

6. Consider the significant differences between *Malone* and the problem. List specific legal and factual differences.

_____

_____

_____

_____

_____

_____

7. Based on these differences, explain why it may be an incorrect application of the law if a court used the reasons in *Malone* to support a similar ruling in the problem.

_____

_____

_____

_____

_____

_____

_____

EXERCISE B6   Reconcile the apparent discrepancies in the case law

Purpose: to establish how a court may be persuaded to follow one line of legal reasoning over another OR to predict why a court might adopt one particular interpretation of the law over another.

1. In *Malone* and *Mills-Hughes*, the courts found that employees of bankrupt companies were entitled to bonuses and vacation pay, but not to termination and severance pay. In *Rizzo*, *Eland*, and *Royal Dressed Meats*, the courts ruled that termination and severance pay were claims provable in bankruptcy. Which group of cases supports a favourable outcome for your clients in problem B?

   _____

   _____

2. What accounts for the apparent inconsistency in the case law?

   _____

   _____

   _____

   _____

   _____

   _____

3. When deciding the issue in problem B, how should a court treat the decisions in *Malone* and *Mills-Hughes*?

   _____

   _____

   _____

   _____

   _____

   _____

   _____

   _____

STEP 4 PREDICTIVE WRITING SKILLS: REPORT THE ANALYTICAL RESULTS

Predictive writing organizes the information gathered through legal analysis to forecast the likely outcome of a case and to identify the strengths and weaknesses of legal arguments. Generally, lawyers expect to see information presented in a certain order.

a. *Predict the outcome*   First, predict the result when the law is applied to the problem at hand.

b. *State the applicable principle*   Second, state the general legal principle likely to be applied (or distinguished) in reaching the prediction. The synthesis of the case law prepared in legal analysis provides this information.

c. *Provide justification*   Third, prove why the prediction is a likely outcome. Use examples from analogous and distinguishable cases to show how the law applies to the problem at hand.

d. *Deal with potential trouble spots*   Use the reconciliation of the case law prepared in legal analysis to deal with any inconsistencies found in the governing case law and explain how unfavourable case law will apply to the problem. Keep in mind that it will be easier to reconcile favourable case law to the problem at hand, more difficult to reconcile inconsistent or incomplete case law, and most difficult to reconcile unfavourable case law. In the exercises that follow, emphasis is placed on practising the most difficult task: "dealing with trouble spots."

e. *Conclude the findings*   Fifth, emphasize the strengths and weaknesses of the prediction in a final summary of the analytical findings.

This pattern is followed whether writing short paragraphs on specific legal issues or organizing the material in a legal memorandum or brief. The pattern is adapted when preparing legal arguments.

Prediction, proof, reconciliation, and conclusion are written more easily when the law is favourable to the client's situation. The skills of legal analysis and predictive writing are put to the test when the law is unfavourable, or the situation is different from precedent cases. In all circumstances, predictive writing must never misrepresent the law; nevertheless, the tools of legal analysis may be used to outline legal reasons favourable to the client's position.

EXERCISE B7   Scenario A: Legal analysis indicates that a favourable decision is likely

Step 4a: Predict

1. First, PREDICT how the law applies.

   In an opening sentence, predict the likelihood of the former employees of Hats & Ts Ltd. receiving termination and severance pay.

   _____

   _____

   _____

   _____

   _____

   _____

Step 4b: State the applicable law

2. Second, STATE the applicable legal principle(s).

   Drawing on the synthesis of the relevant case law, state the general legal principle in question.

   _____

   _____

   _____

   _____

   _____

   _____

Step 4c: Proof

3. Third, PROVE why the prediction is likely.

   a. Supporting cases: Give reasons why a court may apply the rulings from the analogous cases to the problem at hand. First, group analogous cases together and write a general statement about the pattern in the law established by these cases.

   _____

   _____

   _____

   _____

   _____

b. Next, for the purposes of this exercise, use a specific example from each of these analogous cases to illustrate the factual and legal similarities between the problem and the case law.

_____

_____

_____

_____

_____

_____

_____

_____

_____

_____

_____

_____

_____

_____

_____

_____

_____

_____

_____

_____

_____

_____

Step 4d: Deal with trouble spots

4. Fourth, DEAL with potential trouble spots: Demonstrate how cases that undermine the prediction may be distinguished. For example, the rulings in *Malone* and *Mills-Hughes* are unfavourable to the client's situation. Give reasons why a court may not apply these rulings. If necessary, use a specific example from each case that illustrates the factual and legal similarities between the problem and the case law.

_____

_____

_____

_____

_____

_____

_____

_____

_____

_____

_____

_____

_____

_____

_____

_____

_____

_____

_____

_____

5. Fifth, CONCLUDE the analytical findings. Step 4e: Conclude

In a brief summary statement, highlight the strongest reasons that support the prediction.

_____

_____

_____

_____

_____

_____

EXERCISE B8 Scenario B: Legal analysis indicates that a favourable decision is not likely

How would a lawyer use the applicable case law to represent Smith, Carter & Associates (the trustees of Hats & Ts Ltd.)? Even though the law appears to go against the trustees, they wish to dispute the employees' claims to severance and termination pay. A lawyer's job is to find the plausible legal arguments to support the trustees' position. This is done in two ways. First, by emphasizing the reasons why the law should not be applied to the circumstances at hand and second, by demonstrating the differences between the precedent cases and the problem at hand. Throughout this process, the lawyer must not misrepresent or twist the law in any way.

Step 4a: Predict

1. First, PREDICT how the law applies.

   In an opening sentence, predict the likelihood of the Trustee of Hats & Ts Ltd. blocking the payment of termination and severance pay to the employees.

   _____

   _____

   _____

   _____

   _____

   _____

Step 4b: State the
applicable law

2. Second, STATE the applicable legal principle(s).

   Drawing on the synthesis of the relevant case law, state the general legal principle in question. What are the factual circumstances unique to this case that would allow the lawyer to argue a plausible exception to the applicable law?

   _____

   _____

   _____

   _____

   _____

   _____

3. Third, PROVE why the prediction is likely.

Supporting cases: Grouping the analogous cases together, demonstrate how you can support your prediction. Where appropriate, illustrate the factual and legal similarities between the problem at hand and the strongest analogous case(s). Give reasons why a court may apply these rulings.

_____

_____

_____

_____

_____

_____

Step 4d: Deal with trouble spots

4. Fourth, DEAL with potential trouble spots: Demonstrate how cases that undermine the prediction may be distinguished. Give reasons why a court may not apply these rulings. (Note that in trying to build a favourable case for the trustees, the lawyer here will emphasize the factual differences between the problem at hand and the case law. To do this, the lawyer must prepare material that clearly illustrates how the governing cases may be distinguished from the problem at hand).

_____

_____

_____

_____

_____

_____

_____

_____

_____

_____

_____

_____

_____

_____

_____

_____

_____

_____

_____

THE LAW WORKBOOK: Developing skills for legal research and writing

5. Fifth, CONCLUDE the analytical findings.   Step 4e: Conclude

In a brief summary statement, highlight the strongest reasons that support the prediction.

_____

_____

_____

_____

_____

_____

Note: Even when preparing background material, the trustees' lawyer has an ethical duty to point out that the governing cases are against the trustees. However, the lawyer should still give a brief summary statement, highlighting the strongest reasons why an exception to that law might be made in the problem at hand. These reasons are especially important because the employees have appealed the decision of the General Division in favour of the trustee and the matter is now before a higher court.

Problem C: The estates of two friends

Josie Campanili and Wanda Betournay were close friends and regular spa companions. On November 9, 1990, they left Kelowna, BC for a week-long trip to their favourite spa. The trip was a day's drive from Kelowna. On November 13, 1990, they were reported missing. Their bodies were found on February 15, 1991 in Betournay's car. The two women were still buckled in their seats. The car in which they were sitting belonged to Wanda Betournay, who was driving at the time the incident occurred. The car was found lying in a creek bed adjacent to the highway, approximately 70 kilometres east of Kelowna. The vehicle was badly damaged, and had been washed along a flood-swollen creek flowing alongside a mountain highway. Since no one saw the accident occur, it was difficult for the investigators to discern precisely when it happened.

The investigators did know that between 10:00 p.m. on November 8 and 10:00 p.m. on November 10, 1990, the area in and around Kelowna received approximately 32 mm of rain. The three highways that lead into and out of the area in which Betournay's vehicle was found were all closed sometime during the weekend. One was cut off by a major landslide, a second was closed when a large culvert washed out, and two bridges over the third were both closed because of heavy river flooding and potential damage to the bridges' under structures.

Police investigators concluded that, at the time of the accident, the Betournay car had been travelling westbound and left the roadway near the entrance to a rest area with sufficient momentum to break a path through some small alder trees. The vehicle then tumbled down a rock-covered embankment into the swollen floodwaters of Dead Horse Creek, and was swept downstream. At the presumed time of the accident, the creek was in flood condition, the wind was gusting to "extremely high velocities," and a rainstorm was raging.

Investigators testified at trial that there is a dip in the highway at the point where the vehicle is believed to have left the road, and that rain may have collected in the dip. In their opinion, if Betournay had driven straight through the water, no loss of control would have occurred. However, if she suddenly turned the wheels of her car, for whatever reason, or attempted to avoid the pool of water, the vehicle might have hydroplaned, especially if its tires were badly worn. The police determined that the two front tires of the vehicle showed "excessive" wear. They also found that damage to the left front tire was consistent with hitting a rock or other solid object on the road. Investigators could not determine whether or not a flat tire might have caused the vehicle to go out of control and leave the roadway.

Campanili's estate filed an action against Betournay's estate pursuant to the *Family Compensation Act*, RSBC 1979, c. 120. The trial judge found that negligence could not be proved and dismissed the suit filed by Campanili's estate. Campanili's estate now appeals this decision.

EXERCISE C1   Identify the key words, facts, and legal concepts raised by the problem

1. Who is taking whom to court and why?

_____

_____

_____

_____

_____

_____

_____

_____

2. What is the legal problem (or issues)?

_____

_____

_____

_____

_____

_____

_____

_____

3. What are the material facts?

_____

_____

_____

_____

_____

_____

_____

4. Are there any background or remedial facts important to this case?

_____

_____

_____

_____

_____

_____

_____

STEP 2 RESEARCH THE LEGAL PROBLEM

Normally, at this stage, the lawyer follows the research methodology developed in chapters 2 and 3 to find the legislation and case law that will govern the problem. The research has been provided. You may wish to brief the cases, however.

Step 2: Research the legal problem (chapters 2 and 3)

STEP 3 READ AND ANALYZE THE APPLICABLE LAW

Relevant legislation

Step 3: Read and analyze the applicable law (chapters 2 and 4)

- *Family Compensation Act*, RSBC 1979, c. 120

    Action may be brought against estate of deceased person:

    5(1) When any person dies who would have been liable in an action for damages under this *Act* had he continued to live, then, whether he died before or after or at the same time as the person whose death was caused by wrongful act, neglect or default, an action, may be brought and maintained, or, if pending, may be continued, against the personal representative of the deceased person, and the damages and costs recovered in the action are payable out of the estate of the deceased in the same order of administration as the simple contract debts of the deceased.

EXERCISE C2   Brief the relevant case law

Use the "underline-and-margin-note method" to brief the cases as you read them. Remember to state the ratio briefly at the top of the first page.

Toneguzzo-Norvell (Guardian ad litem of) v. Burnaby Hospital, [1994] 1 SCR 114

Ratio: _____

_____

The infant appellant suffered severe disabilities due to oxygen deprivation during her birth. The respondent physician and hospital admitted liability for her injuries and the only issue before the trial judge was the assessment of damages. The appellant's main expert witness testified that, with the continuation of the level of care she currently enjoyed, the appellant could expect to live to 25 or 30 years of age. The respondents' expert witness, relying on an American study on the life expectancy of profoundly handicapped persons, was of the view that her life expectancy was 7.6 years. The trial judge assessed the differing expert opinions and concluded that the best estimate of the appellant's life expectancy was 25 years. He awarded $1,981,879 in damages, including $292,758 for future income loss. The Court of Appeal found that the trial judge had misapprehended the significance of the study as well as attributing greater weight than was warranted to the evidence of the appellant's main expert witness. The court reduced the award, concluding that the trial judge had overestimated the appellant's life expectancy by seven years and had failed to make a deduction for personal living expenses from the portion of the award relating to future income loss for the years after her death. The court also dismissed the appellant's cross-appeal that the damages awarded for future income loss were too low.

Held: The appeal should be allowed in part.

The Court of Appeal erred in interfering with the trial judge's conclusion on life expectancy. The different conclusions of the trial judge and the Court of Appeal arise mainly from the differing weight they put upon the American study. Although the principle of non-intervention of a court of appeal in a trial judge's findings of facts does not apply with the same force to inferences drawn from conflicting testimony of expert witnesses where the credibility of these witnesses is not in issue, this does not change the fact that the weight to be assigned to the various pieces of potentially conflicting evidence is essentially the province of the trier of fact. It was far from clear what weight the study should carry and, in the absence of a palpable or overriding error, the Court of Appeal should not have intervened. Further, the trial judge did not fail to consider, or misapprehend, some obvious feature of the evidence. The trial judge carefully considered the evidence of all the experts on the question of life expectancy, as well as the study. His concerns with respect to the applicability of that study, which led him to discount it to a greater degree than the Court of Appeal would have, do not support a conclusion that he ignored the study, in the absence of a demonstration that his concerns were totally without foundation. Finally, it was open to the trial judge to accept the evidence of the appellant's main expert witness, despite the adverse inference drawn from the appellant's counsel's failure to call the treating neurological pediatrician that the latter's evidence as to life expectancy would not favour the appellant. The trier of fact may accept such evidence as he finds convincing, and an appellate tribunal ought not to interfere unless it is persuaded that the result amounts to a palpable or overriding error.

Owing to the manner in which the case was presented at trial, this Court is not in a position to entertain the appellant's new arguments that the future income loss award should be calculated on male earnings tables.

The Court of Appeal did not err in deducting 50 per cent for living expenses in the "lost years" from the award for loss of future earning capacity. A deduction for personal living expenses must be made not only for the years the appellant will actually live but also for the years after her projected death.

Fontaine v. British Columbia (Official Administrator of), [1998] 1 SCR 424

Ratio:

_____

_____

This was an appeal from a decision of the Court of Appeal dismissing Fontaine's appeal from the dismissal of her action for damages under the *Family Compensation Act*. Appellant claimed damages with respect to the death of her husband who was found several weeks after his expected return from a hunting trip. His body and that of his hunting companion (which was still buckled in the driver's seat) were in the companion's badly damaged truck, which had been washed along a flood-swollen creek flowing alongside a mountain highway. No one saw the accident and no one knew precisely when it occurred. A great deal of rain had fallen in the vicinity of the accident the weekend of their hunting trip and three highways in the area were closed because of weather-related road conditions. The trial judge found that negligence had not been proven against the driver and dismissed the appellant's case. An appeal to the Court of Appeal was dismissed. At issue here was when *res ipsa loquitur* applies and the effect of invoking it.

Held: The appeal should be dismissed.

Since various attempts to apply *res ipsa loquitur* have been more confusing than helpful, the law is better served if the maxim is treated as expired and no longer a separate component in negligence actions. Its use had been restricted to cases where the facts permitted an inference of negligence and there was no other reasonable explanation for the accident. The circumstantial evidence that the maxim attempted to deal with is more sensibly dealt with by the trier of fact, who should weigh the circumstantial evidence with the direct evidence, if any, to determine whether the plaintiff has established on a balance of probabilities a *prima facie* case of negligence against the defendant. If such a case is established, the plaintiff will succeed unless the defendant presents evidence negating that of the plaintiff.

The circumstantial evidence here did not discharge the plaintiff's onus. Many of the circumstances of the accident, including the date, time and precise location, were not known. There were minimal, if any, evidentiary foundations from which any inference of negligence could be drawn. Although severe weather conditions impose a higher standard of care on drivers to take increased precautions, human experience confirms that severe weather conditions are more likely to produce situations where accidents occur and vehicles leave the roadway regardless of the degree of care taken. In these circumstances, it should not be concluded that the accident would ordinarily not have occurred in the absence of negligence. Any inference of negligence, which might be drawn in these circumstances, would be modest. Most of the explanations offered by the defendants were grounded in the evidence and were adequate to neutralize whatever inference the circumstantial evidence could permit to be drawn. The trial judge's finding that the defence had succeeded in producing alternative explanations of how the accident may have occurred without negligence on the driver's part was not unreasonable and should not be interfered with on appeal.

Hellenius et al. v. Lees, [1972] SCR 165

Ratio:

_____

_____

The plaintiffs' action for damages for personal injuries arising out of a motor vehicle accident was dismissed at trial. The cause of the accident was a blowout of a tire on the defendant's car and the jury found that the injuries sustained by the plaintiffs when travelling as passengers for hire in the said vehicle were not caused or contributed to by any act or omission on the part of the defendant. An appeal from the trial judgment having been dismissed by the Court of Appeal, the plaintiffs then appealed to this Court.

Counsel for the plaintiffs submitted that the trial judge erred in failing to charge the jury that the onus of disproving negligence was on the defendant. It was contended that this was a case of _res ipsa loquitur_ and that on this ground there was an initial burden upon the defendant to disprove negligence.

It was also contended that a new trial should be ordered because the defendant's counsel, while addressing the jury, had made some statement to the effect that if the verdict was in favour of the plaintiffs, the defendant would have to bear that verdict for the rest of his life. This statement would serve to indicate to the jury that the defendant was uninsured and this was a factor which should be considered in assessing damages.

Held: The appeal should be dismissed.

The central question as to whether the condition of the tire and its subsequent blow-out were caused or contributed to by a failure of the defendant to exercise reasonable care to ensure that his vehicle and its equipment were in a safe condition for the contemplated journey was adequately stated by the trial judge.

A trial judge in instructing a jury, after all the evidence has been heard from both sides, is not required to enter into any discussion of the way in which the burden of proof shifted from one side to the other as the trial progressed. In this case all the facts were before the jury when the judge addressed them and it was for the jurors to decide on the evidence as a whole whether or not the defendant was guilty of negligence.

As to the alternative submission, there was no prejudicial error that could warrant a new trial.

Gauthier Co. v. Canada, [1945] SCR 143

Ratio: _____

_____

Appeal by the suppliant from the judgment of Thorson J, President of the Exchequer Court of Canada dismissing its claim, made by way of petition of right, for damages caused by a collision between its motor ambulance and a Bren gun carrier owned by the Crown and driven in the course of his duties by a member of the armed forces of Canada.

A Bren gun carrier owned by the Crown and driven in the course of his duties by a member of the armed forces of Canada, while proceeding westerly on a highway in Ontario about 1.45 p.m. on January 11, 1943, skidded so that its rear part was across the south side of the road in the path of the suppliant's motor ambulance which was proceeding easterly on its right side of the road; and a collision resulted. The suppliant's claim against the Crown for damages were dismissed by Thorson J., who held that the suppliant had not established a case of negligence against the Crown. The suppliant appealed.

Held: (Kerwin and Rand JJ dissenting): The appeal should be allowed and the suppliant should have judgment for damages.

The driver of a vehicle meeting another vehicle on a highway has a duty under s. 39 (7) of the *Highway Traffic Act* (RSO 1937, c. 288), and there is a similar duty at common law, to allow to the other vehicle one half of the road free; and a breach of that duty, occasioning damage, will establish a prima facie case of negligence against such driver, casting upon him the onus of explanation (the nature of this onus discussed). Such explanation should (in the words of Lord Dunedin in *Ballard v. North British Ry. Co.*, 60 Sc. LR 441, at 449) "show a way in which the accident may have occurred without negligence." Such a way was not, in the circumstances of this case shown by the mere fact of the skidding (which, by itself, is a "neutral fact," equally consistent with negligence or no negligence) nor by the evidence (on proper inference from the facts established by evidence accepted by the trial judge). (The phrase *res ipsa loquitur* is applicable to a claim against the Crown under s. 19(c) (as enacted by 2 Geo. VI, c. 28) of the *Exchequer Court Act*. The negligence spoken of in section 19(c) may be established by legitimate inference from facts proved by the application of the phrase).

Per Kerwin and Rand JJ, dissenting: The evidence did not justify a finding of negligence on the part of the driver of the carrier. Skidding on a slippery road cannot be taken *per se* as negligence on a driver's part. Even if the doctrine *res ipsa loquitur* applies to the Crown (which it was unnecessary to determine), the explanation by a witness (who considered that the skid had been caused by the left tread striking a smooth or icy patch on the road, though he could not find any), taken in the light of the circumstances, was sufficient to displace any onus resting upon the Crown.

Jackson v. Millar, [1976] 1 SCR 225

Ratio: _____

_____

_____

The plaintiff appealed from the judgment of the Court of Appeal for Ontario that dismissed his action for damages.

M, a sixteen year old youth with very limited driving experience borrowed his father's car and after ten o'clock p.m. set out with two friends to drive from Toronto to Lake Simcoe in order to attend an all night movie. M had spent the day in active outdoor pursuits and undertook to sleep at a friend's cottage should he feel it necessary and return to Toronto the following morning. Having fallen asleep during the performance, he was aroused, started out to Toronto, detoured to the cottage and then failed to take advantage of resting there. On the way back to Toronto, both passengers slept. At a point just beyond an intersection and over-pass, where the pavement had widened somewhat, M realized that his right wheels were on gravel and off the pavement. He attempted to regain the pavement but skidded, lost control of the vehicle and in the accident J, one of the friends, was very seriously injured. The trial judge found that J was a gratuitous passenger but that the negligence of M was gross negligence and awarded damages of $223,785.07 to J, the infant plaintiff, and of $24,118.08 to the adult plaintiff. The Court of Appeal felt that the facts that established M's negligence fell short of establishing gross negligence and were of the opinion that the *res ipsa loquitur* rule was not applicable.

In the result the judgment in the Court of Appeal dismissed J's action but that Court indicated that, in any event, it would have reduced considerably the amount of the damages.

Held: The appeal should be allowed.

The circumstances leading up to the accident and actual accident itself, sparsely as it was described by M, the infant defendant, quite justified the conclusion by the trial judge that the negligence was gross negligence and since such evidence had been given the trial judge's finding should not be disturbed and further that, even if the trial judge had failed to find that the plaintiffs had established acts which constituted gross negligence, the maxim *res ipsa loquitur* could be used by him in finding gross negligence against the driver M.

The Court of Appeal was not justified in its reduction of the award of the trial judge on the basis of failure to take into account the contingencies of life and to allow a discount to reflect present values. The trial judge did work out present value and, while no allowance was made for contingencies of life, in the particular case of this infant plaintiff the only appropriate reduction would be too diminutive to justify interference on appeal.

Taylor Estate v. Wong Aviation Ltd., [1969] SCR 481

Ratio: _____

_____

An aircraft owned by the second respondent and leased by him to the respondent company was rented by the company to one T for the purpose of flying, solo, "in a tight flight circuit around Toronto Island Airport." T, a licensed but inexperienced pilot, took off from the airport and neither he nor the aircraft was ever seen again. In an action brought by the respondents against the executor of T's estate for damages for the loss of the aircraft, the claim of the respondent company was framed in both contract and tort and that of the second respondent in tort only. The action was dismissed at trial. On appeal, the Court of Appeal allowed the appeal and awarded the respondents $10,500. The executor then appealed to this Court.

> **bailment**
> the deposit of goods with an other according to conditions express or implied regarding the level of care expected

Held: The appeal should be allowed.

Adopting the views of the trial judge that it had been satisfactorily demonstrated the loss of the aircraft could have been caused by many other factors as equally consistent with no negligence as with negligence on the part of T and that, accordingly, the maxim *res ipsa loquitur* did not apply, the claims in negligence, based as they were solely on the application of that maxim, should be dismissed.

Both the bailee and the bailed chattel having disappeared and there being no evidence of negligence on the part of the bailee, the rule of evidence whereby the onus is placed on the bailee to disprove negligence was not applicable and the general rules governing proof where performance of a contract has become impossible due to the destruction of the subject-matter should be applied. As the respondents had not adduced any evidence to "establish a fault or default in the defendant," the bailment action depended upon the application of the rule embodied in the maxim *res ipsa loquitur*. As there were factors which might well have caused the loss of the aircraft without any negligence on T's part, that maxim was not applicable.

The appellant had produced an explanation from which it would be just as reasonable for a Court to conclude that the happening occurred without the negligence of the bailee as to conclude that he was negligent. Where there was no direct evidence of negligence, no more could be required of the executor of a deceased bailee who perished with the chattel.

ANALYZE THE CASE LAW

Use the following exercises to analyze the case law. The exercises present the tools of legal analysis (synthesis, analogy, distinction, and reconciliation), according to the general outline used to present the results of legal analysis in predictive writing.

Purpose: To summarize the applicable law.

1. What legal issue is raised in problem C?

    _____

    _____

2. Consider the trend or pattern in the law. How has the law developed between
    1945 and today?

    _____

    _____

3. Summarize the law on point. Write a short statement that summarizes the legal
    principles as they apply to the legal issues and questions raised in problem C.

    _____

    _____

    _____

    _____

    _____

EXERCISE C4   Identify binding authorities

Purpose: To understand how the general law applies to specific circumstances and legal issues.

A thorough analysis of the case law requires an examination of each case and an assessment of how each one affects the problem at hand. It is important to begin with a clear idea about which cases are the most important. Begin by identifying the most recent case from the highest level court, and then proceed to assess the relevance of that case to the problem. Rank the cases according to their court level, jurisdiction, and date. Complete the following chart for a helpful summary of each case and its relevance to the legal issues and facts raised in problem C.

Rank	Legal issue	Facts

1. Study the results of this chart. Which one of these cases most resembles the legal issue raised in problem C and is from the highest court (or the most relevant jurisdiction)?

   _____

   This case is the most analogous case.

2. Of the remaining cases, which cases deal with circumstances or legal issues in a manner consistent with the ruling in the analogous case?

   _____

   _____

   _____

3. Which cases raise legal issues that are somewhat different from the analogous case?

   _____

   _____

   _____

   It may be possible to distinguish these cases from the problem at hand.

   Proceed with the following exercises to complete the analysis of analogous and distinguishable cases.

EXERCISE C5 Analyze analogous and distinguishable cases

Gauthier Co. v. Canada, [1945] SCR 143

PART 1 Identify the analogous cases.

1. Identify the legal and factual similarities between *Gauthier* and the problem.

_____

_____

_____

_____

_____

_____

_____

2. If the facts and legal issues in *Gauthier* are analogous to the problem, what is the result if a court applies the ruling in *Gauthier* to the situation in problem C?

_____

_____

_____

_____

_____

_____

_____

3. Is the result favourable to your clients? Circle "yes" or "no."

               YES   NO

        If yes, proceed to part 2   If no, proceed to part 3

PART 2   Test the strength of the analogy.

4. Identify the differences between *Gauthier* and the problem.

_____

_____

_____

_____

_____

_____

5. Are these differences more important than the similarities between *Gauthier* and the problem? If the answer is "yes," proceed to part 3 to test whether *Gauthier* can be distinguished from the problem.

PART 3   Identify the grounds for distinguishing this case from the problem at hand.

6. Consider the significant differences between *Gauthier* and the problem. List specific legal and factual differences.

_____

_____

_____

_____

_____

_____

7. Based on these differences, explain why it may be an incorrect application of the law if a court used the reasons in *Gauthier* to support a similar ruling in the problem.

_____

_____

_____

_____

_____

_____

_____

Taylor Estate v. Wong Aviation Ltd., [1969] SCR 481

PART 1   Identify the analogous cases.

1. Identify the legal and factual similarities between *Taylor* and the problem.

   _____

   _____

   _____

   _____

   _____

   _____

2. If the facts and legal issues in *Taylor* are analogous to the problem, what is the result if a court applies the ruling in *Taylor* to the situation in problem C?

   _____

   _____

   _____

   _____

   _____

   _____

3. Is the result favourable to your clients? Circle "yes" or "no."

YES	NO
If yes, proceed to part 2	If no, proceed to part 3

PART 2 Test the strength of the analogy.

4. Identify the differences between *Taylor* and the problem.

_____

_____

_____

_____

_____

_____

5. Are these differences more important than the similarities between *Taylor* and the problem? If the answer is "yes," proceed to part 3 to test whether *Taylor* can be distinguished from the problem.

PART 3 Identify the grounds for distinguishing this case from the problem at hand.

6. Consider the significant differences between *Taylor* and the problem. List specific legal and factual differences.

_____

_____

_____

_____

_____

_____

7. Based on these differences, explain why it may be an incorrect application of the law if a court used the reasons in *Taylor* to support a similar ruling in the problem.

_____

_____

_____

_____

_____

_____

_____

Hellenius et al. v. Lees, [1972] SCR 165

PART 1   Identify the analogous cases.

1. Identify the legal and factual similarities between *Hellenius* and the problem.

_____

_____

_____

_____

_____

_____

2. Is *Hellenius* analogous to the problem?

_____

3. If the facts and legal issues in *Hellenius* are analogous to the problem, what is the result if a court applies the ruling in *Hellenius* to the situation in problem C?

_____

_____

_____

_____

_____

_____

4. Is the result favourable to your clients? Circle "yes" or "no."

YES   NO

If yes, proceed to part 2   If no, proceed to part 3

PART 2 Test the strength of the analogy.

5. Identify the differences between *Hellenius* and the problem.

_____

_____

_____

_____

_____

_____

6. Are these differences more important than the similarities between *Hellenius* and the problem? If the answer is "yes," proceed to part 3 to test whether *Hellenius* can be distinguished from the problem.

PART 3 Identify the grounds for distinguishing this case from the problem at hand.

7. Consider the significant differences between *Hellenius* and the problem. List specific legal and factual differences.

_____

_____

_____

_____

_____

_____

8. Based on these differences, explain why it may be an incorrect application of the law if a court used the reasons in *Hellenius* to support a similar ruling in the problem.

_____

_____

_____

_____

_____

_____

_____

Jackson v. Millar, [1976] 1 SCR 225

PART 1   Identify the analogous cases.

1. Identify the legal and factual similarities between *Jackson* and the problem.

_____

_____

_____

_____

_____

_____

2. Is *Jackson* analogous to the problem?

_____

3. If the facts and legal issues in *Jackson* are analogous to the problem, what is the result if a court applies the ruling in *Jackson* to the situation in problem C?

_____

_____

_____

_____

_____

_____

4. Is the result favourable to your clients? Circle "yes" or "no."

| YES | NO |

| If yes, proceed to part 2 | If no, proceed to part 3 |

THE LAW WORKBOOK: Developing skills for legal research and writing

PART 2 Test the strength of the analogy.

5. Identify the differences between *Jackson* and the problem.

_____

_____

_____

_____

_____

_____

6. Are these differences more important than the similarities between *Jackson* and the problem? If the answer is "yes," proceed to part 3 to test whether *Jackson* can be distinguished from the problem.

PART 3 Identify the grounds for distinguishing this case from the problem at hand.

7. Consider the significant differences between *Jackson* and the problem. List specific legal and factual differences.

_____

_____

_____

_____

_____

_____

8. Based on these differences, explain why it may be an incorrect application of the law if a court used the reasons in *Jackson* to support a similar ruling in the problem.

_____

_____

_____

_____

_____

_____

_____

Toneguzzo-Norvell (Guardian ad litem of) v. Burnaby Hospital, [1994] 1 SCR 114

PART 1   Identify the analogous cases.

1. Identify the legal and factual similarities between *Toneguzzo-Norvell* and the problem.

   _____

   _____

   _____

   _____

   _____

   _____

2. Is *Toneguzzo-Norvell* analogous to the problem?

   _____

3. If the facts and legal issues in *Toneguzzo-Norvell* are analogous to the problem, what is the result if a court applies the ruling in *Toneguzzo-Norvell* to the situation in problem C?

   _____

   _____

   _____

   _____

   _____

   _____

4. Is the result favourable to your clients? Circle "yes" or "no."

   YES   NO

   If yes, proceed to part 2   If no, proceed to part 3

PART 2 Test the strength of the analogy.

5. Identify the differences between *Toneguzzo-Norvell* and the problem.

_____

_____

_____

_____

_____

_____

6. Are these differences more important than the similarities between *Toneguzzo-Norvell* and the problem? If the answer is "yes," proceed to part 3 to test whether *Toneguzzo-Norvell* can be distinguished from the problem.

PART 3 Identify the grounds for distinguishing this case from the problem at hand.

7. Consider the significant differences between *Toneguzzo-Norvell* and the problem. List specific legal and factual differences.

_____

_____

_____

_____

_____

_____

8. Based on these differences, explain why it may be an incorrect application of the law if a court used the reasons in *Toneguzzo-Norvell* to support a similar ruling in the problem.

_____

_____

_____

_____

_____

_____

Fontaine v. British Columbia (Official Administrator of), [1998] 1 SCR 424

PART 1   Identify the analogous cases.

1. Identify the legal and factual similarities between *Fontaine* and the problem.

_____

_____

_____

_____

_____

_____

2. Is *Fontaine* analogous to the problem?

_____

3. If the facts and legal issues in *Fontaine* are analogous to the problem, what is the result if a court applies the ruling in *Fontaine* to the situation in problem C?

_____

_____

_____

_____

_____

4. Is the result favourable to your clients? Circle "yes" or "no."

<table>
<tr><td>YES</td><td>NO</td></tr>
<tr><td>If yes, proceed to part 2</td><td>If no, proceed to part 3</td></tr>
</table>

PART 2 Test the strength of the analogy.

5. Identify the differences between *Fontaine* and the problem.

_____

_____

_____

_____

_____

_____

6. Are these differences more important than the similarities between *Fontaine* and the problem? If the answer is "yes," proceed to part 3 to test whether *Fontaine* can be distinguished from the problem.

PART 3 Identify the grounds for distinguishing this case from the problem at hand.

7. Consider the significant differences between *Fontaine* and the problem. List specific legal and factual differences.

_____

_____

_____

_____

_____

_____

8. Based on these differences, explain why it may be an incorrect application of the law if a court used the reasons in *Fontaine* to support a similar ruling in the problem.

_____

_____

_____

_____

_____

_____

_____

EXERCISE C6   Reconcile the apparent discrepancies in the case law

Purpose: To establish how a court may be persuaded to follow one line of legal reasoning over another OR to predict why a court might adopt one particular interpretation of the law over another.

1. Have the courts applied the *Family Compensation Act* and the legal principle of *res ipsa loquitur* in a consistent manner? If you believe they have, explain why. If you find a discrepancy in the court rulings, what accounts for the apparent inconsistency?

_____

_____

_____

_____

_____

_____

_____

_____

_____

_____

_____

_____

_____

EXERCISE C7   Scenario A: Legal analysis indicates that a favourable decision is likely

1. First, PREDICT how the law applies.

   In an opening sentence, predict who is most likely to win this appeal, the Campanili family or the Betournays?

Step 4a: Predict

_____

_____

_____

_____

_____

_____

2. Second, STATE the applicable legal principle(s).

   Drawing on the synthesis of the relevant case law, state the general legal principle that supports the prediction.

Step 4b: State the
applicable law

_____

_____

_____

_____

_____

_____

3. Third, PROVE why the prediction is likely.

    a. Supporting cases: Give reasons why a court may apply the rulings from the analogous cases to the problem. First, group analogous cases together and write a general statement about the pattern in the law established by these cases.

_____

_____

_____

_____

_____

_____

    b. Next, for the purposes of this exercise, use a specific example from each of these analogous cases to illustrate the factual and legal similarities between the problem and the case law.

_____

_____

_____

_____

_____

_____

_____

_____

_____

_____

_____

_____

_____

4. Fourth, DEAL with potential trouble spots: Demonstrate how cases that undermine the prediction may be distinguished. If necessary, use a specific example from each case that illustrates the factual and legal dissimilarities between the problem at hand and the case law.

Step 4d: Deal with trouble spots

_____

_____

_____

_____

_____

_____

_____

_____

_____

_____

_____

_____

_____

_____

_____

_____

_____

_____

_____

_____

_____

Step 4e: Conclude

5. Fifth, CONCLUDE the analytical findings.

In a brief summary statement, highlight the strongest reasons that support the prediction.

_____

_____

_____

_____

_____

_____

EXERCISE C8 Scenario B: Legal analysis indicates that a favourable decision is not likely

The Campanilis are determined to appeal the trial judge's decision. Based on your analysis of the case law, what legal principles may be used to support the Campanilis' appeal? Remember to emphasize the reasons why the law should not be applied to the circumstances at hand and to demonstrate the differences between the precedent cases and the problem.

1. First, PREDICT how the law applies.

   In an opening sentence, predict the likelihood of the Campanilis' winning their appeal. Qualify your prediction by indicating whether they have a strong or weak case in light of your analysis of the case law.

   Step 4a: Predict

   _____

   _____

   _____

   _____

   _____

   _____

2. Second, STATE the applicable legal principle(s).

   Drawing on the synthesis of the relevant case law, state the general legal principle in question.

   Step 4b: State the applicable law

   _____

   _____

   _____

   _____

   _____

   _____

   What are the factual circumstances or legal issues unique to this case that provide grounds for a plausible exception to the applicable law?

   _____

   _____

   _____

   _____

   _____

3. Third, PROVE why the prediction is likely.

    a. Supporting cases: A particular law or legal principle cannot be ignored, but a lawyer may want to argue that it should not be applied to the problem at hand. In the problem here, the "supporting cases" (the cases most authoritative and analogous to the problem), do not support the Campanilis' appeal. The challenge for the Campanilis' lawyer is to demonstrate how these cases can in fact be distinguished from the problem. To do this, a lawyer must give reasons why a court may not apply these rulings. There are two types of reasons that can be prepared:

        i. Point to specific examples of factual and legal dissimilarities between the problem and the strongest analogous case(s) to illustrate why it would not be appropriate for a court to treat the *Campanili* case in the same way.

> **Note:** In preparing these reasons, a lawyer draws on the analysis and reconciliation of the case law in different ways to support a possible answer. By proposing alternatives, the lawyer is dealing with the trouble spots. As a result, step 4d is followed in a slightly different manner.

ii. Focus attention on a more favourable legal theme: Are there other cases here that deal with a similar theme or legal issue but when applied to the situation at hand, render a more favourable outcome? On what basis might the rulings in these cases be applied to the problem?

_____

_____

_____

_____

_____

_____

_____

_____

_____

_____

_____

_____

_____

4. Fourth, CONCLUDE the analytical findings.

Step 4e: Conclude

In a brief summary statement, highlight the strongest reasons why an exception to the governing case law should be made.

_____

_____

_____

_____

_____

_____

_____

The previous exercises emphasized a step-by-step practice of the various analytical skills used to prepare legal materials. The following exercises offer different methods of condensing and preparing analysis of the applicable case law, focusing attention on how to use the tools of legal analysis in predictive writing.

Problem D: The Curvesco affair

Marc Curvesco tested positive for HIV in October 1995. When a public health nurse advised him to use condoms and to inform prospective sexual partners that he was HIV-positive, Marc became verbally abusive. He told her that he had no intention of following her advice. No one would have sex with him if his condition were known, he argued. Two weeks later, he met Kitty Hawk. Their relationship lasted 18 months during which time the couple had unprotected sexual intercourse. Before the couple had intercourse, Kitty expressed her concern about sexually transmitted diseases to Marc, although she did not ask him specifically whether he had HIV or AIDS. He assured her that he had tested negative for HIV eight months earlier.

Kitty developed hepatitis and she was advised to have an HIV test. She and Marc were both tested for HIV in January 1996. In February, Kitty was informed that her test was negative, but that her partner had tested HIV-positive. She was advised to undertake subsequent tests to determine whether she had developed the virus. At this time, the public health nurse told Marc again that he must use condoms and inform his sexual partners that he was HIV-positive. This time, he argued that he would not use condoms until Kitty underwent another test. If she was not HIV-positive at that point, he claimed that he would end their relationship and start a relationship with an HIV-positive woman.

For several more months Kitty and Marc continued to have unprotected sex. Kitty explains that she continued the relationship because she loved him and because she did not want to put another woman at risk. Their relationship ended in April 1996. Kitty maintains that had she known that Marc was HIV-positive, she would never have consented to unprotected sexual intercourse with him in the first place.

When the public health nurse heard that the relationship between Kitty and Marc had ended, she delivered a letter to Marc ordering him to inform future partners that he was HIV-positive, and to use condoms. Shortly thereafter, Marc began to arrange dates through an escort service. He began to have regular appointments with one of the escorts, Holly Berry, for which he paid $150 a visit. Before engaging in sexual activities, however, Holly questioned Marc closely about sexually transmitted diseases. When Holly asked Marc about HIV specifically, he told her he was worried and was thinking about having the HIV test. Nevertheless, the couple had unprotected sex. When Holly discovered that Marc had HIV and had known that he had it, she confronted him. He apologized for lying. Holly claims that if she had known that Marc was HIV-positive, she would never have engaged in unprotected sexual intercourse with him.

At the time this problem comes to your attention, neither Holly Berry nor Kitty Hawk has tested positive for the virus.

STEP 1 ANALYZE THE PROBLEM

EXERCISE D1 Identify the key words, facts, and legal concepts raised by the problem

1. Identify the relevant parties to the dispute and state their relationship to the case.

_____

_____

_____

_____

_____

_____

_____

_____

2. List the relevant legal problem(s) or issue(s) raised in the Curvesco affair:

_____

_____

_____

_____

_____

_____

_____

_____

3. What are the material facts?

_____

_____

_____

_____

_____

_____

_____

_____

_____

4. Are there any background or remedial facts important to this case?

_____

_____

_____

_____

_____

_____

STEP 2   RESEARCH THE LEGAL PROBLEM

Normally, at this stage, the lawyer follows the research methodology developed in chapters 2 and 3 to find the legislation and case law that will govern the problem. The research has been provided here in order to practise the tools of legal analysis. You may wish to brief the cases, however.

Step 3: Read and analyze
the applicable law
(chapters 2 and 4)

STEP 3   READ AND ANALYZE THE APPLICABLE LAW

Relevant legislation

- *Criminal Code*, RSC 1985, c. C-46, as amended:

Causing bodily harm by criminal negligence

221. Every one who by criminal negligence causes bodily harm to another person is guilty of an indictable offence and liable to imprisonment for a term not exceeding ten years.

Assault

265(1) A person commits an assault when

(a) without the consent of another person, he applies force intentionally to that other person, directly or indirectly;

(b) he attempts or threatens, by an act or a gesture, to apply force to another person, if he has, or causes that other person to believe on reasonable grounds that he has, present ability to effect his purpose; or

(c) while openly wearing or carrying a weapon or an imitation thereof, he accosts or impedes another person or begs.

Application

(2) This section applies to all forms of assault, including sexual assault, sexual assault with a weapon, threats to a third party or causing bodily harm and aggravated sexual assault.

Consent

(3) For the purposes of this section, no consent is obtained where the complainant submits or does not resist by reason of

(a) the application of force to the complainant or to a person other than the complainant;

(b) threats or fear of the application of force to the complainant or to a person other than the complainant;

(c) fraud; or

(d) the exercise of authority.

Accused's belief as to consent

(4) Where an accused alleges that he believed that the complainant consented to the conduct that is the subject-matter of the charge, a judge, if satisfied that there is sufficient evidence and that, if believed by the jury, the evidence would constitute a defence, shall instruct the jury, when reviewing all the evidence relating to the determination of the honesty of the accused's belief, to consider the presence or absence of reasonable grounds for that belief.

Aggravated assault

268(1) Every one commits an aggravated assault who wounds, maims, disfigures or endangers the life of the complainant.

Punishment

(2) Every one who commits an aggravated assault is guilty of an indictable offence and liable to imprisonment for a term not exceeding fourteen years.

EXERCISE D2   Brief the relevant case law

Use the "underline-and-margin-note method" to brief the cases as you read them. Remember to state the ratio briefly at the top of the first page.

R v. Jobidon, [1991] 2 SCR 714

Ratio: _____

_____

The accused was charged with manslaughter, through the offence of assault, following a fistfight. The fight started in a bar. The victim had been prevailing when the owner separated them and told the accused to leave. He left and waited outside in the parking lot. When the victim came out, a crowd of people gathered around them to see the fight. While both men stood facing each other, the accused struck the victim with his fist, hitting him with great force on the head, knocking him backwards onto the hood of a car. The accused continued forward and, in a brief flurry, struck the victim repeatedly on the head. The victim rolled off the hood and lay limp. He was taken to the hospital where he died.

At trial, the accused was found not guilty of manslaughter. The judge held that the victim's consent to a "fair fight" negated assault, and held further that the accused had not been criminally negligent. The Court of Appeal set aside the acquittal and substituted a guilty verdict on the charge of manslaughter. This appeal raises the issue as to whether absence of consent is an element, which must be proved by the Crown in all cases of assault under section 265 of the *Criminal Code*, or whether there are common law limitations that restrict or negate the legal effectiveness of consent in certain types of cases. A secondary issue is whether the accused could be convicted of manslaughter on a basis other than that of an unlawful act of assault.

Held: The appeal should be dismissed.

Per La Forest, L'Heureux-Dubé, Gonthier, Cory and Iacobucci JJ: Section 265 of the *Code* should be read in light of the common law limitations on consent. Section 265 sets out a general rule that one cannot commit assault if the other person agrees to the application of force. However, while section 265 states that all forms of assault, including assault causing bodily harm, are covered by the general rule, it does not define the situations or forms of conduct or eventual consequences which the law will recognize as being valid objects of consent for the purpose of the offence. The common law has generated a body of law to illuminate the meaning of consent and to place certain limitations on its legal effectiveness in the criminal law. It has also set limits on the types of harmful actions to which one can validly consent, and which can shelter an assailant from the sanctions of the criminal law. Section 8 of the *Code* indicates that common law principles continue to apply to the extent that they are not inconsistent with the *Code* or other Act of Parliament and have not been altered by them. In particular, section 8(3) of the *Code* expressly provides that exculpatory defences continue so to operate to exclude criminal liability.

Limits on consent to assault have long been recognized by English and Canadian courts. Although there is no clear position in the modern Canadian common law, when one takes into account the combined English and Canadian jurisprudence, when one keeps sight of the common law's persistence to limit the legal effectiveness of consent to a fist fight, and when one understands that section 265 has always incorporated that persistence, the scale tips heavily against the validity of a person's consent to the infliction of bodily injury in a fight. The relevant common law policy considerations also support that conclusion. It is not in the public interest that adults should willingly cause harm to one another without a good reason. There is no social value in fistfights or street brawls. These activities may even lead to serious breaches of the public peace.

Here, the victim's consent to a fair fight did not preclude commission of the offence of assault under section 265 of the *Code*. The limitation demanded by section 265 vitiates consent between adults intentionally to apply force causing serious hurt or non-trivial bodily harm to each other in the course of a fistfight or brawl. This is the extent of the limit which the common law requires in the factual circumstances of this appeal. This formulation will not affect the validity or effectiveness of freely given consent to rough sporting activities carried out according to the rules of the game, medical or surgical treatment, or dangerous exhibitions by qualified stuntmen.

The provisions of the *Code* have not ousted the common law limitations on consent. First, Parliament, by setting out factors that may vitiate consent in section 265(3) of the *Code*, did not intend to replace any common law rules that might have negated the legal effectiveness of consent to an act which would otherwise constitute assault. That list merely made concrete basic limits on the legal effectiveness of consent which had for centuries formed part of the criminal law in England and in Canada. The history of our criminal law reveals that codification did not replace common law principles of criminal responsibility, but in fact reflected them. That history also reveals that limitations on consent based on public policy existed before the codification of Canada's criminal law and they have not been ousted by statutory revisions and amendments made to the *Code*. Accordingly, even if it could be concluded that section 265(3) negated the applicability of common law rules which describe when consent to assault will be vitiated for involuntariness or defects in the will underlying the apparent consent, it would not follow that those amendments erased limitations based on public policy. Parliament, if it had so intended, would have stated that intention. Section 8(3) of the *Code* strongly suggests preservation of the common law approach to consent in assault. Second, by specifying in section 265(2) that section 265 is to apply to all forms of assault, Parliament did not intend to eliminate the common law prescription of objects or forms of conduct to which legally effective consent may not be given. Rather, Parliament sought to ensure that the basic elements of the offence of assault in section 265 (1)(a) to (c), the circumstances listed in section 265(3) for vitiating consent due to a coerced or misinformed volition, and the required state of mind for raising a defence in section 265(4), would be applied without exception, irrespective of the peculiar form of assault.

While a fistfight constitutes a situation in which the concept and term "assault" fit quite naturally, criminal negligence is less well tailored to that kind of situation. In a fistfight, there is an obvious intention to apply force to the other person. This conscious regard for some level of harmful consequence to the physical integrity of another person distinguishes assault from criminal negligence, where there is actually a disregard for the likely impact of one's conduct on the other's physical safety.

Per Sopinka and Stevenson JJ (dissenting): Consent cannot be read out of the offence: it is a fundamental element of many criminal offences, including assault, and the statutory provision creating the offence of assault explicitly provides for the element of consent. The victim's consent, while it cannot transform a crime into lawful conduct, is a vital element in determining what conduct constitutes a crime. The absence of consent is an essential ingredient of the actus reus and is often confused with the defence of honest belief in consent which relates not to the actus reus of the offence but to the mens rea or mind state of the accused. An honest belief that there was consent may constitute a defence even though there was no consent.

Parliament extended the principle that an absence of consent is necessary to all assaults, except murder, in order to make the criminal law more certain. Section 265 was neither to outlaw consensual fighting nor to allow it if the trial judge thought it socially useful in the circumstances. Rather, s. 265 makes the absence of consent a requirement in the offence and restricts that consent to situations where force has been intentionally applied and where the victim has clearly and effectively consented free of coercion and misrepresentation. The scope of consent to an assault must be closely scrutinized. The trial judge must decide whether that consent applied to the activity which is the subject of the charge instead of evaluating the utility of the activity. The more serious the assault, the more difficult it should be to establish consent.

The absence of consent cannot be swept away by a robust application of judge-made policy. Use of the common law to eliminate an element of the offence that is required by statute is more than interpretation and is contrary to the letter and spirit of s. 9(a) which provides that no person should be convicted of an offence at the common law.

Given the danger inherent in the violent activity in this case, the scope of the consent required careful scrutiny. The trial judge found that the victim's consent did not extend to a continuation of the fight once he had lost consciousness. The accused, by continuing to pummel the victim after he knew the victim was unconscious, knowingly acted beyond the ambit of the victim's consent. Given the finding that the accused committed an assault and given that the victim died as a result of that unlawful act, the accused is guilty of manslaughter under ss. 222(5)(a) and 234 of the *Criminal Code*.

R v. Bolduc and Bird, [1967] SCR 677

Ratio: _____

_____

The two appellants, one a medical doctor and the other a layman friend of the doctor, were convicted of indecent assault, contrary to section 141 of the *Criminal Code*. The doctor represented to a female patient that his friend was a medical intern in need of further experience and in this way obtained the patient's consent to the friend's presence in the examining room during the course of an examination of the patient's intimate parts. During the examination, the friend stood by and observed but at no time did he touch the patient. The Court of Appeal affirmed their convictions. The appellants were granted leave to appeal to this Court.

Held (Spence J dissenting): The appeal should be allowed and a verdict of acquittal entered for both appellants.

Per Cartwright, Fauteux, Ritchie and Hall JJ: The appellants were not guilty of an indecent assault within the meaning of section 141 of the *Criminal Code*. The conduct of the doctor was unethical and reprehensible in the extreme. However, the consent of the patient was not obtained by false and fraudulent representations as to the nature and quality of the act to be performed by the doctor. The fraud was as to the friend being a medical intern. His presence as distinct from some overt act by him was not an assault. The friend was acting as a "peeping tom," and such conduct is not an offence.

Per Spence J, dissenting: Under section 230 of the *Criminal Code*, the application of force, however slight, is an assault when it is "without the consent of another person or with consent when it is obtained by fraud." In this case, the patient consented to be touched by the doctor in the presence of a doctor and not a mere layman. The indecent assault upon her was not the act to which she consented and therefore the two appellants were guilty under the provisions of section 141(1) of the *Code* when considered with sections 21 and 230 of the *Code* without recourse to the provisions of section 141(2).

R v. Ssenyonga (1993), 81 CCC (3d) 257, 21 CR (4th) 128 (Gen. Div.)

Ratio: _____

_____

The accused, Charles Ssenyonga, is charged with three counts of aggravated sexual assault and three counts of criminal negligence causing bodily harm. There is evidence that he knew he was infected with the human immuno-deficiency virus, (HIV), and without telling the three complainants of that fact, engaged in sexual intercourse with them, thereby exposing them to the risk of HIV infection, which they have now contracted. Counsel for the accused moved to dismiss the charges of aggravated sexual assault on the grounds that each of the three complainants freely and voluntarily engaged in sexual intercourse with the accused without the use of a condom. Mr. Dawson submits in the case of each complainant that the Crown has failed to negative consent and, therefore, no assaults were committed. The only element of the charges of aggravated sexual assault in issue on this motion is the issue of consent.

Held: Appeal allowed; a new trial was ordered.

The court reviewed the evidence to assess grounds for conviction. The court noted the circumstances under which the accused and the complainants engaged in sexual intercourse:

1. he already knew he was infected with HIV;

2. he knew of the risk of transmitting the virus to the complainants through unprotected sexual intercourse, i.e., sexual intercourse without the use of a condom;

3. none of the complainants knew he was HIV positive;

4. none of the complainants would have consented to have sexual intercourse with him had they known he was HIV positive.

There is evidence that after having sexual intercourse with the accused, each of the complainants tested positive for HIV.

The defence admitted, pursuant to section 655 of the *Criminal Code*, that the men with whom the complainants had engaged in sexual intercourse before becoming involved with the accused, were tested and determined to be HIV negative, after the three complainants were found to be HIV positive.

The crown's position was as follows. Because of the unique characteristics of HIV, consent to sexual intercourse is vitiated where a person who knows he is infected with HIV engages in sexual intercourse with another person without disclosing his HIV positive status, whether or not the complainant in fact contracts HIV from such sexual intercourse. In these circumstances, the consent of the complainant may be vitiated on any one of three legal grounds, which are independent of each other. If consent is vitiated on any single ground, the offence of aggravated sexual assault is made out and the motion must fail. The three grounds are:

(1) Unprotected sexual intercourse with a person who knows and fails to disclose that he is infected with HIV is so inherently dangerous that it exceeds the scope of the complainants' implied consent;

(2) Fraud, as specified in section 265(3)(c);

(3) Public policy limits on consent.

(1) UNPROTECTED SEXUAL INTERCOURSE AND IMPLIED CONSENT:

The position of defence was as follows. In considering the case at bar, one must be very mindful of the distinction between the *actus reus* and the *mens rea* of the offence of assault. The *actus reus* of the general intent offence of assault is the application of force, directly or indirectly, without the consent of the person to whom the force is being applied. If there is consent to the application of force, there is no *actus reus* and therefore no assault. If there is no assault, there can be no sexual assault and no aggravated sexual assault. Each of the three complainants consented to the application of force incidental to the acts of sexual intercourse in question and, therefore, there is no assault in law.

The accused's failure to disclose his HIV positive status does not constitute fraud within the meaning of section 265(3)(c) because it does not go to the nature and quality of the act of sexual intercourse. Public policy limitations on consent have been confined traditionally to activities lacking social utility, such as fistfights. Sexual intercourse is an activity that has social utility. Where an activity has social utility, the courts have allowed substantial risks to be assumed by participants.

With respect to the *actus reus* of assault, the purpose of section 265(1)(a) of the *Criminal Code* is to control the non-consensual direct or indirect application of force by one person to another. However, not all such applications or transmissions of force will constitute the *actus reus* of the offence. Consent to the application of force may be express or implied. Where the consent is not express, such excusals flow from employing the concept of implied consent. However, the law recognizes that there are limits to the nature or degree of force to which people impliedly consent.

Apart from the fact that he was HIV positive, there is no suggestion that the accused applied any force per se during sexual intercourse with the complainants that was in any way dangerous in nature or excessive in degree. What created the danger to the complainants was not the application of force but the presence of the virus. The complainants may not have consented to the transmission of the virus, nor even to the risk of that occurring, but the evidence is indisputable that they did consent to the application of force inherent in the acts of sexual intercourse, which force was not in itself excessive or dangerous.

The final requirement of informed consent is that the victim must have been given sufficient information to make a valid determination. In the absence of clear and binding authority, this branch of the Crown's argument must fail.

---

(2) FRAUD:

Although the majority in *R v. Clarence* (1888), 22 QBD 23 (CCR) found that failing to disclose a venereal disease did not vitiate the consent of the accused's wife to engage in sexual intercourse with him, two earlier English cases held that failing to disclose a venereal disease constituted fraud that did vitiate consent.

The court ruled that the word "fraud" in the former section 244(3)(c), now section 265(3)(c) of the *Criminal Code* means fraud as to "the nature and quality of the act," and should not be extended to all frauds causally connected with consent. Parliament must determine whether fraud in sexual offences should be expanded to include any fraud which has a causal connection with consent or to what extent, if any, it should be expanded.

Fraud sufficient to vitiate consent must relate to the "nature and quality" of the act. In this case, the complainants were under absolutely no misapprehension as to the nature of the acts in which they were engaging. They were fully aware that they were consenting to participate in acts of sexual intercourse with the accused. Nothing he said or did induced them to believe otherwise. Accordingly, the Court found no evidence of fraud.

(3) PUBLIC POLICY:

There is no good reason on moral grounds for permitting a person to have sexual intercourse without disclosing his HIV positive status. If an infected person chooses to engage in sexual activity, which he is under no duty to do, the privacy interest of the infected person should yield to the physical safety and autonomy of the partner.

The purpose of the *Criminal Code* is to control the non-consensual direct or indirect application of force by one person to another. The law of assault is too blunt an instrument to be used to excise AIDS from the body politic. Although public interests may well be served by the criminalization of this kind of conduct, the legislature has not yet done so. Legally, there are no grounds to support the charges of aggravated sexual assault in this case.

R v. Cuerrier, [1998] 2 SCR 371

Ratio:

_____

_____

The accused was charged with two counts of aggravated assault pursuant to section 268 of the *Criminal Code*. Even though a public health nurse had explicitly instructed him to inform all prospective sexual partners that he was HIV-positive and to use condoms every time he engaged in sexual intercourse, the accused had unprotected sexual relations with the two complainants without informing them he was HIV-positive. Both complainants had consented to unprotected sexual intercourse with the accused, but they testified at trial that if they had known that he was HIV-positive they would never have engaged in unprotected intercourse with him. At the time of trial, neither complainant had tested positive for the virus. The trial judge entered a directed verdict acquitting the accused. The Court of Appeal upheld the acquittals.

Held: The appeal should be allowed and a new trial ordered.

Per Cory, Major, Bastarache and Binnie JJ: To prove the offence of aggravated assault, the Crown must establish (1) that the accused's acts "endanger[ed] the life of the complainant" (section 268(1)) and (2) that he intentionally applied force without the consent of the complainant (section 265(1)(*a*)). The first requirement is satisfied in this case by the significant risk to the lives of the complainants occasioned by the act of unprotected intercourse. It is unnecessary to establish that the complainants were in fact infected with the virus. With respect to the second requirement, it is no longer necessary, when examining whether consent in assault or sexual assault cases was vitiated by fraud under section 265(3)(*c*), to consider whether the fraud is related to "the nature and quality of the act." The repeal in 1983 of statutory language imposing this requirement and its replacement by a reference simply to "fraud" indicates that Parliament's intention was to provide a more flexible concept of fraud in assault and sexual assault cases. To that end, principles that have historically been applied in relation to fraud in criminal law can be used with appropriate modifications.

In the context of the wording of section 265, an accused's failure to disclose that he is HIV-positive is a type of fraud which may vitiate consent to sexual intercourse. The essential elements of fraud in commercial criminal law are dishonesty, which can include non-disclosure of important facts, and deprivation or risk of deprivation. The dishonest action or behaviour must be related to the obtaining of consent to engage in sexual intercourse — in this case unprotected intercourse.

The accused's actions must be assessed objectively to determine whether a reasonable person would find them to be dishonest. The dishonest act consists of either deliberate deceit respecting HIV status or non-disclosure of that status. Without disclosure of HIV status there cannot be a true consent. The consent cannot simply be to have sexual intercourse. Rather, it must be consent to have intercourse with a partner who is HIV-positive. The extent of the duty to disclose will increase with the risks attendant upon the act of intercourse. The failure to disclose HIV-positive status can lead to a devastating illness with fatal consequences and, in those circumstances, there exists a positive duty to disclose.

The nature and extent of the duty to disclose, if any, will always have to be considered in the context of the particular facts presented. To establish that the dishonesty results in deprivation, which may consist of actual harm or simply a risk of harm, the Crown needs to prove that the dishonest act had the effect of exposing the person consenting to a significant risk of serious bodily harm. The risk of contracting AIDS as a result of engaging in unprotected intercourse meets that test. Further, in situations such as this, the Crown is still required to prove beyond a reasonable doubt that the complainant would have refused to engage in unprotected sex with the accused if she had been advised that he was HIV-positive. Therefore, a complainant's consent to sexual intercourse can properly be found to be vitiated by fraud under section 265 if the accused's failure to disclose his HIV-positive status is dishonest and results in deprivation by putting the complainant at a significant risk of suffering serious bodily harm.

An approach to the concept of fraud in section 265(3)(c) of the *Code* that includes any deceit inducing consent to contact would bring within the sexual assault provisions of the *Code* behaviour which lacks the reprehensible character of criminal acts and would trivialize the criminal process by leading to a proliferation of petty prosecutions instituted without judicial guidelines or directions. Some limitations to the concept of fraud in that section are necessary. The fraud required to vitiate consent for sexual assault must carry with it the risk of serious harm. This standard is sufficient to encompass not only the risk of HIV infection but also other sexually transmitted diseases which constitute a significant risk of serious harm. However, the standard is not so broad as to trivialize a serious offence.

Where public health endeavours fail to provide adequate protection to individuals like the complainants, the criminal law can be effective. The criminal law has a role to play both in deterring those infected with HIV from putting the lives of others at risk and in protecting the public from irresponsible individuals who refuse to comply with public health orders to abstain from high-risk activities.

R v. Petrozzi, [1987] 5 WWR 71, 13 BCLR (2d) 273 (CA)

Ratio:

_____

_____

The appellant appeals his conviction on a charge of sexual assault. The appellant testified that he had agreed to pay a prostitute, the complainant, $100.00 for sex. Sex was performed but the appellant indicated that he did not have the funds to pay and that moreover, the prostitute had agreed that he did not have to pay her until she had satisfied him. Prior to charging the jury the trial Judge told both counsel that when charging the jury on assault with respect to section 244 of the *Code*, he intended to instruct them to determine whether the accused had obtained the complainant's consent by fraud when he had agreed to pay $100.00 to her for sexual services but had never intended to pay her anything. The trial judge instructed the jury that if the accused obtained consent without in a fraudulent manner then the consent to the sexual act was vitiated. If the accused never intended to pay for the sexual act then he obtained the sexual services of the prostitute by fraudulent means.

Held: Appeal allowed, new trial ordered.

The issue is whether section 244(3)(c) is limited to false and fraudulent representations as to the nature and quality of the act or to the identity of the offender or whether it covers any fraud which has a causal connection with the giving of consent.

The Courts have always restricted fraud insofar as assault is concerned to fraud as to the nature and quality of the act or to the identity of the offender, and the Court is unable to say that in enacting section 244(3)(c), parliament intended to enable the Courts to give an expanded interpretation to the word "fraud." Parliament must determine whether fraud in sexual offences should be expanded to include any fraud that has a causal connection with consent or to what extent, if any, it should be expanded. Although there was ample evidence upon which the jury could convict the accused of sexual assault, the Court is unable to say that the Judge's charge on fraud as it related to the issue of consent did not have a significant effect on the decision of the jury. Accordingly, the appeal must be allowed and a new trial held.

R v. Thornton, [1993] 2 SCR 445

Ratio: _____

_____

_____

The accused knowingly donated HIV infected blood to the Red Cross. The judgment of the Court was delivered orally by:

Lamer CJ: We are all of the view that this appeal fails. Section 216 imposed upon the appellant a duty of care in giving his blood to the Red Cross. This duty of care was breached by not disclosing that his blood contained HIV antibodies. This common nuisance obviously endangered the life, safety and health of the public.

ANALYZE THE CASE LAW

Use the following exercises to analyze the applicable case law and to organize your analysis in the order in which it will be used to predict how the courts will rule on the legal issues raised in the problem.

EXERCISE D3 Synthesize the applicable law

Purpose: To provide a general statement of the law applicable to a legal question or issue. Patterns and trends in law are important to note.

1. Use the chart below to summarize an analysis of the applicable case law and to present an overview of the case law in this area. Rank the cases, beginning with the most authoritative case. Be sure to identify the legal issues in the case that are of importance to the case at hand.

Case	Issue(s)	Holding	Ratio

THE LAW WORKBOOK: Developing skills for legal research and writing

Review the table. In preparing your rough notes on problem D, you may also find it helpful to reorganize the list of cases, grouping the cases that decided similar issues in the same way together. Seeing the information in this way can help to identify a pattern or trend developing in the law.

Case	Issue(s)	Holding	Ratio
R v. Jobidon			
R v. Bolduc and Bird			
R v. Ssenyonga			
R v. Cuerrier			
R v. Petrozzi			
R v. Thornton			

2. Write a statement that synthesizes the law applicable to problem D.

Based on your analysis of the case law, write a general statement of the law as it pertains to problem D. Indicate if the law appears to be changing or if there is a predictable general pattern in the way the courts have applied the legal principle.

_____

_____

_____

_____

_____

_____

_____

_____

_____

EXERCISE D4 Analyze analogous and distinguishable cases

Step 3c: Identify binding authorities

Step 3d: Analyze analogous and distinguishable cases

In the following exercises, use the case law to predict how the courts are likely to deal with the problem at hand. Be sure to consider how the law will affect each of the individuals involved in this case.

This time, instead of distinguishing or analogizing each case to the problem, group the cases that deal with similar issues in a similar manner together. Work on establishing the basis for analogizing or distinguishing the group of cases to the problem.

Grouping analogous cases together is one way to deal with a large number of cases, and to demonstrate the strength of a precedent, as well as the likelihood that it will be applied again in similar circumstances. Specific reference to the similar or distinguishable facts (or issues) in individual cases are used to provide the most effective example of what the law is and how it applies to the problem.

1. Identify the cases that have decided the legal issues raised in problem D in the same way. For each issue, list the names of cases that that can be dealt with as a group. You may identify more or fewer than five issues.

Issue: _____   Case: _____

_____   Case: _____

_____   Case: _____

Issue: _____   Case: _____

_____   Case: _____

_____   Case: _____

Issue: _____   Case: _____

_____   Case: _____

_____   Case: _____

Issue: _____   Case: _____

_____   Case: _____

_____   Case: _____

Issue: _____   Case: _____

_____   Case: _____

_____   Case: _____

2. For each issue, identify the grounds for drawing an analogy between the group of cases and the problem at hand. You may have more or fewer than five issues.

Issue: _____

_____

Issue: _____

_____

Issue: _____

_____

Issue: _____

_____

Issue: _____

_____

3. Suppose that someone was skeptical about generalizing the law in this way. Choose a specific example from one of the cases listed that best demonstrates to that person the strength of the factual analogy.

_____

_____

_____

_____

_____

_____

4. What would be the outcome if a court applied the reasons used to support the ruling in these cases to the situation in problem D?

_____

_____

_____

_____

_____

_____

_____

_____

_____

_____

_____

_____

_____

5. Test the strength of the analogy.

    a. Identify any significant differences between the group of cases and the problem at hand.

_____

_____

_____

_____

_____

_____

_____

_____

b. Are these differences more important than the similarities? List only the most significant legal and factual differences.

_____

_____

_____

_____

_____

_____

_____

_____

6. Test the grounds for possible distinction of the analogous cases.

A lawyer must analyze the law and its application to a problem keeping in mind the possibility that someone else might want to argue for another interpretation. It is good practice to anticipate what reasons someone might have for arguing that the case law should or should not apply.

a. Is there a group of cases that can be distinguished from the problem at hand? List the names of similar cases that may be dealt with as a group.

_____

_____

_____

_____

_____

_____

b. Identify the significant legal and factual differences between the group of cases and the problem at hand.

_____

_____

_____

_____

_____

_____

c. Use an example from one of the distinguishable cases listed that best illustrates why these differences are important to consider in applying the law to the problem at hand.

_____

_____

_____

_____

_____

_____

_____

_____

_____

_____

d. Are there any other reasons why someone might think that a court would be applying the law incorrectly if it were to use the reasons given in these cases to support a similar finding in problem D? If there are no good reasons, explain why.

_____

_____

\ _____

_____

_____

_____

_____

_____

Step 3e: Reconcile discrepancies in case law

7. Reconcile any legal discrepancies found in the case law.

Purpose: To establish how a court may be persuaded to follow one line of legal reasoning over another, or to predict why a court might adopt one particular interpretation of the law over another.

What reasons explain apparent inconsistencies in the case law?

_____

_____

_____

_____

_____

_____

_____

_____

8. Prepare a final overview of the results of legal analysis. For each person involved in this problem, summarize how you would use each case if you were his or her lawyer. Indicate the factual or legal basis of the analogy or distinction.

Case	Marc Curvesco	Kitty Hawk	Holly Berry
R v. Jobidon			
R v. Bolduc and Bird			
R v. Ssenyonga			
R v. Cuerrier			
R v. Petrozzi			
R v. Thornton			

STEP 4   REPORT THE ANALYTICAL RESULTS

EXERCISE D5   Scenario A: Kitty Hawk's case

Prepare the results of legal analysis as though you were the Crown preparing Kitty Hawk's case.

Step 4a: Predict

1. First, PREDICT how the law applies.

   In an opening sentence, predict the likelihood of a court convicting Marc Curvesco of having sexually assaulted Kitty Hawk.

   _____

   _____

   _____

   _____

   _____

   _____

Step 4b: State the
applicable law

2. Second, STATE the applicable legal principle(s).

   State the general legal principle(s) applicable to the problem at hand, drawing on the synthesis of the relevant case law, prepared in exercise D3.

   _____

   _____

   _____

   _____

   _____

   _____

3. Third, PROVE why the prediction is likely.

Step 4c: Proof

Supporting cases: Give reasons why a court may apply the rulings from the analogous cases to the problem at hand. For each relevant legal issue, group the analogous cases together to write a general statement about the pattern in the law established by these cases. For each legal issue, use the best example from one of these cases to illustrate the factual and legal similarities between the problem and the case law.

_____

_____

_____

_____

_____

_____

_____

_____

_____

_____

_____

_____

_____

_____

_____

_____

_____

_____

_____

_____

_____

_____

_____

Step 4d: Deal with
trouble spots

4. Fourth, DEAL with potential trouble spots: Demonstrate how cases that undermine the prediction may be distinguished.

_____

_____

_____

_____

_____

_____

_____

_____

_____

_____

_____

_____

_____

_____

_____

_____

_____

_____

_____

_____

_____

_____

THE LAW WORKBOOK: Developing skills for legal research and writing

5. Fifth, CONCLUDE the analytical findings. Step 4e: Conclude

In a brief summary statement, highlight the strongest reasons that support the prediction.

_____

_____

_____

_____

_____

_____

EXERCISE D6   Scenario B: Holly Berry's case

Report on the results of legal analysis of the law as though you were the Crown preparing Holly Berry's case.

Step 4a: Predict

1. First, PREDICT how the law applies.

   In an opening sentence, predict the likelihood of a court convicting Marc Curvesco of having sexually assaulted Holly Berry.

   _____

   _____

   _____

   _____

   _____

   _____

Step 4b: State the applicable law

2. Second, STATE the applicable legal principle(s).

   State the general legal principle(s) applicable to the problem, drawing on the synthesis of the relevant case law, prepared in exercise D3.

   _____

   _____

   _____

   _____

   _____

   _____

3. Third, PROVE why the prediction is likely. Step 4c: Proof

Supporting cases: Give reasons why a court may apply the rulings from the analogous cases to the problem at hand. For each relevant legal issue, group the analogous cases together to write a general statement about the pattern in the law established by these cases. For each legal issue, use the best example from one of these cases to illustrate the factual and legal similarities between the problem and the case law.

_____

_____

_____

_____

_____

_____

_____

_____

_____

_____

_____

_____

_____

_____

_____

_____

_____

_____

_____

_____

Step 4d: Deal with
trouble spots

4. Fourth, DEAL with potential trouble spots: Demonstrate how cases that undermine the prediction may be distinguished.

_____

_____

_____

_____

_____

_____

_____

_____

_____

_____

_____

_____

_____

_____

_____

_____

_____

_____

_____

_____

_____

THE LAW WORKBOOK: Developing skills for legal research and writing

5. Fifth, CONCLUDE the analytical findings. Step 4e: Conclude

In a brief summary statement, highlight the strongest reasons that support the prediction.

_____

_____

_____

_____

_____

_____

Exercise D7 Scenario C: Marc Curvesco's case

Prepare the results of your legal analysis as though you were defence counsel preparing Marc Curvesco's case.

Step 4a: Predict

1. First, PREDICT how the law applies.

   In an opening sentence, predict the likelihood of a court convicting Marc Curvesco of having sexually assaulted Kitty Hawk and Holly Berry.

   _____

   _____

   _____

   _____

   _____

   _____

Step 4b: State the applicable law

2. Second, STATE the applicable legal principle(s).

   State the general legal principle(s) applicable to the problem, drawing on the synthesis of the relevant case law, prepared in exercise D3.

   _____

   _____

   _____

   _____

   _____

   _____

3. Third, PROVE why the prediction is likely.

Supporting cases: Give reasons why a court may apply the rulings from the analogous cases to the problem at hand. For each relevant legal issue, group the analogous cases together to write a general statement about the pattern in the law established by these cases. For each legal issue, use the best example from one of these cases to illustrate the factual and legal similarities between the problem and the case law.

_____

_____

_____

_____

_____

_____

_____

_____

_____

_____

_____

_____

_____

_____

_____

_____

_____

_____

_____

Step 4d: Deal with
trouble spots

4. Fourth, DEAL with potential trouble spots: Demonstrate how cases that undermine the prediction may be distinguished.

_____

_____

_____

_____

_____

_____

_____

_____

_____

_____

_____

_____

_____

_____

_____

_____

_____

_____

_____

_____

THE LAW WORKBOOK: Developing skills for legal research and writing

5. Fifth, CONCLUDE the analytical findings.

Step 4e: Conclude

In a brief summary statement, highlight the strongest reasons that support the prediction.

_____

_____

_____

_____

_____

_____

Problem E: Treaties and taxes

Charles Shingoose is a status Indian and a prominent community figure among the First Nations. He resides and works on an Indian reserve. The reserve is located in the province of New Brunswick, and has been in existence since 1905. It has long been the custom to do grocery shopping off the reserve. Prior to 1993 such purchases were exempt from all federal and provincial taxes.

New Brunswick's *Social Services and Education Tax Act* levies a tax on items sold for consumption, and the tax is payable at the time of sale. In 1993, the province passed an amendment to the act that repealed the provision exempting status Indians from paying provincial sales tax on goods purchased off-reserve for on-reserve use. According to the amendment, only goods and services purchased on reserve lands or delivered there by the vendor are sales tax exempt.

To test the constitutional validity of the amendment, Charles Shingoose decided to order groceries from an online grocery service that provides home delivery of groceries ordered from the company's Web site. Even though he ordered the groceries from the computer at his home on the reserve, the Web-based grocery store was located physically off the reserve. He purchased a number of items intended for his personal use and had them delivered to his home on the reserve, where he proceeded to consume what he had purchased.

He refused to pay sales tax on the items, however, citing s. 87 of the *Indian Act*. The Web manager notified the appropriate provincial government office, and the respondent was charged under the *Social Services and Education Tax Act*.

At trial, the presiding judge held that s. 87 of the *Indian Act*, which exempts goods on reserves from taxation, applies only to property actually purchased on a reserve. He convicted Charles Shingoose and levied a small fine.

Charles Shingoose appealed that decision and, by a majority vote, the New Brunswick Court of Appeal reversed the trial decision. The Court of Appeal held that as a matter of statutory interpretation, s. 87 of the *Indian Act* was in conflict with the 1993 amendment to the provincial *Social Services and Education Tax Act*. The Appeal Court ruled that the amendment was inoperative to the extent that it was inconsistent with s. 87.

The province of New Brunswick has now appealed that decision.

EXERCISE E1   Identify the key words, facts, and legal concepts raised by the problem

1. Identify the relevant parties to the dispute and state their relationship to the case.

_____

_____

_____

_____

_____

_____

_____

_____

2. List the relevant legal problem(s) or issue(s) raised in the Shingoose problem.

_____

_____

_____

_____

_____

_____

_____

_____

3. What are the material facts?

_____

_____

_____

_____

_____

_____

_____

_____

4. Are there any background or remedial facts important to this case?

_____

_____

_____

_____

_____

_____

STEP 2   RESEARCH THE LEGAL PROBLEM

Step 2: Research the legal problem (chapters 2 and 3)

Normally, at this stage, the lawyer follows the research methodology developed in chapters 2 and 3 to find the legislation and case law that will govern the problem. The research has been provided. You may wish to brief the cases, however.

STEP 3   READ AND ANALYZE THE APPLICABLE LAW

Step 3: Read and analyze the applicable law (chapters 2 and 4)

Relevant legislation

- *Indian Act*, RSC 1970, c. I-6, s. 87; SC 1980-81-82-83, c. 47, s. 25:

Property exempt from taxation

87(1) Notwithstanding any other Act of Parliament or any Act of the legislature of a province, but subject to section 83, the following property is exempt from taxation, namely,

(a) the interest of an Indian or a band in reserve lands or surrendered lands; and

(b) the personal property of an Indian or a band situated on a reserve.

Idem

(2) No Indian or band is subject to taxation in respect of the ownership, occupation, possession or use of any property mentioned in paragraph (1)(a) or (b) or is otherwise subject to taxation in respect of any such property.

Idem

(3) No succession duty, inheritance tax or estate duty is payable on the death of any Indian in respect of any property mentioned in paragraphs (1)(a) or (b) or the succession thereto if the property passes to an Indian, nor shall any such property be taken into account in determining the duty payable under *the Dominion Succession Duty Act*, chapter 89 of the Revised Statutes of Canada, 1952, or the tax payable under the *Estate Tax Act*, chapter E-9 of the Revised Statutes of Canada, 1970, on or in respect of other property passing to an Indian.

- *Social Services and Education Tax Act*, RSNB 1973, c. S-10:

Deposit

10. When a vendor sells goods or services to a person who alleges that he is not purchasing them as a purchaser within the meaning of this Act, such person shall deposit with the vendor an amount equivalent to the amount of the tax for which he would be liable if he were purchasing the goods or services as such a purchaser, and the amount so deposited shall be refunded to him upon application to the Minister and upon furnishing the Minister with proof that he did not purchase the goods or services as such a purchaser.

EXERCISE E1 Brief the relevant case law

Use the "underline-and-margin-note method" to brief the cases as you read them. Remember to state the ratio briefly at the top of the first page.

Williams v. Canada, [1992] 1 SCR 877

Ratio: _____

_____

The appellant, a member of an Indian Band, received regular unemployment insurance benefits in 1984 for which he qualified because of his former employment with a logging company, and his employment by the Band in a "NEED" project. In both cases, the work was performed on the reserve, the employer was located on the reserve, and the appellant was paid on the reserve. In addition to regular benefits, the appellant also received "enhanced" unemployment insurance benefits paid in respect of a job creation project administered on the reserve by the Band, pursuant to a written agreement between the Band and the Canada Employment and Immigration Commission. The regular and enhanced benefits were paid by the Commission's regional computer centre in Vancouver.

The appellant received a notice of assessment by the Minister of National Revenue that included in his income for 1984 the regular and enhanced unemployment insurance benefits. The appellant contested the assessment but the Minister overruled his objection. The appellant then appealed to the Federal Court, Trial Division, which concluded that, under the *Indian Act*, both the regular and enhanced unemployment insurance benefits were exempt from taxation. The Federal Court of Appeal set aside the judgment holding that only the enhanced portion of those benefits was exempt. The issue in this case is the *situs* of unemployment insurance benefits received by an Indian for the purpose of the exemption from taxation provided by section 87 of the *Indian Act*.

Held: The appeal should be allowed and the cross-appeal should be dismissed.

The *situs* of the receipt of unemployment insurance benefits cannot be determined in the same way the conflict of laws determines the *situs* of a debt. To simply adopt general conflicts of law principles and to apply the "residence of the debtor" test in the present context would be entirely out of keeping with the scheme and purposes of the *Indian Act* and *Income Tax Act*. While the residence of the debtor may remain an important factor, or even the exclusive one, this conclusion cannot be directly drawn from an analysis of how the conflict of laws deals with such an issue.

The proper approach to determining the *situs* of intangible personal property is for a court to evaluate the various connecting factors that tie the property to one location or another. In the context of the exemption from taxation in the *Indian Act*, the connecting factors which are potentially relevant should be weighed in light of three important considerations: the purpose of the exemption; the type of property in question; and the incidence of taxation upon that property. Given the purpose of the exemption, the ultimate question is to what extent each connecting factor is relevant in determining whether taxing the particular kind of property in a particular manner would erode the entitlement of an Indian *qua* Indian to personal property on the reserve.

The location of the employment, which gave rise to the qualification for the unemployment insurance benefits, is a particularly relevant factor in identifying the *situs* of the benefits. The connection between the previous employment and the benefits is a strong one. The benefits are based on premiums arising out of previous employment, not general tax revenue, and the duration and extent of the benefits are tied to the terms of employment during a specified period. The manner in which unemployment insurance benefits are treated for the purposes of taxation further strengthens this connection, as there is symmetry of treatment in the taxation of premiums and benefits, since premiums are tax-deductible and benefits are taxed. For an Indian whose qualifying employment income was on the reserve, however, the symmetry in the tax implications of premiums and benefits breaks down. The original employment income was tax-exempt and the taxation paid on the subsequent benefits does more than merely offset the tax saved by virtue of the premiums. It is an erosion of the entitlements created by the Indian's employment on the reserve.

In this case, since the location of the qualifying employment was on the reserve, the benefits received by the appellant were also located on the reserve. This conclusion also applies to the enhanced benefits. The appellant only qualified for participation in the job-creation program because he had been receiving regular unemployment insurance benefits, that is, because of his prior employment that had ceased. It follows that both the regular and enhanced benefits were exempt from taxation pursuant to section 87 of the *Indian Act*.

The question of the relevance of the residence of the recipient of the benefits at the time of receipt does not arise in this case since it was also on the reserve. The residence of the debtor and the place where the benefits are paid are connecting factors of limited weight in the context of unemployment insurance benefits.

Simpsons-Sears Ltd. v. NB (Secretary), [1978] 2 SCR 869

Ratio:

During 1972, S Ltd., a retail merchandising company, distributed catalogues to prospective customers in New Brunswick. Some of the catalogues were mailed from Ontario to persons in New Brunswick who had previously purchased goods from the company and others were delivered by various means to customers' homes in New Brunswick. Simpson Sears Ltd. (referred to here as "S Ltd.") was assessed for tax on the basis that the free distribution of catalogues constituted consumption of these catalogues within the meaning of the *Social Services and Education Tax Act*. S Ltd. appealed arguing that the free distribution of the catalogues did not constitute consumption of the catalogues and that the tax constituted an indirect tax since it would be passed on to the individuals who purchased goods from the catalogues. The Supreme Court, Queens Bench Division, allowed the appeal. The New Brunswick Court of Appeal reversed this decision. The taxpayer appealed further.

Held (Pigeon, Martland, Beetz, de Grandpré JJ dissenting): The appeal was allowed.

The taxpayer was not a consumer within the meaning of the *Social Services and Education Tax Act*. Subsections 5(1) and 7(1) of the *Act* were applicable to cases where there has been "a retail sale within the province" and when read in conjunction could only be construed as imposing a tax on the consumer when goods were purchased. When section 4, the charging section, was read in light of subsection 5(1), the word "consumption" in section 4 must be construed as meaning a consumption after sale if the goods were to be purchased at retail within the province. There was no sale of catalogues within the province and in the circumstances subsection 5(2) which imposed a tax on the consumption of goods "not purchased at a retail sale within the Province" was not applicable. The word consumption in the phrases "consumption by use" and "consumption otherwise than by use" in paragraphs 5(2)(a) and (2)(b) respectively must be construed as meaning "ultimate use" and did not include the distribution of the catalogues which was merely an incidental use of the catalogues. Furthermore, the tax which the province sought to impose in these circumstances was not a *direct tax within the meaning of subsection 92(2) of the BNA Act*. There was no sale of any kind involved in the distribution of catalogues and the statute did not convert the distributor into a final purchaser, consumer, or user required to bear the burden of the tax. Since the taxpayer ultimately recovered the cost of producing and distributing the catalogues, in the price it charged for its goods the taxpayer was not bringing goods into the province for consumption by another at its own expense within the meaning of subsection 7(2).

R v. Louis Francis, [1956] SCR 618

Ratio:

_____

_____

The Chief Justice: This is an appeal against a decision of the Exchequer Court dismissing the Petition of Right of the suppliant (an Indian resident in a reserve in Canada) and the question is whether three articles, a washing machine, a refrigerator and an oil heater, brought by him into Canada from the United States of America are subject to duties of customs and sales tax under the relevant statutes of Canada. None was paid and in fact the articles were not brought into this country at a port of entry; they were subsequently placed under customs detention or seizure and in order to obtain their release, the appellant, under protest, paid the sum demanded by the Crown. The Petition of Right claims the return of this money and a declaration that no duties or taxes were payable by the appellant with respect to the goods.

Held: The appeal should be dismissed with costs.

The date of importation of the washing machine is December 1948; of the refrigerator April 24, 1950, and of the oil heater September 7, 1951. The relevancy of the dates is that section 49 of the Statutes of Canada, 1949, 2nd session, c. 25, relied upon by the respondent, was assented to on September 10, 1949, and was, therefore, in effect at the time the suppliant brought into Canada the refrigerator and oil heater, but was not in force when the washing machine was imported. Further more section 87 of _The Indian Act_, RSC 1951, c. 29, also referred to on behalf of the respondent, was first enacted in the revision of _The Indian Act_ in 1949 by section 87 of c. 29 of the statutes of that year, which chapter was brought into force on September 4, 1951, so that even if applicable, its provisions would affect only the importation of the oil heater and I find it unnecessary to express any opinion upon the matter.

The appellant falls within the definition of "Indian" in section 2(1)(g) of RSC 1951, c. 29 and at all relevant times he resided on the St. Regis Indian Reserve in St. Regis village in the westerly part of the Province of Québec, which adjoins an Indian reserve in the State of New York in the United States of America — the residents of both reserves belonging to the St. Regis Tribe of Indians. The articles were brought into Canada in the manner already described in order to lay the foundation for the present proceeding as a test case.

The first claim advanced on behalf of the appellant is that these imposts need not be paid because of the following provisions of Article III of the _Treaty of Amity, Commerce and Navigation_, between His Britannic Majesty and the United States of America signed on November 19, 1794, and generally known as the _Jay Treaty_:

> — No Duty on Entry shall ever be levied by either Party on Peltries brought by Land, or Inland Navigation into the said Territories respectively, nor shall the Indians passing or repassing with their

own proper Goods and Effects of whatever nature, pay for the same any Impost or Duty whatever. But Goods in Bales or other large Packages unusual among Indians shall not be considered as Goods belonging bona fide to Indians.

In view of the conclusion at which I have arrived, it is unnecessary to deal with the question raised by the respondent that the articles imported by the appellant were not his "own proper goods and effects."

The *Jay Treaty* was not a Treaty of Peace and it is clear that in Canada such rights and privileges as are here advanced of subjects of a contracting party to a treaty are enforceable by the Courts only where the treaty has been implemented or sanctioned by legislation. This is an adaptation of the language of Lamont J, speaking for himself and Cannon J. in *Arrow River & Tributaries Slide & Boom Co. Ltd. v. Pigeon Timber Co. Ltd.*, [1932] SCR 495, and is justified by a continuous line of authority in England. Although it may be necessary in connection with other matters to consider in the future the judgment of the *Judicial Committee in The Labour Conventions Case*, [1937] AC 326, so far as the point under discussion is concerned it is there put in the same sense by Lord Atkin. It has been held that no rights under a treaty of cession can be enforced in the Courts except in so far as they have been incorporated in municipal law: *Vajesingji Joravarsingji v. Secretary of State for India* (1924), LR 51 Ind. App. 357; *Hoani Te Heuheu Tukino v. Aotea District Maoria Land Board*, [1941] AC 308. The case of *Sutton v. Sutton* (1830), 1 Russ. & M 664, relied upon by the appellant, dealt with the construction of another provision of the *Jay Treaty* and of the *Statute of 37 Geo. III*, c. 97 that was passed for the purpose of carrying certain terms of the *Treaty* into execution. This is not a case where vested rights of property are concerned and it is unnecessary to consider the question whether the terms of the *Jay Treaty* were abrogated by the war of 1812.

I agree with Mr. Justice Cameron that clause (b) of section 86 of The *Indian Act* does not apply, because customs duties are not taxes upon the personal property of an Indian situated on a Reserve but are imposed upon the importation of goods into Canada. I also agree that, so far as the refrigerator and the oil heater are concerned, section 49 of c. 25 of the 1949 statutes is a complete bar. This is "An Act to amend the *Income Tax Act* and the *Income War Tax Act*." While it is true that in section 48 there are references to residents in Newfoundland and in sections 49 and 50 to Newfoundland, most of the sections deal with income tax throughout all of Canada. The words are clear that no one is entitled to any deduction, exemption or immunity from, or any privilege in respect of any duty or tax imposed by an Act of the Parliament of Canada; and the *Customs Act* of Canada certainly provides for a duty on all the goods brought into the country by the appellant. Counsel for the appellant points to the words "notwithstanding any other law heretofore enacted" and argues that the rights upon which the appellant bases his claim under the *Jay Treaty* do not arise under any enactment. For the reasons already given, I cannot agree that any relevant rights of the appellant within that *Treaty* are judicable in the Courts of this country.

Leighton v. British Columbia (1989), 57 DLR (4th) 657, [1989] 4 WWR 654 (BC CA) [alternate case name: *Metlakatla Band v. British Columbia*]

Ratio:

LAMBERT JA: The provincial Crown would like the provincial sales tax to apply to Indians in the same way as it applies to non-Indians, to the greatest extent that provincial legislation can achieve that purpose. So, as counsel for the Crown said in argument, the provincial Crown is trying to impose the provincial sales tax right up to, but of course not over, the limits of the exemption conferred by s. 87 of the *Indian Act*, RSC 1970, c. I-6.

Held: Appeal allowed.

It is the use of tax-free goods off the reserve that the provincial Crown finds particularly abhorrent. So to try to overcome those two decisions, the provincial legislature, in 1987, enacted two new subsections of the *Social Service Tax Act*, RSBC 1979, c. 388, sections 2 and 2.1. The Metlakatla Band and the Kitamaat Band brought an action to challenge the constitutionality of the new subsections. The parties agreed on a special case under Rule 33, confined to the constitutional question. Mr. Justice Meredith decided that the subsections were constitutional and effective. This appeal is from his decision. The two subsections read in this way:

Section 2

2(4.2) Where tangible personal property that is purchased by an Indian or a band, as defined in the *Indian Act* (Canada), is exempt, but for this subsection, from the tax that would be payable under this *Act*, and that tangible personal property is, while owned by that Indian or band, used at a place where the exemption would not have applied, the Indian or band is, at the time it is so used, liable to pay the tax on the purchase price of that tangible personal property at the rate under this *Act*.

Section 2.1

2.1(3.1) Where an Indian or a band, as defined in the *Indian Act* (Canada), is a lessee of tangible personal property that is exempt, but for this subsection, from the tax that would be payable under this *Act*, and that tangible personal property is, while leased by that lessee, used during a rental period under the lease at a place where the exemption would not have applied, the Indian or band is, at the time it is so used, liable to pay the tax under this section for that rental period and, if applicable, under section 2.2.

The first ground of appeal advanced on behalf of the Indian bands is that the two subsections are in pith and substance laws in relation to matters coming within the class of subject, "Indians," as enumerated in section

91(24) of the *Constitution Act, 1867,* and, as such, their enactment is out-side the powers of the provincial legislature.

A provincial law of general application may apply to Indians on or off a reserve. But even a law of general application may be unconstitutional in its application to Indians if it affects their essential character as Indians. On the other hand, a provincial law which applies specifically to Indians and to Indians alone may still be a law that is not in pith and substance of law in relation to matters coming within the class of subject.

To those general statements of principle, I add that, in characterizing the pith and substance of a law, consideration must be given to the language in which the law is expressed and also to the concepts that it embodies. Both the language and the concepts must be considered in their context.

In this case the two new subsections refer only to Indians, and apply only to Indians. What is more, they impose a new tax which has as its subject-matter either the use of tangible personal property, or the combi-nation of the purchase and use or lease and use of tangible personal property. The general charging sections in the *Social Service Tax Act* show that, in its general application, the tax under that *Act* is imposed either on a purchaser in respect of his purchase or on a lessee in respect of his lease. The only other provision in the *Act* which imposes a tax on a user in respect of use of tangible personal property is section 2(3.4) which imposes a use tax on farmers, aquaculturists and commercial fishermen when they use exempt property for a non-exempt use.

The two new subsections single out Indians to pay a special tax that is not payable by anyone else. The fact that non-Indians pay an equivalent tax, from which Indians are exempt, does not alter the characterization of the concepts expressed in the subsection. In my opinion, the two subsections are, in their legislative character, laws in relation to matters coming within the class of subjects, "Indians," and their enactment is therefore beyond the power of the provincial legislature.

The second ground of appeal is an alternative ground. It is that the new subsections are ineffective because they impose a tax that is prohib-ited by section 87 of the *Indian Act,* and because, where federal and pro-vincial laws conflict, federal law must prevail.

At the time the writ was issued in this case, section 87, in its relevant part, read:

Taxation

> 87. Notwithstanding any other Act of the Parliament of Canada or any Act of the legislature of a province, but subject to section 83, the following property is exempt from taxation, namely:
>
> > (b) the personal property of an Indian or band situated on a reserve; and no Indian or band is subject to taxation in respect of the ownership, occupation, possession or use of any property mentioned in paragraph ... (b) or is otherwise subject to taxation in respect of any such property;

Section 87 has been slightly changed in the 1985 revision of the *Statutes of Canada,* but no change in substance has been made.

If property is "situated on a reserve" it is exempt from tax and no Indian or band may be taxed in respect of the use of that property. The word "situated" does not mean that the property must be permanently on the reserve. But "situated on" means more than merely "on."

The application of section 87 will depend on the kind of property being considered. The characteristics of being "situated on a reserve" may be different for electricity than they are for cigarettes, or than they are for automobiles, or than they are for intangible property.

The word "situated" has been taken back in the cases to its root in the word "*situs*," and help has been gained from other areas of law which deal with the establishment of a *situs* for property. In dealing with the circumstances in which an automobile may be said to be situated on a reserve, in *Danes v. The Queen*, Mr. Justice Macfarlane, for the court, said this, at p. 259:

> I do not think that property is without a *situs* just because it is mobile. From the point of view of the Indian owner of a motor vehicle it would be reasonable to say that the *situs* of the vehicle would be at his residence, which is the place where the vehicle is kept when not in use, and to which, habitually, it returns.

In that passage, Mr. Justice Macfarlane linked the *situs* of property with the residence of an individual. For the purposes of determining whether property is "situated on a reserve," the pattern of use and safekeeping of the property must be examined to establish its paramount location. If the location is on a reserve then the property itself is "situated on a reserve."

So I do not consider that either tangible personal property or its Indian owner can be taxed with respect to the use of the property off the reserve if the paramount location of the property remains on the reserve.

We were urged by Crown counsel to "read down" the two new subsections by giving them an interpretation that would prevent them from conflicting with section 87. That would require significant rewriting in order to ensure that any tax on use only reached property that was situated off the reserve. The subsections themselves, in their present form, cannot carry an interpretation that would restrict their application so that there was no conflict with section 87. So, quite apart from the issue of constitutionality dealt with on the first ground of appeal, this is not a proper case for "reading down."

The reasons set out require that this appeal be allowed. In my opinion the two new subsections are unconstitutional. I would allow the appeal.

reading down
a narrow interpretation
of a statutory provision

R v. Lewis, [1996] 1 SCR 921

Ratio: _____

_____

All three appellants, who are members of the Squamish Indian Band and reside at the Cheakamus Reserve, were charged with contravening the British Columbia Fishery (General) Regulations. On three different occasions in 1985 and 1986, two of the appellants engaged in "net fishing" on the Squamish River in an area immediately contiguous to the reserve. In the case of the third appellant, the fishing took place on the west side of the Squamish River, opposite the reserve. All three appellants claimed that they were authorized by Squamish Indian Band By-law No. 10 to fish at the time and in the manner in question. The by-law authorizes band members to fish "upon Squamish Indian Band waters," which are defined as "water situate upon or within the boundaries of Reserves." The by-law was passed pursuant to section 81(1)(o) of the *Indian Act*, which authorizes a band council to make by-laws for "the preservation, protection and management of ... fish ... on the reserve." The appellants were convicted. On appeal, the County Court judge applied the presumption *ad medium filum aquae*, and found that the boundary of the reserve extended to the midline of the Squamish River. He concluded that By-law No. 10 constituted a complete defence in cases where the fishing took place on the east (or reserve) side of the river. The appeals of the first two appellants were allowed, since they had been fishing on the east side of the Squamish River, while the third appellant's appeal was dismissed because he had been fishing on the west side. The Court of Appeal allowed the Crown's appeals against the acquittals and dismissed the third appellant's appeal against his conviction.

Held: The appeal should be dismissed.

By-law No. 10, enacted by the Squamish Band Council pursuant to section 81(1)(o) of the *Indian Act*, does not apply to the fishery in the Squamish River at the Cheakamus Reserve and therefore cannot constitute a defence to the charges against the appellants pursuant to the British Columbia Fishery (General) Regulations.

The fishery itself is not part of the Cheakamus Reserve. A desire of both the provincial and federal governments to support and protect native fishing does not amount to granting exclusive fisheries. In fact, statements and legislation both before and after Confederation demonstrate that the Crown's policy was to treat Indians and non-Indians equally as to the use of the water and not to grant exclusive use of any public waters for the purpose of fishing. The Crown's general policy of not granting exclusive fisheries to Indians equally extends to the allotment of the Cheakamus Reserve. A brief review of the historical circumstances surrounding this particular grant clearly evinces an intention to allocate land, such as fishing stations, but not the Squamish River as forming part of the reserve. Assuming, without deciding, that the Crown had a fiduciary duty to include the river as part of the reserve in order to secure the fishery for the Band, that duty was fulfilled. First, it appears from the historical evidence that any fiduciary obligation on the part of the Crown to secure access to the fishery for the Band was honoured by providing fishing stations for their use. Furthermore, the fact that the Crown did not secure a larger access to the fishery for the Band, in addition to the fishing stations, did not amount to exploitation.

The *ad medium filum aquae* presumption is a common law rule by which ownership of the bed of a non-tidal river or stream belongs in equal halves to the owners of riparian land. This presumption can be rebutted either by the terms of the instrument, or circumstances surrounding the grant or conveyance indicating a different intention. Assuming without deciding that the *ad medium filum aquae* presumption applies to Indian reserves, in western Canada at least it does not apply to navigable rivers. Since the Squamish River is navigable, as explicitly found by the trial judge, the *ad medium filum* presumption cannot apply, and the question whether in the circumstances the presumption was rebutted does not arise. Consequently, the natural boundary of the Squamish River, and not the middle thread of the river limit the boundaries of the reserve.

riparian
riverbank

The phrase "on the reserve" in the context of section 81(1)(*o*) of the *Indian Act* should receive its ordinary and common sense meaning and be interpreted as "within the reserve" or "inside the reserve" or "located upon or within the boundaries of the reserve." Parliament's intention in enacting section 81(1) as a whole and in particular para. (*o*) was to provide a mechanism by which Band Councils could assume management over certain activities within the territorial limits of their constituencies. These considerations, together with the fact that By-law No. 10 defines "Squamish Indian Band waters" to be those which are "situate[d] upon or within the boundaries of Reserves," lead to the conclusion that Parliament never intended that such a fishing by-law should have an extra-territorial effect. While treaties and statutes relating to Indians should be liberally construed and doubtful expressions resolved in favour of the Indians, the word "on" used in the connection of "on the reserve," in its ordinary and natural meaning, signifies "within the reserve," not "adjacent to the reserve." The phrase "on the reserve" should receive the same construction wherever used within the *Indian Act*. When the *Act* is considered in its entirety, it is clear that Parliament never intended that a by-law passed by the Band Council should have an extra-territorial effect. Furthermore, an examination of the French text supports "on the reserve" as meaning in or within the boundaries of the reserve. If Parliament had intended to grant regulatory powers to Indian Band Councils beyond the limits of their reserves, it would have specifically provided for such powers. Accordingly, it is the *Fisheries Act* and its Regulations, not the By-law, which apply to the Squamish River.

Nowegijick v. The Queen, [1983] 1 SCR 29

Ratio:

_____

_____

Appellant, a registered Indian living on a reserve, objected to the income tax assessment on his wages. He was employed by an Indian corporation having its head and administrative offices on the reserve and was paid at the corporation head office. The actual work was done off the reserve. Appellant claimed that that income was exempted from taxation by virtue of section 87 of the *Indian Act*. That section provides that personal property of an Indian situated on a reserve is exempt from taxation and that no Indian is subject to taxation in respect of any such property. The *Income Tax Act* makes tax payable upon taxable income — *i.e.* income minus deductions. The Federal Court Trial Division ruled in appellant's favour but the Court of Appeal reversed the judgment holding that the tax imposed under the *Income Tax Act* was not taxation in respect of personal property within the meaning of section 87 of the *Indian Act*.

Held: The appeal should be allowed.

Treaties and statutes relating to Indians should be liberally construed and doubtful expressions resolved in favour of the Indians. The Crown conceded that the *situs* of the wages was on the reserve. The primary task in this case is to construe the words "no Indian ... is ... subject to taxation in respect of any such [personal] property." Income is personal property; taxable income is equally personal property. A tax in respect of wages is a tax in respect of personal property. The effect of section 87 is not only to exempt what can properly be described as direct taxation on property; it also exempts persons from taxation.

Analyze the case law

Use the following exercises to analyze the case law. The exercises present the tools of legal analysis (synthesis, analogy, distinction, and reconciliation), according to the general outline used to present the results of legal analysis in predictive writing.

Exercise E2   Synthesize the applicable law

Purpose: To provide a general statement of the law applicable to a legal question or issue. Patterns and trends in law are important to note.

1. Use the chart below to summarize an analysis of the applicable case law and to present an overview of the case law in this area. Rank the cases, beginning with the most authoritative case. Be sure to identify the legal issues in the case that are of importance to the case at hand.

Case	Issue(s)	Holding	Ratio

Review the table. In preparing your rough notes on problem E, you may also find it helpful to reorganize the list of cases, grouping the cases that decided similar issues in the same way together. Seeing the information in this way can help to identify a pattern or trend developing in the law.

Case	Issue(s)	Holding	Ratio
Williams v. Canada			
Simpsons-Sears Ltd. v. NB (Secretary)			
R v. Louis Francis			
Leighton v. British Columbia			
R v. Lewis			
Nowegijick v. The Queen			

2. Write a statement that synthesizes the law applicable to problem E.

Based on your analysis of the case law, write a general statement of the law as it pertains to problem E. Indicate whether the law appears to be changing or whether there is a predictable general pattern in the way the courts have applied the legal principle.

_____

_____

_____

_____

_____

_____

_____

_____

_____

EXERCISE E3 Analyze analogous and distinguishable cases

Step 3c: Identify binding authorities

Step 3d: Analyze analogous and distinguishable cases

In the following exercises, use the case law to predict how the courts are likely to deal with the problem. Be sure to consider how the law will affect each of the individuals involved in this case.

This time, instead of distinguishing or analogizing each case to the problem, group the cases that deal with similar issues in a similar manner together. Work on establishing the basis for analogizing or distinguishing the group of cases to the problem.

Grouping analogous cases together is one way to deal with a large number of cases, and to demonstrate the strength of the precedent, as well as the likelihood that it will be applied again in similar circumstances. Specific reference to the similar or distinguishable facts (or issues) in individual cases are used to provide the most effective example of what the law is and how it applies to the problem.

1. Identify the cases that have decided the legal issues raised in problem E in the same way. For each issue, list the names of cases that that can be dealt with as a group. You may identify more or fewer than five issues.

Issue: _____   Case: _____

_____   Case: _____

_____   Case: _____

Issue: _____   Case: _____

_____   Case: _____

_____   Case: _____

Issue: _____   Case: _____

_____   Case: _____

_____   Case: _____

Issue: _____   Case: _____

_____   Case: _____

_____   Case: _____

Issue: _____   Case: _____

_____   Case: _____

_____   Case: _____

2. For each issue, identify the grounds for drawing an analogy between the group of cases and the problem. You may have more or fewer than five issues.

Issue: _____

_____

Issue: _____

_____

Issue: _____

_____

Issue: _____

_____

Issue: _____

_____

3. Suppose that someone was skeptical about generalizing the law in this way. Choose a specific example from one of the cases listed that best demonstrates to that person the strength of the factual analogy.

_____

_____

_____

_____

_____

_____

_____

_____

_____

4. What would be the outcome if a court applied the reasons used to support the ruling in these cases to the situation in problem E?

_____

_____

_____

_____

_____

_____

_____

_____

_____

_____

_____

5. Test the strength of the analogy.

   a. Identify any significant differences between the group of cases and the problem.

_____

_____

_____

_____

_____

_____

_____

b. Are these differences more important than the similarities? List only the most significant legal and factual differences.

_____

_____

_____

_____

_____

6. Test the grounds for possible distinction of the analogous cases.

A lawyer must analyze the law and its application to a problem keeping in mind the possibility that someone else might want to argue another interpretation. It is good practice to anticipate what reasons someone might have for arguing that the case law should or should not apply.

a. Is there a group of cases that can be distinguished from the problem? List the names of similar cases that may be dealt with as a group.

_____

_____

_____

_____

_____

b. Identify the significant legal and factual differences between the group of cases and the problem.

_____

_____

_____

_____

_____

_____

c. Use an example from one of the distinguishable cases listed that best illustrates why these differences are important to consider in applying the law to the problem.

_____

_____

_____

_____

_____

_____

_____

_____

d. Are there any other reasons why someone might think that a court would be applying the law incorrectly if it were to use the reasons given in these cases to support a similar finding in problem E? If there are no good reasons, explain why.

_____

_____

_____

_____

_____

_____

_____

_____

Step 3e: Reconcile
discrepancies in
case law

7. Reconcile any legal discrepancies found in the case law.

Purpose: To establish how a court may be persuaded to follow one line of legal reasoning over another, or to predict why a court might adopt one particular interpretation of the law over another.

What reasons explain apparent inconsistencies in the case law?

_____

_____

_____

_____

_____

_____

_____

_____

THE LAW WORKBOOK: Developing skills for legal research and writing

8. Prepare a final overview of the results of legal analysis. For each party involved in this problem, summarize how you would use each case if you were their lawyer. Indicate the factual or legal basis of the analogy or distinction.

Case	Shingoose	Provincial authorities
Williams v. Canada		
Simpsons-Sears Ltd. v. NB (Secretary)		
R v. Louis Francis		
Leighton v. British Columbia		
R v. Lewis		
Nowegijick v. The Queen		

STEP 4 PREDICTIVE WRITING SKILLS: REPORT THE ANALYTICAL RESULTS

EXERCISE E4   Scenario A: Charles Shingoose's case

Prepare the results of your legal analysis as though you were the lawyer representing Charles Shingoose.

1. First, PREDICT how the law applies.

   In an opening sentence, predict the likelihood of a court upholding the Appeal Court's decision that the provincial government's amendment to s. 87 of the *Indian Act* was in conflict with the 1993 amendment to the provincial *Social Services and Education Tax Act*.

   _____

   _____

   _____

   _____

   _____

   _____

2. Second, STATE the applicable legal principle(s).

   State the general legal principle(s) applicable to the problem, drawing on the synthesis of the relevant case law, prepared in exercise E2.

   _____

   _____

   _____

   _____

   _____

   _____

3. Third, PROVE why the prediction is likely.

In a brief summary statement, highlight the strongest reasons that support the prediction.

Supporting cases: Give reasons why a court may apply the rulings from the analogous cases to the problem at hand. For each relevant legal issue, group the analogous cases together to write a general statement about the pattern in the law established by these cases. For each legal issue, use the best example from one of these cases to illustrate the factual and legal similarities between the problem and the case law.

_____

_____

_____

_____

_____

_____

_____

_____

_____

_____

_____

_____

_____

_____

_____

_____

_____

_____

_____

Step 4d: Deal with trouble spots

4. Fourth, DEAL with potential trouble spots: Demonstrate how cases that undermine the prediction may be distinguished.

_____

_____

_____

_____

_____

_____

_____

_____

_____

_____

_____

_____

_____

_____

_____

_____

_____

_____

_____

_____

_____

THE LAW WORKBOOK: Developing skills for legal research and writing

5. Fifth, CONCLUDE the analytical findings. Step 4e: Conclude

In a brief summary statement, highlight the strongest reasons that support the prediction.

_____

_____

_____

_____

_____

_____

REFERENCES

Romeo and Juliet demonstration

Bujold v. Dempsey (1996), 181 NBR (2d) 111 (QB).

Canadian General Insurance Co. v. Rowsell (1996), 140 Nfld. & PEIR 329, 438 APR 329 (Nfld. TD).

Eales v. James (1977), 17 Nfld. & PEIR 242 (Nfld. Dist. Ct.).

Fleming v. Atkinson, [1959] SCR 513, 18 DLR (2d) 81.

Rowe v. Canning (1994), 117 Nfld. & PEIR 353, 4 MVR (3d) 269 (Nfld. TD).

Ruckheim v. Robinson, [1995] 4 WWR 284, 1 BCLR (3d) 46 (CA).

Problem A

Labour Relations Act, RSO 1990, c. L.2, s. 64.

Ajax (Town) v. CAW, Local 222, [2000] 1 SCR 538.

Canada (Attorney General) v. Public Service Alliance of Canada (PSAC), [1993] 1 SCR 941.

Canadian Broadcasting Corp. v. Canada (Labour Relations Board), [1995] 1 SCR 157.

UES, Local 298 v. Bibeault, [1988] 2 SCR 1048.

W.W. Lester (1978) Ltd. v. United Assn. of Journeymen and Apprentices of the Plumbing and Pipefitting Industry, Local 740, [1990] 3 SCR 644.

Problem B

Bankruptcy Act, RSC 1985, c. B-3 [now the *Bankruptcy and Insolvency Act*], s. 121(1).

Employment Standards Act, RSO 1980, c. 137.

Eland Distributors Ltd. (Trustee of) v. British Columbia (Director of Employment Standards), [1996] 7 WWR 652, 21 BCLR (3d) 91 (SC).

Mills-Hughes et al. v. Raynor et al. (1985), 63 OR (2d) 343, 25 OAC 248, 47 DLR (4th) 381 (CA).

Re Malone Lynch Securities Ltd., [1972] 3 OR 725 (SC).

Rizzo & Rizzo Shoes Ltd. (Re), [1998] 1 SCR 27.

UFCW, Local 617P v. Royal Dressed Meats Inc. (Trustee of) (1989), 70 OR (2d) 455, 63 DLR (4th) 603 (HCJ).

Problem C

Family Compensation Act, RSBC 1979, c. 120.

Fontaine v. British Columbia (Official Administrator of), [1998] 1 SCR 424.

Gauthier Co. v. Canada, [1945] SCR 143.

Hellenius et al. v. Lees, [1972] SCR 165.

Jackson v. Millar, [1976] 1 SCR 225.

Taylor Estate v. Wong Aviation Ltd., [1969] SCR 481.

Toneguzzo-Norvell (Guardian ad litem of) v. Burnaby Hospital, [1994] 1 SCR 114.

Problem D

Criminal Code, RSC 1985, c. C-46, as amended.

R v. Bolduc and Bird, [1967] SCR 677.

R v. Cuerrier, [1998] 2 SCR 371.

R v. Jobidon, [1991] 2 SCR 714.

R v. Petrozzi, [1987] 5 WWR 71, 13 BCLR (2d) 273 (CA).

R v. Ssenyonga (1993), 81 CCC (3d) 257, 21 CR (4th) 128 (Ont. Gen. Div.).

R v. Thornton, [1993] 2 SCR 445.

Problem E

Indian Act, RSC 1970, c. I-6, s. 87; SC 1980-81-82-83, c. 47, s. 25.

Social Services and Education Tax Act, RSNB 1973, c. S-10.

Leighton v. British Columbia (1989), 57 DLR (4th) 657, [1989] 4 WWR 654 (BC CA)
[alternate case name: *Metlakatla Band v. British Columbia*].

Nowegijick v. The Queen, [1983] 1 SCR 29.

R v. Lewis, [1996] 1 SCR 921.

R v. Louis Francis, [1956] SCR 618.

Simpsons-Sears Ltd. v. NB (Secretary), [1978] 2 SCR 869.

Williams v. Canada, [1992] 1 SCR 877.

Choosing databases on Quicklaw, Westlaw, and Lexis

The chart on the following pages shows how to choose databases on Quicklaw, Westlaw, and Lexis when searching for different kinds of legal information. For more detailed explanations and complete database lists, consult the training guides and database directories of Quicklaw, Westlaw, and Lexis.

	QL database (examples)	Lawschool.Westlaw.com database (examples)	Lexis.com database* (examples)
• Finding case law (full-text)	1. ORP (for Ontario Reports and judgments) 2. TAX (for tax cases)	1. ALLCASES (US federal and state cases) 2. ALLFEDS (US federal cases) 3. ALLSTATES (state cases)	1. US federal and state cases 2. English cases 3. Selected Commonwealth cases
• Finding case law (summaries/digests)	1. DRS (Dominion Report Service) 2. ACWS (All Canada Weekly Summaries) 3. WCB (Weekly Criminal Bulletins)	not available	1. All Canada Weekly Summaries 2. Lawyers Weekly Digest 3. Weekly Criminal Bulletin 4. Canadian Labour Arbitration Summaries
• Updating cases (using case citators)	QC works with Canadian cases	Keycite works with US cases, statutes, and regulations	Shepard's works with Canadian cases and US cases, statutes, and regulations
• Finding acts/regulations	1. RSC 2. RSO	1. USC (US Code) 2. CFR (Code of Federal Regulations) 3. FR (Federal Register)	1. US Code 2. Code of Federal Regulations and Federal Register 3. Current Public and General Acts of England and Wales
• Finding cases that have judicially considered a statute	CJ (for all Canadian cases)	Keycite works with US statutes	Shepard's works with US statutes

	QL database (examples)	Lawschool.Westlaw.com database (examples)	Lexis.com database* (examples)
• Finding journal articles (full-text)	JOUR (about 16 Canadian law journals)	1. TP-ALL (ALRs, all journals included in WL, mainly US, some international) 2. TX-TP (Tax, a topical subset of TP-ALL; there are other topical subsets) 3. TP-CANADA (10 Canadian law journals)	1. US law journals, bar journals, ALRs 2. About 28 Canadian law journals
• Finding citations to journal articles (index)	ICLL (Index to Canadian Legal Literature)	1. LJI-INDX (UK journals) 2. CILP (Current Index to Legal Periodicals, most recent 8 weeks) 3. LRAC (Library Review Abstract Clearinghouse, abstracts of not-yet-published scholarly works)	not available
• Finding news	CPN (Canadian Press Newstex, 1984–)	Westnews (including major US newspapers and Globe and Mail)	Legal news
• Finding recent Supreme Court and precedent-setting decisions from other courts and tribunals	LNET (LAW/NET) Topical Netletter	Westclips	Eclipse

* Based on free student password access.

Source: Louise Tsang, Reference Law Librarian (Osgoode Hall Law School), York University Law Library.